ANOTHER KIND OF
COURAGE

Other recent books by the same author:

RAF Fighter Command
Valiant Wings
Tempest Pilot
Fighter Pilot's Summer
Spitfire Offensive
Above The Trenches
Over The Front
Above The Lines
Claims To Fame – The Lancaster

Patrick Stephens Limited, an imprint of Haynes Publishing, has published authoritative, quality books for enthusiasts for over a quarter of a century. During that time the company has established a reputation as one of the world's leading publishers of books on aviation, maritime, military, model-making, motor cycling, motor racing, railway and railway modelling subjects. Readers or authors with suggestions for books they would like to see published are invited to write to: The Editorial Director, Patrick Stephens Limited, Sparkford, Nr. Yeovil, Somerset, BA22 7JJ.

ANOTHER KIND OF COURAGE

Stories of the UK-based Walrus Air-Sea Rescue Squadrons

Norman L.R. Franks

PSL
Patrick Stephens Limited

First published 1994

© Norman L.R. Franks 1994

British Library Cataloguing-in-Publication Data:
A catalogue record for this book
is available from the British Library.

ISBN 1 85260 441 7

Library of Congress catalog card no. 94 77765

Typeset by G&M, Raunds, Northamptonshire
Printed in Great Britain by
Butler & Tanner Ltd, London and Frome

Contents

TO THE WALRUS

She is not a thing of beauty,
All a-tangle in her struts,
Looking like she was assembled,
From a box of bolts and nuts.

When she's sitting in a hangar,
And she's folded back her wings,
She is not the 'joy forever',
Heard of when poets sing.

You would never call her pretty,
Pulchritudinuous or fair,
With her old front-backwards engine,
Pushing at her through the air.

She's no charm, except her virtue,
But that's plenty charm enough,
When you're sitting in a dinghy,
And the sea is getting rough.

When you spot her in the distance,
Like a box kite in the sky,
There's no plane in all creation,
More attractive to the eye.

If you see her from a dinghy,
That is pitching on the blue,
Coastal's awkward ugly duckling,
Will look mighty good to you.

Acknowledgements

Over the last few years while researching this book, I have been deeply privileged to meet or correspond with many men who served so valiantly with the Air-Sea Rescue squadrons during the Second World War and saw duty in both the UK and the Mediterranean. In addition, I have been pleased to have had the opportunity of meeting or corresponding with an equal number of men who have these same men, or others like them, to thank for their lives. They know only too well what measure of men were those who risked their own lives to save others.

To both these rescuers and rescuees, I am extremely grateful for your recollections and the time taken to impart them to me.

Rescuers:

Lt Cdr L.A. Cox	275 Squadron
FO K.S. Butterfield DFC	276 Squadron
WO A.V. Dorman	276 Squadron
W. Elder DFM	276 Squadron
WO L. Ewens	276 Squadron
The late FL R. Hughes DFM	276 Squadron
FL R.V. Renvoize DFC	276 Squadron
WC A.T. Vacquier	276 Squadron
FO J.L. Barber DFM	277 Squadron
FO H.M. Chalmers	277 Squadron
FO R. Eccles	277 Squadron
FL T. Fletcher DFC, DFM & bar	277 Squadron
The late FL D.R. Hartwell	277 Squadron
The late FL L.R. Healey DFC, DFM	277 Squadron
The late WO G.N. Leighton	277 Squadron
WO J. Mallinson	277 Squadron
WO W.A. Rance	277 Squadron
FL A.K. Saunders DFC	277 Squadron
FO L.H. Seales	277 Squadron
FO P.C. Stanton	277 Squadron

WO P.W. Weeden	277 Squadron
SL V.A. Hester DFC	278 Squadron
FO T.H. Humphrey	278 Squadron
FL W.A. Land MBE AFC	278 Squadron
The late FO G.B. Reeder DFC	278 Squadron
WO R.C. Whittaker	278 Squadron
Cdr M.B.P. Francklin DSC RN	764 Squadron, FAA

Rescuees:

FL T.A.H. Slack	41 Squadron RAF
Air Cde G.A. Mason DFC	64 Squadron RAF
WO H.F. Ross	80 Squadron RAF
FL E.B. Karran	119 Squadron RAF
WC E.C. Deanesly DFC	152 Squadron RAF
FO R.H. Milne RCAF	254 Squadron RAF
WO I.C.M. Dunlop	263 Squadron RAF
FL H.J. Voorspuy	320 (Dutch) Squadron RDNAS/RAF
PO J.H. Ot	320 (Dutch) Squadron RDNAS/RAF
FO J.L. Hickson RCAF	420 Squadron RCAF
FO A.J. MacDonald RCAF	420 Squadron RCAF
SL W.G.M. Hume RCAF	442 Squadron RCAF
WO J.W. Hough RNZAF	464 Squadron RNZAF
SL C.J. Sheddan DFC RNZAF	486 Squadron RNZAF
FO T.S. Turek	609 Squadron RAuxAF
Capt E.D. Beatie	336th FS, 4th FG USAAF
Lt Wm H. Turcotte	332nd BS, 91st BG USAAF

Thanks are also due to the following, all of whom gave generous help to the project: Mrs Joyce Smith (ex LACW); Mr Joe French, Secretary of the Goldfish Club of Great Britain; Mrs A.D. Grace; fellow historians and writers, Chaz Bowyer, Roger Freeman, Ray Sturtivant and Chris Ashworth. The Air-Sea Rescue Association and the Keeper and staff of the Public Records Office, Kew. And as always, to Heather; she knows why.

Introduction

The fall of France in June 1940 changed the face of the war for Britain. That it happened so quickly was one thing; that it happened at all was another. The immediate implications were that if, or more correctly, when, the German Air Force – the Luftwaffe – began its attacks against Britain, their aeroplanes would come from French bases and not from Germany.

Much of the Royal Air Force's peacetime training for air defence was centred around the understanding that, just as in the First World War, Britain, France and perhaps some, if not all, the Low Countries, would be fighting a land war on European soil. Also, and again similar to the Great War, Britain would only be attacked from the air, just as the Zeppelin and Schutte-Lanz airships and Gotha bombers had done in that war.

That all changed when France was defeated. Now, not only could the Luftwaffe's aircraft have a better range by flying from captured French airfields just across the English Channel, but they would be able to have fighter escort. With fighter escort, the air battles would no longer be the long-trained for, simple section or squadron formation attacks on a few lumbering bombers, but a fight to the death because the Spitfire and Hurricane fighter pilots would now have to contend with Messerschmitt fighters protecting the bombers.

RAF Fighter Command was a defensive instrument, not designed for fighting long, arduous battles out over the English Channel or North Sea, and certainly not for engaging hostile aircraft virtually out of sight of the British coast. Their first such encounter came with the evacuation of the British Expeditionary Force from Dunkirk during May and early June of 1940. For the first time, the peacetime-trained fighter pilots had to fly sorties they had not envisaged, in a battle they had not expected and what was more, they had to fly over to the French coast and even over northern France, in order to engage the enemy and try to protect the escaping British Army.

This in itself brought problems, but one main one reared its head when fighter pilots were shot down and baled out into the sea, anywhere from just off the French beaches, to mid-Channel, or to just off the English coast. That the pilots wore a life preserver – the famed 'Mae West', so named because when it was inflated, it made the airmen instantly think of the generous proportions of that erstwhile buxom American actress, whose line, 'Come up and see me some time', had become famous – only ensured a period of buoyancy in the water. Unless someone came along and plucked the downed airmen from the sea, the Mae West only prolonged the inevitable.

As the year of 1940 and then 1941 progressed, the RAF, and in those early years, Fighter Command's pilots in particular, found themselves fighting more and more over the sea. During the Battle of Britain, the fighter pilots often engaged German raiders over the coast of southern England, or, with brave enthusiasm, chased fleeing raiders back across the English Channel towards France. If in those air battles they had the misfortune to find it necessary to jump or crash-land into the sea, they needed to be rescued.

During the spring and summer of 1941, with the daylight attacks on Britain largely at an end, the Royal Air Force began to 'take the war to the enemy', flying all manner of operations over France and Belgium, even Holland. That necessitated two sea crossings, and a faulty engine could just as easily deposit them into the water as either German fighters or anti-aircraft fire.

During 1941, the fighter pilots began to be equipped with rubber dinghies so that if they were unlucky enough to find themselves bobbing on the ocean, they could at least have the chance of getting themselves out of the water. This, of course, always assumed that they were unwounded, or at least not too badly wounded as to inhibit their efforts to clamber into this means of surviving a little longer than merely being supported by their Mae West.

Bomber and Coastal Command aircraft carried dinghies from the beginning; after all, the bomber was designed to attack, so crews would obviously need to cross water, and Coastal Command, by its very nature, was closely associated with the sea! In bomber aircraft, the dinghy was of a size to accommodate the number of men in the crew, and the pack was usually stowed in the wing, where it would eject itself and inflate when the aircraft hit the sea. In the larger aircraft, more than one dinghy would be carried.

Fighter Command began to be issued with dinghies in the early summer of 1941, the single-seat K-type forming part of the pilot's parachute pack, on which he sat during flight. It was attached to him by means of a lanyard so that in normal circumstances, he would stay attached to the dinghy when he hit the water and discarded his parachute. If he ditched, he would still be attached to the dinghy, even though he had not used the parachute.

It is recorded that the date the first fighter pilot was rescued from a K-type dinghy was 16 June 1941.

★   ★   ★   ★   ★

In the final analysis, however, it was of no value to have airmen down in the sea, in either Mae Wests or dinghies, unless someone was going to go out and rescue them. The chances of being picked up by some lucky ship, either friendly or hostile, – while it did happen – were generally slim. Initially the Royal Navy was the obvious service, for they had boats! The British, being a sea-going nation, obviously had any number of ports and naval bases around its hundreds of miles of coastline, where light naval vessels were stationed. Therefore, in the early days of the Second World War, anyone seen or known to be in the water was reported to the naval authorities, who would be able to send out a boat.

The first rescue service was started from the Dover area during the Dunkirk evacuation. The Royal Navy used launches or pinnaces (tenders). By the autumn of 1940, some 30 airmen, both British and German, had been rescued by this method, but it was believed that a great many more must have come down in the sea and had simply not been rescued. Obviously, a properly run organization was needed to both find and then pick up these downed men. Quite apart from the humane aspects, the Royal Air Force could not afford to lose highly trained aircrew in this way, and confidence in their probable survival was a boost to morale.

The Royal Air Force had, of course, given some thought to rescue craft in the 1930s. Indeed, the RAF, quite apart from having grown from the amalgamation of the Royal Flying Corps and Royal Naval Air Service in the First World War, had seaplanes and flying boats. Thus they had tenders – small launches – to take men to and from these types of aircraft, from the very early days. These boats had developed slowly over the peacetime years and by 1936, the High-Speed Launch was in being. The first, known initially as a Crash Boat, reached the Marine Unit at RAF Calshot in that same year, and having accepted this type of vessel for various duties, the RAF ordered a further 16.

With a world war on the horizon, some thought was given to the possible problem of rescuing men from the sea by using these launches, and on 28 February 1939, Air Vice Marshal Sholto Douglas MC, DFC, the Assistant Chief of the Air Staff, presided over a meeting which placed the responsibility for Air-Sea Rescue under the control of RAF Coastal Command. Following this decision, a further 13 High-Speed Launches were ordered.

The embryo Air-Sea Rescue Service stumbled on into war, and did its very best to rescue as many downed airmen as was possible, given the lack of proper coordination with other elements of the various air and naval organizations, and the rather hit-and-miss nature of their work. Air Vice Marshal Keith Park, AOC No 11 Group, Fighter Command, whose pilots it was who were about to take the brunt of the Battle of Britain, co-operated with the Vice Admiral, Dover, and had managed to borrow a few Westland Lysander aircraft to work with the naval launches. It was an amazingly simple but mammoth advance.

Then on 22 August 1940, at the very height of the Battle of Britain, Air Vice Marshal Arthur Harris OBE, AFC, AOC No 5 Bomber Group (and the future C-in-C of Bomber Command), presided over a meeting to draft out a proposed Air-Sea Rescue Service, which was brought about because of the concern felt about the number of aircrew who were being lost over the English Channel.

At this meeting, it was proposed to continue the service controlled by
Coastal Command, with boats from the Naval Auxiliary Patrol, while
the new RAF rescue launches would come under the control of the local
naval authorities. However, the RAF would retain responsibility for 12
Lysander aircraft, while Fighter Command would take control of all
search and rescue operations.

Despite these agreements, there were no further major developments
until the Directorate of Air-Sea Rescue was formed in mid-February
1941.

The dozen Lysander aircraft had been borrowed from Army Co-
Operation Command, as they were all but unemployed following the
fall of France, there being no land battles in which to use them. In any
event, the type was now obsolete as a front-line aircraft, designed for
battle-front operations. So with these few aircraft, the promise of a new
organization, and some naval and RAF High-Speed Launches at various
coastal bases, the Air-Sea Rescue Service slowly began to take shape. If
the new formation proved successful, it would not be because of the
aeroplanes, the boats or the organization. It would be due to the courage
of the men in those planes and boats.

Of all the aspects of Air-Sea Rescue, this book will cover, in the main,
the operations of the Supermarine Walrus amphibious seaplanes, and, of
course, the men who flew in them. It is a spectacular story.

Chapter One

The Early Days

It is always interesting to see how things develop, and the way Air-Sea Rescue (ASR) developed during the war years is fascinating. Having begun to establish the boat side of the Service at ports around the coast of Britain, as we saw in the Introduction, it quickly followed that aircraft searching for missing airmen would have a far better chance of spotting them than men standing on the heaving decks of a High-Speed Launch (HSL).

To the layman, most things seem simple. What, for instance, is more simple than speeding out to sea in a powerful speedboat, the wind in your hair, the powerful roar and surge of the engines, the white frothing water trail left behind, and the gentle rise and fall of the boat as it crests a wave. From miles away, you spot your man, sitting expectantly in his dinghy, waving merrily, a smile of relief on his face, and gratitude in his heart. That really is the layman's view!

Reality is somewhat different. As any seaman will tell you, one can never judge the sea from the 'civilian's' perspective, which is either standing ankle-deep in the surf on a holiday beach, the sun warming his body, the gentle breeze of summer caressing his brow as he watches children play, or the odd yacht skimming along just a few hundred yards off the balmy shore.

Perhaps the more adventurous have had the experience of a 'heaving' deck under their feet as they enjoyed a week or two on the Norfolk Broads, or the canals of central England! All good experience, but not in the least like anything the men of the rescue service experience, either during the Second World War or now, so let us forget the romantic pictures that one can so easily conjure up.

The sea, whether it is the English Channel, the North Sea, the Bristol Channel or perhaps the Irish Sea, is generally rougher than one might suppose when standing safely on shore. The winds whip up the waves, the currents can be dangerous, and when the waves do get up, the view from the comparatively low level of an HSL is very restricted. Even if the boat's crew had been given an accurate positional fix, by the time they had sped to that location, the man in his dinghy could have drifted several miles, and even if he had only gone a short distance, he might still be invisible to them.

So he fires his distress flares, or flashes his signal mirror, I hear you cry. Very good, provided they have not been lost overboard, or he is unwounded and in full command of his faculties, or he has not been in his tiny rubber liferaft for several days, with hardly the strength to remain in his dinghy. Cold, wet through, miserable, hungry, anxious, possibly suffering from exposure, let alone any injuries, he is not bubbling with enthusiasm even if he realizes that rescue is at hand. Indeed, he may be only minutes away from death, so the men in the HSL do not expect him to jump up and down, blowing a whistle and calling for them to come his way!

It did not, therefore, take very long to appreciate that if the man or men could be spotted more easily from the air, a rescue boat could then be directed quickly to the spot and pick up whoever they had found. So in early 1941, a few ASR Flights were established.

Among the first were Flights at RAF Hawkinge, Shoreham and Martlesham Heath. These locations covered the south-east of England, approximately from the Suffolk coast to the Isle of Wight. This, as far as the air war in 1941 was concerned, was the main battle zone, so this would be where the majority of 'customers' would be. The men in the water were always known as customers, sometimes 'kippers'!

As mentioned in the Introduction, the first aircraft that were made available were Lysanders. The Westland Lysander, known affectionately as the 'Lizzie', was designed as a two-seat Army Co-operation aircraft and entered RAF service in 1938. The high-winged configuration made the aircraft ideal for Army reconnaissance, and it was this same quality that made them perfect for searching the seas for missing aircrew. The two-man crew did not have to contend with the normal blind spots of a low-winged aeroplane, and they were slow enough – their maximum speed was only around 230 m.p.h. – to be able to search adequately, the sea not rushing by in a blur!

★　★　★　★　★

Perhaps at this stage we should view how one downed pilot had been rescued in the very early days, in 1940, during the Battle of Britain. Flight Lieutenant Christopher Deanesly was a Spitfire pilot with No 152 Squadron in that struggle. He was rescued twice from the sea during that fateful summer:

I believe I was the only pilot pulled out of the Channel twice in 1940. Most of 152 Squadron's casualties were in the sea and while a few were picked out once, I was much luckier.

On the first occasion, when I ditched about three miles off Portland Bill, I had been put out of action by a bullet through the header tank. The squadron had been attacking a number of Ju 87s bombing a small convoy. This included the *Empire Henchman*, which was towing a lighter of ammunition to Falmouth, and whose captain picked me up; and as he didn't want to bring his hazardous cargo into Lyme Regis, he radioed for the RAF air-sea rescue launch stationed there to come out and take me off. The transfer and landing on the Cobh at Lyme Regis was carried out very smoothly and after a period in hospital I returned to the squadron in August.

Late in the afternoon of 26th September, I was one of a Flight from 152 intercepting a number of German bombers returning after dropping their loads. Just as I was closing in on a Heinkel 111, either his rear gunner, or an Me 109 escort, hit me with probably a cannon shell and the aircraft immediately lost power and caught fire. I baled out at about 8,000 feet and landed comfortably in the sea about 10 miles off Swanage. One of the squadron pilots saw me jump and helped by the pad of fluorescene dye which spread a trail in the sea, he was able to fly a northerly bearing to RAF Warmwell.

Some weeks before, as no use could be found for an Army Co-Operation Lysander squadron, two Lysanders were posted to several fighter stations to provide some sort of air-sea rescue, though they had no dinghies and only smoke floats. My brother pilot was able to give the Lysander pilot an approximate bearing to fly and an estimate of distance. All worked out to pattern and the old Lysander arrived about three-quarters of an hour after I went into the sea. He dropped a smoke float and guided a small RN launch to me which came out from Swanage.

Flight Lieutenant E.C. Deanesly, No 152 Squadron

★   ★   ★   ★   ★

The Flights which were established in 1941 had their first successes in the summer, with Fighter Command's offensive over Northern France coming to its height. One of the first recorded successes came on 5 July. Flying from Hawkinge, Sergeant David Waddington and his gunner, Sergeant R.S. 'Sticky' Glew, flying Lysander V9488, located a Polish fighter pilot five miles off Dunkirk. He had been in his dinghy for three days, and once spotted, the Lysander crew were able to direct a launch to him.

Because at this stage the dinghy was only just coming into use by the fighter pilots, the Lysander had been rigged up with a dinghy pack attached to its fixed undercarriage spats, where, in its earlier role, the aircraft had carried six small bombs. Once they located a pilot, who might only be in his Mae West – or not – or whose dinghy might be damaged, etc., they could drop a dinghy to him. Hopefully he would be able to inflate it and climb into it. Sergeant Waddington and Sergeant Patterson, in V9483, did just that two days later, while calling up an HSL.

The Martlesham Flight had a success on 10 July. Sergeant S.A. Morrison and Sergeant Moule, in V9545, searched for a missing pilot four miles north-east of Foulness, off the Kent coast, flying at 50 ft because of dense low cloud. Eventually they spotted him some 10 miles north of Herne Bay, in his dinghy. Being unable to make contact with their ground control, they spotted a small fishing boat six miles away and diverted it to the man, who was picked up. Two days later the same crew located a man in a Mae West south of Dungeness. They dropped a dinghy which landed 30 ft from him, but he made no attempt to reach it. A rescue launch was guided in, but the boat crew found the man was dead. Rescue had come too late.

This was the other aspect of the ASR service. If found earlier, could that man have still been alive? Was he dead when he hit the sea? Would he have died even if he had been rescued earlier?

It was these questions which often faced the ASR men, and although difficult to answer with any certainty, from the very beginning they determined that to be effective, they had to do certain things. They must react quickly to a rescue call, fly out accurately to the position given and search at a height that would allow them maximum coverage, but not so high that they might miss spotting just the head, arms and shoulders of a man who might or who might not be conscious. Time was the priority. The longer they took to find that man in the sea, the greater the danger he would not survive.

If we again look at the problem from the layman's point of view, we can quite easily convince ourselves that, although the sea may be cold, surely a man can hang on and will himself to live. The same layman will recall that swim in the sea off Brighton, last summer. Sure, the water was not all that warm, but it was not unpleasant! Forget it.

The flyers in the Second World War flew all year round, generally in all sorts of weather, or changeable and deteriorating weather. They could not operate just on days when they thought the sea might prove warm enough for them to survive should they be unlucky enough to have to ditch. In any event, the sea around Britain's coasts is never 'warm'. Out in the English Channel or North Sea, it is cold – bitterly cold. In some conditions, and especially during the winter months, survival in the sea might be counted in minutes, certainly not in hours. Without a dinghy, death would be fairly swift and unpleasant. Even in a dinghy, it was no picnic. Being in a dinghy, you were still completely soaked to the skin, and however much you baled out the water, even supposing you were uninjured and able to bale, you were generally sitting in several inches of water all the time.

The waves, even on a good day, were enough to make even the best 'sailors' seasick. Being wet, the wind, or even a gentle breeze, would raise the chill factor. If you were nursing a bullet or shrapnel wound, or perhaps a broken limb, a badly gashed head or face, smashed or broken fingers, a broken pelvis – the list is endless – one's ability to fight back was greatly reduced. You were facing death, either through your injuries, or the cold – or both. And even if you were unwounded, uninjured, and reasonably secure in your little rubber home, and the weather was not being totally unkind, you still had to be found. As the hours stretched into days, perhaps a week, hunger, thirst and despair became your companions.

If you were extremely lucky, a ship might come along and spot you, even a submarine might pop up next to you. A fighting aircraft on its way to or from a target might just see you and report the sighting. If they see you, if they get your position right, if, when you had ditched or baled out you were able to send out a distress Mayday call, if, if . . . There were a lot of 'ifs'.

Whatever the circumstances, the main chance of rescue came from the Air-Sea Rescue services. The lucky ones were rescued. The unlucky ones – well, they still appear on the missing lists, now presumed lost.

★　★　★　★　★

Eventually, there were HSL bases covering the whole of the British Isles, from Scotland, the east coast of England, round the south-east corner, the south, south-west and Wales. This is the story of the flying side of Air-Sea Rescue, but the HSLs were a main part of that story and featured in many rescues involving the Lysander aircraft, and the aircraft that superseded the Lysander.

One of the first HSL units was No 27, at Ferry Dock, Dover – right at the apex of the early battle zone. It was formed in December 1940, the first boat, *HSL 143* commanded by Flight Lieutenant Revell, arriving five days before Christmas. *HSLs 122* and *123* arrived from Calshot in January 1941 (Sir Algernon Guiness and Pilot Officer Blake-Smith commanding). One of their first rescues was that of Squadron Leader J.A. O'Neill DFC, commanding officer of No 601 Squadron. His squadron engaged Me 109s over France and O'Neill shot one down, only to be hit by another. He almost made it back across the English Channel, but then ditched.

As there was a known Fighter Command operation taking place, the ASR stations had been alerted, and the form was to send out a couple of boats to patrol in the Channel, in case any of the RAF boys got into trouble. Being out on patrol cut the rescue time. *HSL 143* had left Dover at 4 p.m. to patrol between Hastings and Dungeness, and actually saw O'Neill's Hurricane go into the sea, four miles away from them. Although wounded in the legs, O'Neill was quickly rescued and taken back to Dover.

This was perhaps the typical HSL type of operation, being on patrol and in more or less the right place in anticipation of any RAF pilots running out of airspace, but not out of water! Over the next five years the HSLs were to rescue hundreds of men by this method and, of course, by being sent out in response to specific Mayday calls.

A life is a life, be it a squadron leader, as in O'Neill's case, or a sergeant pilot. It made no difference to his rescue, although it must be said that the higher the rank the more, perhaps, insistent the Group controllers might be. The Hawkinge Flight had a high-ranker on 9 July 1941. Wing Commander John Peel DFC, leader of the Kenley Wing, went into the sea south of Dungeness after operations over France. The Wing had escorted three Stirling bombers to Mazingarbe and had been engaged near Hardelot where one Me 109 was shot down. On the return flight, 20 Me 109s were encountered and No 312 Squadron claimed a couple more, but lost two of their own.

A Lysander was Scrambled, crewed by Sergeants Hurst and 'Sticky' Glew. They located a customer in his K-type dinghy, waving his small signal flag (part of the dinghy equipment). Hurst called up an HSL and a Royal Navy patrol boat picked the Wing Leader up.

It became clear to the crews of the Lysanders that while they might find the men in the water, they were then helpless to do more once they had called out a rescue boat. They could drop a dinghy, even supplies if it was thought necessary; otherwise, all they could do was to circle the position, make sure they kept the customer in sight and watch out for both hostile air and sea craft, whilst awaiting the first sighting of the approaching HSL.

More than once, they discovered that a man had died soon after rescue by the HSLs, either through exposure or through wounds that could not be tended until the HSL arrived. Two Lysanders from Hawkinge found a pilot 60 miles east of Deal on 17 July 1941, but he died soon after the boat got to him. A comment was made then that a Walrus aircraft would have been useful.

The Supermarine Walrus came from a good stable of flying boats, for it had been Supermarine and R.J. Mitchell who had combined to produce the famous S.6 and S.6B racing seaplanes which had successfully secured for Britain the Schneider Trophy in 1931. Mitchell, of course, went on to design Britain's most famous fighter aeroplane – the Spitfire.

Initially a private venture, the Walrus had been designed as a machine capable of being catapulted from Royal Navy warships. Originally named the Seagull, it first flew in 1933, and the Fleet Air Arm (FAA) had some on strength in the mid-1930s. In 1935 it was renamed the Walrus.

Over 200 were built, an original order for 12 by the RAF in May 1935 being increased by a further 204 the following year. A high-wing biplane, the Walrus saw considerable service with the FAA. It had a single Bristol Pegasus VI, 775 h.p. engine of the pusher-design, a wooden hull, and a range of 600 miles. A cruising speed of 95 m.p.h. was ideal for slow spotting of water-borne objects. It was also an amphibian, which meant it could land and take off on both land and water.

The early Mk Is were built by Supermarine, but the Mk IIs, which were used by the RAF, were built by Saunders-Roe (Saro) at Cowes, on the Isle of Wight. In RAF service it could carry a crew of four, with two defensive Vickers 'K' guns in the bows and amidships; but when it was used by the Air-Sea Rescue Service, it had a crew of three although later two became more usual. More often than not, the guns were removed to reduce weight which, as the Walrus crews found, was often the difference between getting airborne or not, once someone had been rescued. A final total of 741 Walruses were built, 453 by Saro and 288 by Supermarine.

The Walrus became an ideal vehicle for the Air-Sea Rescue Service which was now being organized onto a proper footing.

The three Flights continued to fly Lysander search missions during the latter half of 1941, and had a number of successes, especially Hawkinge. The HSLs, too, were now regularly picking up downed pilots. The Dover HSLs picked up nearly 30, including one man twice.

Co-operating with a Lysander, *HSL 123* picked up Pilot Officer Vicki Ortmans, a Belgian pilot flying with No 609 Squadron, on 19 August 1941. On 27 September, *HSL 147* rescued him again! The third time Ortmans was shot down into the English Channel, on 21 October, he was rescued not by the British but by the Germans!

If the ASR Flights could get their hands on a Walrus or two, the crews could not only search and locate downed airmen, but could then land on the water, take them on board and fly them back to safety. If the rescued men were suffering from wounds or the effects of the sea, they could at least be given first aid, certainly a warm blanket and some hot soup or some such. Just being out of the water reduced the effects of hypothermia.

By this time, the Directorate for Air-Sea Rescue was seeing the results

of its early efforts. It was estimated that the proportion of rescued aircrew
had risen from around 20 to over 33 per cent. Plans were now put in
hand to raise the Flights to squadron status and to employ better search
and rescue aircraft. Meanwhile, the Royal Navy had become involved
in the rescue operations, and they, like some of the Lysander men,
suggested the use of Walrus amphibians.

So, by late 1941, the Air-Sea Rescue Service, having more than proved
itself, was about to grow – and continue growing, while the pilots and
gunners would be able to take on a new role. No longer would they be
just a search organization; they would now be able to take an active part
in the actual rescues! For these men the daily routine became
commonplace; only later did it become obvious that each individual act
was one of extreme heroism and courage. Another kind of courage.

Chapter Two

New Status, New Aircraft

In the late summer of 1941, the numbering range of RAF squadrons was in the upper two hundreds, so when the decision was made to make the few ASR Flights up to full squadrons, the first available number was 275.

Thus the Flights at Valley, in North Wales and Andreas on the Isle of Man were formed into No 275 Squadron at RAF Valley, on 15 October 1941. Its first CO was a former Battle of Britain pilot, Flight Lieutenant R.F. Hamlyn DFM, posted in from No 242 (Fighter) Squadron. Its first aircraft were Lysander IIIAs, and the new unit was declared operational by November 1941.

Next came No 276 Squadron, formed on 21 October 1941 from the Flights at Harrowbeer, Fairwood Common, Perranporth, Roborough (where No 16 Squadron's Lysanders combined coastal patrols with ASR duties) and Warmwell. It was to be based at Harrowbeer, Devon, with a detachment at Fairwood Common in South Wales. Its CO was Squadron Leader Hulbert. It was equipped with Lysander IIIAs, but also Walruses, and was soon operational, with its 'A' Flight at Roborough (Plymouth) under Flight Lieutenant P.R.P. Fisher. 'A' Flight then went to Warmwell; 'B' Flight remained at Harrowbeer, where it covered the Exeter Sector with two Walrus amphibians and three 'Lizzies'; while 'C' Flight operated from Perranporth.

No 277 Squadron, which was to become the premier ASR squadron – in terms of rescues – was formed on 22 December 1941, from the detached Flights at Hawkinge, Martlesham Heath, Shoreham, Tangmere, Kenley, and at Stapleford Tawney, Essex. Like most of the ASR squadrons, the Flights remained almost totally autonomous, and little changed from what had gone on before. From time to time the CO would pay each base a visit, and perhaps they would hear of some happening at one of the other airfields, but in the main they were totally separate.

The first CO was Squadron Leader Clark, and the initial equipment consisted of eight Lysanders and four Walruses. The squadron's three Flights continued to operate from Shoreham, near Brighton, Hawkinge, just inland from Folkestone, and Martlesham Heath, just to the north-east of Ipswich. With its prime position, No 277 Squadron covered the south-east corner of England, and was to see almost constant action over the next two and a half years or so.

The fourth squadron, No 278 (actually the first by date), came into being on 1 October 1941, at Matlaske, a satellite airfield in Norfolk. The original No 3 ASR Flight had been operating since July from RAF Coltishall. No 278 had three Lysanders and two Walruses, with three more Lysanders on detachment at North Coates, on the Lincolnshire coast, south of Grimsby. This squadron covered a large area and would have detachments at Woolsington, Acklington, Hutton Cranswick, Ayr, Peterhead and Drem. Pilot Officer P.R. Smith, who had commanded No 3 ASR Flight since August, was given command and promoted to flight lieutenant, while Pilot Officer J.H. Chase commanded the detachment at North Coates in November. Soon after the squadron's formation, a further three Lysanders arrived to bring it up to establishment – nine Lysanders.

In order to cover the wider areas of water, Nos 279 and 280 Squadrons were formed in November and December 1941, respectively, and were equipped with Hudson and Anson aircraft, which were also able to operate on night sorties. They covered the south and north-east respectively. Because of a shortage of Hudsons, No 280 Squadron at Thorney Island re-equipped with Ansons early the following year.

Thus, by the end of 1941 there were six ASR squadrons in being, four equipped or about to be equipped with Walruses as well as Lysanders, and two with twin-engined Hudsons or Ansons. For the Walrus-equipped squadrons and detached Flights, business was about to begin in earnest.

* * * * *

First off the mark was 278 Squadron. On the afternoon of 1 December 1941, Sergeant W.F. Sims with Flight Sergeant S.A. Hurrell as air gunner, searching for a missing crew in Lysander V9609, found six men huddled in a dinghy. A Walrus was called, and Flight Lieutenant P.R. Smith and Flight Sergeant Atkinson, in Walrus L2238, flew to the spot, landed and picked up six Polish airmen.

Seven days into the New Year of 1942, and it was Ronald Hamlyn, the CO of 275 Squadron, who made his unit's first successsful Walrus rescue. Late on 6 January, Sergeant E.W. Peacock took off from Penrhos, Anglesey, in Anson N9822, of No 9 Air Observer's School. He ran into some bad weather, with snow and ice, and suddenly both engines cut dead, for no apparent reason. Peacock made a good forced landing on the sea, although he suffered a cut forehead. They had come down off Llanbedr, but by the time their SOS was received, and also because of the weather, no rescue attempt could be mounted until first light the next morning.

At 9 a.m. on the 7th, Sergeant Hopkinson, a former fighter pilot with No 74 Squadron, took off in a Lysander and found the Anson still afloat one and a half miles off Llanbedr. He called base and Hamlyn was airborne at 9:10 a.m., but over the spot he could see nothing of the crew. He commenced a standard H-square search pattern and located a dinghy in which four men sat huddled. He landed at 9:45 a.m., had two of the men come aboard, then took off and landed them at Penrhos. He then returned and picked up the remaining two. While in the Walrus, the men had their clothes removed and were put into sleeping bags to keep warm.

★　★　★　★　★

These were still early days in the Walrus squadrons' activities, and many Lysander search flights were still being carried out. And not all rescue flights were successful.

A lost friend

On 16 April 1942, Pilot Officer J.V. Renvoize of 276 Squadron, for instance, was sent off from Warmwell when a Hurricane pilot from 175 Squadron went down. Flight Sergeant B.H. Forman had been part of a fighter-bomber raid on Maupertus airfield – his squadron's first operational mission. Bricker Forman had previously flown with 247 Squadron, joining 175, in which Jim Renvoize had also served, in March. On the way back, his Hurricane developed a glycol leak. He got out of his aircraft alright, and his companions saw him climb into his dinghy, but they had to leave him when their fuel began to run low.

His position was given as 45 miles south of Bournemouth and Renvoize headed out with a Spitfire escort. However, the Germans were on the ball this day, and some Me 109s engaged them. One Spitfire was shot down and it was obviously too dangerous to stick around too long, so that was one pilot known to be alive but unable to be found. Jim Renvoise recalls:

I had known 'Happy' Forman in 247 Squadron. I did the first search for him with Flight Sergeant Galloway in a Lysander in the late evening. I did two more searches the next day and during one, a Spitfire from our escort was shot down by Me 109s. We failed to find the dinghy, the position given as 50 miles south of Bournemouth. The whole episode was very annoying, particularly as it was someone I knew. I believe his body was found a few days later, still in the dinghy.

The problem was a fact that we kept asking the powers-that-be to drum into squadrons; to have a section remain circling anyone who was forced to ditch, so that a fix could be obtained, and then send out replacement sections from other squadrons until the chap could be picked up by Walrus or launch. Sometimes, of course, the rest of the squadron would be very short of petrol, and it is possible in this case that someone did give a fix.

Quite often when we got a call to Scramble, we would find that the ditching had occurred some hours earlier – goodness knows what had happened in between.

Flight Lieutenant J.V. Renvoize, No 276 Squadron

Bricker Forman's body was found and buried at Efford, near Exeter.

Back at Hawkinge, 277 Squadron had yet to record their first successful Walrus rescue, but the Lysander sorties were still working well. Flight Lieutenant W.P. Green had taken over command of the squadron in March.

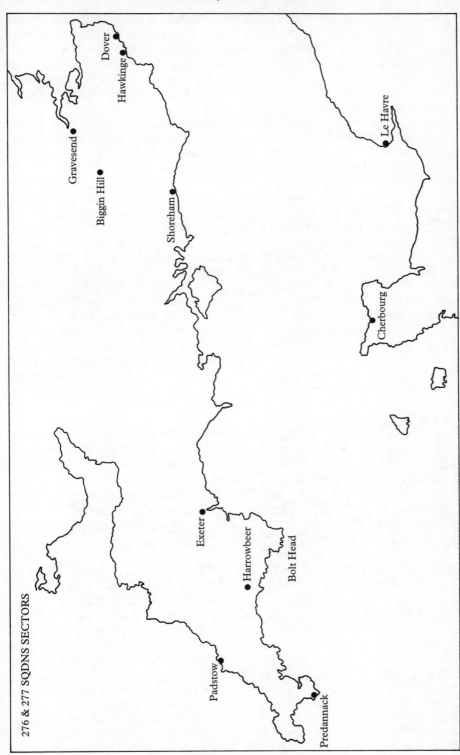

276 & 277 SQDNS SECTORS

Dover
Hawkinge
Gravesend
Biggin Hill
Shoreham
Le Havre
Cherbourg
Exeter
Harrowbeer
Bolt Head
Padstow
Predannack

Another Wing Leader was plucked from the water on 27 April, thanks to a Lysander crew. Wing Commander P.H. 'Dutch' Hugo DFC was leading the Tangmere Wing and was engaged over Ostend by a number of FW 190s. In the fight that followed he probably destroyed one '190 and damaged a second before he was himself hit and wounded in the shoulder. His Spitfire was damaged, forcing him to leave it at 3,000 ft, parachuting down into the sea.

At 2 p.m. Hawkinge were alerted with a 'Top Line' call, meaning that an operation was being carried out and to be ready to Scramble. Pilot Officer Morrison and 'Sticky' Glew were the Readiness crew and 55 minutes later they got their call when control received the Mayday. They headed out, 20 miles from Deal, to find a Spitfire circling Hugo in his dinghy. They radioed back, then flew low to drop two smoke floats to mark his position. He was later picked up by a minelayer. 'Dutch' Hugo was to end the war as one of the RAF's top fighter pilots with 22 victories and a string of damaged.

The Shoreham Flight helped another high-ranker to be rescued on 26 May. Group Captain Richard Atcherley, one of the famous Atcherley twins who gave so much valuable service to the RAF, was the Station Commander of RAF Kenley. Although he was not required to fly, the RAF could never keep the Atcherley brothers on the ground for long, but on this day his Spitfire developed engine trouble over the English Channel and he ditched. Sergeant Tom Fletcher flew out to search for him, although at that time he only knew a Group Captain was in the water, but not who. He spotted him and directed a nearby trawler to his position, which effected a successful rescue.

Tom Fletcher

It is perhaps appropriate that Tom Fletcher is introduced to the reader at this time. He will be mentioned a good deal in this book. He was to become the most decorated ASR pilot and by the war's end held the record for people rescued.

Tom Fletcher was and is very much his own man, who tolerated no nonsense from either his contemporaries or his superiors, which on occasion got him into trouble. However, he was fortunate enough to have more than enough friends and admirers to get him off the various hooks on which he was caught from time to time, and whatever anyone thought of him, he was certainly a very courageous and successful rescue pilot. On one occasion he was even recommended for the Victoria Cross!

In a reserved occupation when the war began, he immediately tried to join the RAF. His single-minded way of doing things put the back up of the first recruiting sergeant he came up against. Tom wanted to be a fighter pilot and to join 43 Squadron. One can understand the sergeant's thoughts. Almost every young hopeful he interviewed wanted to be a fighter pilot, but as for assigning himself to one particular squadron even before he'd joined the RAF, well . . .

Tom Fletcher, however, had met some of 43 Squadron, and felt that if he was going to fight he may as well fight with them. It sounds hard to believe, but Tom eventually did become a fighter pilot, and his first posting was as a sergeant pilot – to No. 43 Squadron, RAF. Some time

later he had a run-in with his CO after a night-fighter sortie, which ended
with him being posted to 91 Squadron.

Now 91 was one of those unusual squadrons in Fighter Command.
Formed initially as No 421 Flight, its specific task was coastal patrols –
called *Jim Crow* sorties. It also had earlier flown over the northern coast
of France at the end of the Battle of Britain, to try and spot raids building
up which perhaps British radar had not picked up. Its role was ideal to
help on search and rescue sorties and to escort the Lysander and Walrus
aircraft of 277 Squadron.

Based at Hawkinge with 91, Tom immediately came into close contact
with the ASR boys of 277, whom he later joined. With 277 he was to
fly all their various types of aircraft and become the main Walrus pilot,
training and converting new pilots onto this type. All this, and he was
still a sergeant pilot. He did receive a promotion to flight sergeant, but
it was not long before he was back to sergeant again. The problem was
that while authority tried to 'keep him down' on the one hand, he was
getting the job done, and people kept decorating him!

★ ★ ★ ★ ★

It doesn't matter how you bring them in . . .

No 276 Squardron made its first successful Walrus rescue on 18 June
1942. A 58 Squadron Whitley V (Z9161/'A'), flown by Sergeant K.W.
Craig RCAF, took off at 3:20 a.m. to fly a convoy patrol south of Ireland.
Returning to his base at St Eval, Craig was instructed to divert to
Chivenor because of the weather. But he was now low on fuel and the
weather had forced him down to 100 ft above the sea, where the 'clag'
became even worse, so he reluctantly decided he must try for Chivenor
after all. However, his luck and his fuel ran out. First the port engine
stopped, and the Whitley didn't usually go far on one engine. Then the
second engine spluttered and died. Craig put the Whitley down onto
the water two miles off Bude, and he and his five crewmen climbed into
the dinghy.

Alerted by Group, 276 Squadron Walrus W3026 was Scrambled,
flown by Sergeant R.C. Yeates, with Flight Sergeant W. Smith and
Sergeant L.G. Badger as crew. They found the dinghy, landed and took
the six men aboard, but found they could not take off with the extra
weight. So Yeates turned the Walrus towards land and taxied it towards
the coast, reaching Bude at 2:25 p.m.

This episode demonstrates one of the drawbacks of the Walrus
operations; that although they could often land in poor conditions and
a roughish sea, a combination of sea and an aircraft full of crew and
survivors could easily make it impossible for the amphibian to take off
again. Whilst seen as a drawback by some, there were to be few
complaints from the men rescued from the sea. Almost anywhere was
better than in the wet and cold of a dinghy in the middle of the sea. At
least they were comparatively safe, in good hands and with hot soup or
coffee inside them, and some dry clothing.

As the war progressed, and aircraft became larger, necessitating bigger
crews, this problem was going to be on the increase. It was something the
Walrus men were going to have to live with, as indeed they did. And

because of it, a good many men lived. Nevertheless, as will be seen, it caused several interesting adventures.

★   ★   ★   ★   ★

A DFM in the morning, a dunking in the afternoon

From Group Captain to NCO pilot, it was all the same to 277 Squadron. On 1 June 1942, Martlesham signalled a successful pick up, Sergeants J.S.G. Arundel and Markey with Flight Sergeant N. Pickles being the crew of Walrus W2735.

Sergeant Ronnie Stillwell of 65 Squadron had been engaged on *Circus 179* that afternoon, 65 putting up eight Spitfires as part of the Debden Wing, who were acting as close escort to 12 Bostons bombing Flushing. They were safely escorted to and from the target without any interference from enemy fighters, although intense flak met them. Then on the return trip, Stillwell's Spitfire (P8789) developed engine trouble and it quickly became obvious that he was not going to get home, so he baled out some 40 miles from Flushing. Flying Officer G.R.G. Sarll circled around, watching Stillwell hit the sea and get into his dinghy, while he gave a Mayday call.

Stillwell hit the water at about 6:45 p.m., Arundel being Scrambled at 7 p.m., escorted by two Spitfires. At first all they found was a patch of oil, Sarll having had to fly home, but then a search located the dinghy. It was only Arundel's third sea landing, but he managed it successfully, taxied up to the dinghy and very soon Norman Pickles was hauling the Spitfire pilot in through the rear hatch, none the worse for his dunking.

It had been a busy day for Stillwell and 65 Squadron. That same morning, Stillwell had received a signal that he had been awarded the DFM. The squadron had then flown on *Circus 177* to Bruges, led by Wing Commander J.A.G. Gordon, a Canadian who had been badly burned in the Battle of Britain commanding 151 Squadron. South of the target the squadron had been attacked by 12 German fighters, and in a running fight to and across the coast they lost three pilots. The Wing Commander was heard to give a Mayday call, but failed to return, and his 'Number Two' was also lost. Pilot Officer J.R. Richards, in the same section, was shot down by a '190 and baled out into the sea, but was picked up by a Royal Navy launch.

Stillwell had been in his dinghy for two hours and after the Walrus landed at Martlesham, he spent the next 24 hours in bed, returning to his squadron on the 3rd. He later presented 277 with an engraved tankard for his safe rescue. Ronnie Stillwell went on to add a DFC to his DFM and become a Squadron Leader.

It had also been a busy day for 277 at Hawkinge, for that morning Flying Officer J.A. Spence and Sergeant Weston, in Lysander V9545, had found a fighter pilot south-east of Dover and guided a boat to him.

Martlesham were again involved on 3 June, and Shoreham had a success two days later. On the 3rd it was the Canadian, Sergeant Arundel, and Markey who were again involved, together with Sergeant Bunn.

The previous night, Flight Sergeants T.A. Gibbs and M.S.J. Waller had been the crew of an 85 Squadron Douglas Havoc, one of several Scrambled to intercept a night raid on Canterbury by a force of Dornier

217s. At about 2:30 a.m., they were pursued and attacked by an aircraft which Gibbs later reported he thought was a 'friendly', as Waller was telling him he was receiving Identification Friend or Foe signals (IFF, an automatic signal transmitted by RAF aircraft, especially at night, in order that friendly aircraft would not attack each other).

They were about nine miles north-east of North Foreland. At about 2:42 a.m., the resident naval officer at Burnham heard gunfire out at sea, and five minutes later a Havoc crashed five miles east of Foulness Point. At approximately the same time, the CO of 85 Squadron claimed to have shot down one of the raiders. The squadron claimed another as damaged.

Gibbs, his aircraft on fire, succeeded in baling out by standing up in his cockpit, opening the hatch and just rolling down the fuselage. Hitting the water, he inflated his dinghy and climbed in, but being uncertain as to his exact position, allowed two rescue launches that came near him to pass in case they were German.

At first light, two Havocs and two Hurricanes of 3 Squadron took off from Hunsdon to search for survivors of either the Havoc or the German bomber. At 5.15 a.m., Flight Lieutenant E. Tappin spotted one man in a dinghy off Foulness Point, and called in its position. Arundel and his crew (in W2735) were already airborne, flew to the spot, landed and picked up Sergeant Gibbs. A couple of hours later the body of Sergeant Waller was found at the mouth of the River Crouch.

And the Station Commander came too

A Walrus of 275 Squadron achieved another success on 26 June. Quite often, search and rescue sorties involved a number of different people. Everyone could sympathize with someone in the water. It could so easily be themselves, so most people wanted to help if they could. One day it might be them in the water, as indeed it proved to be in a few instances, as we shall see.

A Beaufighter of 456 (RAAF) Squadron had been Scrambled from Valley at 11:45 a.m. when a possible German raider was reported over the Irish Sea. Orbiting at 3,000 ft, Pilot Officer P.A. Dey spotted a Ju 88 flying 50 ft below him, going from right to left, in a westerly direction. Dey set off in pursuit and was about to open fire when the '88's rear gunner got in a burst, hitting the 'Beau' (T3014) in the port wing and engine. Dey replied with two bursts but saw no strikes and had just broken away in order for his navigator, Sergeant E.W. Mitchell, to reload the guns, when petrol began to pour into the cockpit and fuselage from a severed fuel pipe. Then the port engine stopped. Dey now found his hydraulics had also been damaged and as he was rapidly losing height knew he would have to ditch.

In the following crash-landing, Mitchell was injured, receiving a scalp wound and two broken ribs, but both men climbed out of their respective hatches and got into the pilot's K-type dinghy as Mitchell's dinghy failed to open. The 'Beau' floated for just about two minutes, but it was time enough for the two men to extricate themselves.

With an emergency call made, 275 Squadron Scrambled a Lysander, while the Station Commander at RAF Valley, Wing Commander Walter

Churchill DSO, DFC, took off in a Spitfire to help and 456 Squadron sent out Sergeant G.F. Gatenby and Sergeant Melrose in a Beaufighter.

Sergeant Lee was in the Lysander but it was the Wing Commander who spotted the dinghy and radioed its position. Soon the Lysander, 'Beau' and Spitfire were circling the men, Lee remaining over them until Pilot Officer R.W.V. Jessett and Flight Sergeant Bryan turned up in a Walrus. A landing was difficult as there was a three- to four-foot swell, but Jessett managed it, got the two men aboard and returned to base at 3:10 p.m., where Churchill welcomed them back.

Chapter Three

Prime Position Squadron

Having introduced the reader to the early beginnings of the ASR Walrus squadrons in the UK, we will now select and record in some detail just some of the rescues which they carried out. The main rescues of each of the ASR squadrons are listed in the Appendices at the end of the book.

It must be borne in mind, however, that the list records just the rescues where the Walrus aircraft played a major part. There are just as many rescues where the Walrus crews were active in either directing HSLs, Royal Navy vessels or other surface craft to the scene of a subsequently successful rescue. These counted just as much as if the Walrus crew themselves had landed and picked up the men. Often there were good reasons for them not to land, but they still shared in the credit for lives saved.

★ ★ ★ ★ ★

No 277 Squadron – *Quaerendo Servamus* (We Save by Seeking)

As we shall see, 277 had what might be regarded as the Prime Position for rescue work, being based at, initially, three airfields which covered the whole area of this busy corner of wartime England: Martlesham, Hawkinge and Shoreham.

All the Walrus squadrons were now beginning to become firmly established and each week brought new experience to their growing skills. There was also a new aircraft.

While the Luftwaffe had interfered little with the squadrons' activities, there was always the danger that they might suddenly do so. While the Lysander was armed, its light defensive armament of one or perhaps two .303 in machine-guns which could be fired from the rear cockpit, would be no real match for an Me 109 or FW 190. There was, however, another aeroplane available, but like the Lysander, it was a cast-off, due to its lack of success in its primary designated role.

The Boulton-Paul Defiant had been designed and built as a two-seat fighter, with a power-operated turret behind the cockpit, in which was mounted four .303 in machine-guns. It was a single-engined, low-wing monoplane, and had in its early encounters with German aircraft been mistaken for a Hurricane. Once the German fighter pilots became more familiar with it, the Defiant, following its initial success, became easy meat for the enemy. Lacking any forward firing armament – a thoughtless omission – the Defiant was subsequently relegated to night-fighting. But it was also obsolete in this role because to be successful at night, one really needed airborne radar, and there was no possibility of radar being carried in the Defiant.

Therefore, Defiants began to be issued to training units and the ASR squadrons, where in the latter they were to be used in both search and escort duties. One of the first to arrive at 277 Squadron was V1117, and this aircraft was involved in the next two rescues – of 277 aircrew!

On the afternoon of 12 July, at Martlesham, Flight Lieutenant A.S. Linney was scheduled to have instruction on flying the Walrus – in this case, W3077 – off Brightlingsea. There were two visiting officers, Flight Lieutenant Gregson and Pilot Officer B.C. Middleton of 124 Squadron, who went along for the ride. Flight Sergeant T.M. Ormiston was at the controls. Meanwhile, Flying Officer Carrillo was air testing the Defiant and saw the Walrus fall into the sea from 20 ft and sink. Carrillo called for help and three of the four men were rescued, but Middleton was drowned.

The first defiant-assisted rescue

The first recorded success of a Defiant in its search role came on 21 July 1942, but oddly, this too was the rescue of one of its own.

On this day, Flight Sergeant Tom Fletcher took off in Walrus W2736 with Sergeant Weston, taking a new pilot, Flight Sergeant P.K. Marsden, for some dual instruction and sea landings. On one take-off, however, the Walrus ran into trouble, a float came off and the seaplane nosed in. Tom Fletcher recalls:

We had made just the one landing and on trying to get off again, the port wheel came down. The wheels on the Walrus came up into the well under the wing, and on the hub there was a fitting which clipped into a spring-loaded catch. These catches, screwed into a wooden section, would perhaps get a bit wet, etc. What must have happened was that the catch gave and the wheel came down. When one pumped the wheels up, the pressure used to decrease gradually. Therefore, what we used to do as we flew along was to give the wheels a couple of pumps now and again, to keep this pressure up and keep the weight off the catches.

So the wheel came down as we were taking off, slewed us round and the float dug in and was torn off. The wing-tip broke and filled with water, and we hadn't the weight to put on the other wing to lift it up. Consequently, we had to get out of it!

I was the only one with my own dinghy, so I told the other two to get on top of the aircraft. I thought Weston would have taken the aircraft dinghy with him, but he didn't. When I saw we had only one personal dinghy and knew that wouldn't be enough for the three of us, I slid my side windows to and yelled to them that I was going back to get the other dinghy. Meantime, the Walrus was slowly turning over.

I grabbed the crew dinghy and when I got back to the pilot's seat with it, the top of the roof was under water, so I couldn't slide the hood back. I opened the one side window which wasn't yet under the water and pushed the dinghy pack out, then started clawing out myself. But Weston started to pull the canopy back in an effort to help me, which it didn't, and I had to yell at him, otherwise I'd have had it.

Nobody knew we were missing, of course, and it took some time for base to realize something had happened. But I think someone on shore might have seen it. Anyway, the HSL from Newhaven and one from Littlehampton were alerted. Littlehampton was the nearest, and all I can remember was these two bows coming straight at us – they seemed to be having a race to see which could get to us first! However, both chopped their throttles and it was Flight Sergeant Rogers from Littlehampton that got to us.

Flight Sergeant T. Fletcher, No 277 Squadron

The squadron had also sent out one of its Defiants (V1117), flown by Warrant Officer A.K. Saunders, from New Zealand, and Sergeant L.H. Healey. They located the dinghies and helped to guide the HSLs to them. Another 'first' was for the Littlehampton boat, for this was their first crash call, and *No 442*, which was in fact a Seaplane Tender, was able to notch up its first rescue.

Len Healey, in the Defiant's gun turret, was later to be crewed more or less permanently with Tom Fletcher, and they made a winning team. Len had earlier been an air gunner, flying in Defiants with 153 Squadron, being posted to 277 in June 1942. He had been involved in a crash in a Defiant in September 1941 when his squadron was in Scotland. He and his pilot had been chasing a German bomber, ran out of fuel and crashed. Len's right eye was pushed out onto his cheek in the crash, and when a local lady arrived and tried to take charge of 'her' casualties, who had been taken to a farmhouse, she took one look at Len and his eye and promptly fainted!

Len eventually went to a rehabilitation centre at Chester where he shared a room with Sergeant George Mason, a fighter pilot who had broken a leg in a crash. They had three weeks of comparatively luxurious care from the people of Chester. The two men were destined to meet each other again in very different circumstances.

Having recovered – with both eyes intact – Len had been posted back to the squadron but was reluctant to fly in Defiants, so he ended up being posted to 277, who needed air gunners for their ASR work. He was equally reluctant to fly in the Defiants that were now arriving for 277. Walruses and Lysanders were alright, but not the Defiants.

The Flight Commander was a bit anxious about this, for all his men had to be proficient on all three types to be effective. Tom Fletcher, knowing that unless Healey got over this problem he was likely to be posted elsewhere, talked him into flying with him in a Defiant. Len trusted Tom as a pilot, so agreed, and although never liking it, he did fly in the Defiant when he had to. He was in one with Keith 'Kiwi' Saunders on the day they helped rescue Tom Fletcher and the others:

'Kiwi' Saunders, who I also flew with on several occasions, had a slight speech impediment. Our call-sign was *Dencot* and every time I flew with

'Kiwi', I heard him call the Control Tower that we were airborne, but it always came out as, 'D . . . D . . . D . . . D . . . – Oh, fuck it, I'm airborne!' After that, he was always known as 'Fuck it, I'm airborne.' by the Ops Room.

Sergeant L.H. Healey, No 277 Squadron

★   ★   ★   ★   ★

The Germans react

There must have been something about Defiant V1117. On the 12th it had seen a Walrus crash; on the 21st it had searched and found the crew of another downed Walrus; then on 25 July . . .

It was a Saturday, and at Martlesham, Flight Sergeant Arundel and Sergeant Bunn took off at 1:05 p.m. in V1117, escorted by two Spitfires, to fly towards Dunkirk where a pilot was reported to be in the 'drink'. The escort was provided by Pilot Officer J.F. Stokes and Flight Sergeant A.C. Kelly of 416 (RCAF) Squadron. This was the third search of the area for the missing pilot. By now the Germans must have been more than suspicious of all the activity, and reacted.

Within sight of the French coast, the three British aircraft were attacked by six FW 190s. John Stokes' Spitfire was hit and went into the sea. As he fought a couple of the '190s, Kelly saw the Defiant shot down, hit the water and blow up. He quickly broke off and headed for England. John Arundel, William Bunn and Stokes were all killed.

The German fighters were from the 9th Staffel of JG26. Unteroffizier Boerner shot down the Defiant for his first victory, while two Spitfires were claimed, one by Oberleutnant Kurt Ruppert, his nineteenth kill, and one by Unteroffizier Edgar Doerre for his first.

The Germans reacted again to a search mission on 12 August, the Shoreham Flight being involved this time. Warrant Officer N. W. Peat, a Canadian, and Flight Sergeant G.G. Wirdnam were in Lysander V9545, having been sent out by Tangmere 30 miles off the south coast where a Hurricane pilot was believed to be in the sea.

They found nothing, but then the Controller warned them of bandits and to head for England. They did so and were about six miles off Littlehampton at about 50 ft when they spotted two FW 190s at 1,000 ft, approaching from the east in line abreast. They dived on the 'Lizzie', making a head-on attack. Norman Peat went into some pretty violent manoeuvres, including several steep 'S' turns, then the '190s separated and began making attacks from opposite sides. The Lysander was hit in the fuselage and tail, Peat now having dived the aircraft down to sea level.

The Focke-Wulfs came in again, this time in line astern, the leader opening fire with cannon at 800 yds. From the rear cockpit, Wirdnam was able to get in a burst at about 60 yds as the '190 banked to starboard. With the underbelly of the '190 plainly in his sights, Wirdnam saw his bullets entering the fighter's wing root and cockpit area. Then he turned his attention to the second '190 which was about 300 yds dead astern. A two-second burst deterred the fighter from coming closer than 200 yds, and then, during the next bit of evasive action, Wirdnam saw a splash and much foam off to the port quarter, where the first '190 would have been. The second '190 now turned and flew off. Wirdnam was credited with a 'probable'.

The other side of the coin

Lest the reader thinks that success was assured once the ASR service got into action, we can record here one of those rescues, and there were to be many, that was not crowned with a successful pick-up. It concerns the first rescue of Pilot Officer W.A. Land of 278 Squadron. Bill Land (usually known as George) had been a fighter pilot, firstly with 504 Squadron and later with 601. It was with 601 that he got his 'new' name, as there were two Bills in the squadron, so he was given George to live with. Following a bad crash in an Airacobra, he joined 278, but on 10 August 1942, with Flight Sergeant C.Hogan in L2268 . . .

We were ordered to search a position 120 degrees, 78 miles from Coltishall for a missing Mosquito. Wreckage was subsequently found covering an extensive area. It consisted of thousands of small pieces of floating wood which I decided was balsa-wood and thus the remains of the missing aircraft. I saw, too, a patch of green fluorescene dye, and between the crests of the waves, caught a glimpse of someone floating in a Mae West.

I had to land some distance from the centre of the area to avoid the wreckage and located the green patch. Unfortunately we only found a floating body in the Mae West, clad in a leather Irvine flying jacket. I lowered the undercarriage and also put out two drogues to reduce the taxying speed. Leaving the cockpit, I helped Paddy Hogan assemble a portable winch which we attached to the Scarff ring of the former 'midships gun position, aft of the trailing-edge of the wing. With the engine just idling in a seven-foot swell, we managed to get a harness on the body. Paddy wound the winch to lift it whilst I tried to swing it into the aircraft.

However, the weight of the soaked flying clothing and the man's severe injuries, which must have occurred on impact with the sea, plus the swell, made our task impossible. After several attempts we were forced to give up.

Among the paraphernalia carried in our aircraft were some spherical hollow glass balls joined by a rope, which were used as buoys for keeping fishing trawling nets afloat. We attached a number of these to the body to ensure it would not sink. I then pumped the undercarriage up, took off and circled the position until the eventual arrival of an HSL. I dropped a smoke float and then returned to base.

We were both emotionally disturbed by our experience and after landing, Paddy took me to the Sergeants' Mess where he persuaded the Mess Steward, although it was mid-morning, to provide us with some very large, free whiskies.

I ascertained later that *HSL 124* recovered the body and that the airman (of 151 Squadron) was buried with full military honours. This gave us some satisfaction in that one of our boys had been returned for a proper Christian burial.

Pilot Officer W.A. Land, No 278 Squadron

★   ★   ★   ★   ★

Dieppe – Operation 'Jubilee'

All three of 277's Flights were briefed for a major operation for 19 August, and both the Shoreham and Hawkinge Flights were on 'Top Line' before dawn. The major 'Op' was the Canadian raid on the French coastal port and town of Dieppe.

The Dieppe raid has gone down in history as one of the bitterest day's fighting in the Second World War, and for the RAF one of its greatest and most intense air battles. From first light till dusk, squadron upon squadron of fighters, fighter-bombers and light bombers flew to and from the port. Over 100 Allied aircraft were lost and 50 German fighters and bombers were shot down. With the planned effort, Fighter Command knew there would be casualties and knew too that the Air-Sea Rescue Service would have their work cut out.

At Hawkinge, 'Top Line' was called for 4:30 a.m., the Flight having been briefed the previous evening by the French CO of 91 Squadron, Squadron Leader Jean Demozay. They knew that the first RAF aircraft would be hitting the gun emplacements on the Dieppe headlands at first light and laying smoke as the Canadian troops went ashore in their landing craft. At 9:00 a.m., David Waddington and Flight Sergeant L.A. Johnson were Scrambled to search 30 miles out to sea, but they only found an oil patch and a drifting, but empty, parachute. Next off were Warrant Officer R. Knowlton and Flight Sergeant J. Rose, who found a dinghy to which they directed an HSL which picked up Sergeant C.H. Evans of 91 Squadron who had baled out when his Spitfire's engine packed up. Waddington and 'Sticky' Glew were out before midday, saw a Spitfire crash, but found no sign of its pilot.

In the early afternoon, Flight Lieutenant Johnny Spence RCAF and Flight Sergeant H.W. Bruck-Horst were Scrambled, but only found wreckage – no pilot. Then they too saw a Spitfire crash, investigated, but only found oil, which is all that Waddington and Glew found on their next patrol. Others on patrol also were only rewarded with oil patches, no survivors.

The Shoreham Flight had early 'customers'. Tom Fletcher and Len Healey were Scrambled when a Boston was reported shot down in flames off Worthing, followed shortly after by a report that a Spitfire or a Hurricane had collided during a dogfight off Worthing.

The Boston was from 418 (RCAF) Squadron, and was in difficulty after take-off as its wheels would not retract – their locking pins had not been removed! The crew had hoped they could be pulled up over the Channel, but they eventually had to abort their mission. Two early FW 190s, roaming around trying to see what was going on, spotted the luckless Boston off Shoreham and shot it down. At about the same time, the French CO of 174 Squadron, Squadron Leader Emile Fayolle DFC, returning from his first sortie to Dieppe, probably ran into the two '190s. Exactly what occurred is uncertain, but he was lost. Whether he was shot down or the Hurricane collided with a '190, is not clear. There was also a suggestion, made by onlookers, that the Frenchman rammed the '190.

However, Fletcher and Healey in Walrus X9526 found some men in a dinghy and directed a nearby HSL to them, but a search for the fighter pilots proved fruitless. Tom Fletcher, of course, usually operated from Hawkinge, not Shoreham. He remembers:

I did three trips on the 19th. Len and I were crewed-up for the day and we had a roster of time on and time off. Each time we were 'on', or about to come off duty, the 'phone would ring. We went off at first light and the Boston crew never made Dieppe. The crew was picked up by an HSL from Littlehampton.

With our wives, Len and I had rented a little bungalow at Lancing, so each time we came back we flew over it to let them know we were safe.

Flight Sergeant T. Fletcher, No 277 Squadron

We were informed that a Boston crew had crashed into the sea. We made a search and finally found them, and it appeared that they had had quite a bit of trouble. As soon as their aircraft had hit the water it had broken into two pieces. The forward portion rolled over and sank with the pilot and navigator trapped inside. Somehow or other, they were torn free and both floated to the surface.

Fifteen yards away the nav was in great peril, with the shrouds of his parachute wrapped around his neck, pulling his head under water. He had been wounded, too. [The gunner swam to the pilot and got him into a dinghy, then went to the navigator.] The air gunner swam to the navigator and having blown up his Mae West, found his dinghy had been torn and would not inflate. By this time both the pilot and navigator were conscious. The gunner then struggled to get the navigator to the pilot's dinghy and having succeeded, told them to hang on. The shore was only a short distance away so he decided to swim for it, but he had only gone a few yards when we appeared, so he decided to remain with his two companions. For nearly an hour they clung together until a rescue launch, which we had notified base was required, picked them up and brought them back.

Sergeant L.R. Healey, No 277 Squadron

All three men, Sergeant W.L. Buchanan, Pilot Officer P.C. McGillicuddy, and Sergeant Clarence G. Scott, who received the DFM for his courage in helping to save his two fellow crew members, survived.

Several Lysander and Defiant trips were flown from Shoreham, but again it was a case of oil patches, empty parachutes or empty dinghies. Flight Sergeant R. Holland and Sergeant Les Seales located a pilot in a half-inflated dinghy, so they dropped another dinghy, a smoke float and then called for a launch. They then had to return due to their fuel running low, but a launch did rescue the pilot, Sergeant F.H. Tyrell of 111 Squadron. This launch was later strafed by German fighters but Tyrell got home, although some of the boat's crew were wounded. Les 'Dizzy' Seales, recalls:

I flew two sorties with Bobby Holland that day. We took a Defiant rather than a Walrus as it was felt there would be too much activity over there. It was felt too that landing would be a bit dicey, so our task was to locate people and then wait for the boats to pick them up.

Sergeant L.H. Seales, No 277 Squadron

As the day progressed and the convoy of ships was returning from Dieppe, so the air battles concentrated over the Channel, and a number of aggressive German fighter pilots flew right to the English coast. Pilot

Officers R.F. Harris and J.D. Adamson, in Defiant AA312, were on a search south of Beachey Head when they found themselves right in the middle of a dogfight.

There were about 80 RAF and German fighters all milling about, and seeing the Defiant, two FW 190s broke away and dived after it. Harris began evasive action, but then Adamson called that two Spitfires had engaged the '190s. Harris then saw an Me 109 attacking a small boat so flew towards it at sea level, but the '109 pilot saw him and climbed up behind the Defiant. More evasive action followed, with shells zipping over the Defiant's wing, but Adamson was calling for Harris to hold the aircraft steady so he could get in a shot.

Harris did as he was asked and heard the rattle of the four .303s behind him, while shells from the German fighter churned up the sea ahead of them. Adamson's fire seemed to score hits on the '109 which pulled up and away into some cloud, leaving a grey vapour trail behind it.

These two men must have impressed someone, for a short while later, when more German fighters were over the south coast, chasing back the last of the raiding force, they were sent up in their Defiant – as aerodrome defence!

Several RAF personnel were rescued that day, all by rescue launches, but 277 Squadron had played their part, even though only a few men had been helped to the safety of the HSLs. Flying in a large battle area in slow and mostly unarmed aircraft was not the best of places to be.

Chapter Four

We'll Meet Again

'Is that you, George? It's me, Len!'
After the excitement of Dieppe, 277 Squadron's three Flights settled down to the more routine search and rescue sorties. That they were in the 'prime area' is confirmed by the fact that over the next few months, it was they who saw the bulk of the 'action'.

Meantime, 277 Squadron had a new CO in mid-August 1942, when Squadron Leader A.S. Linney took command. Tony Linney had been with 229 (Fighter) Squadron in 1940, was shot down over Dunkirk, flew with the squadron in the Battle of Britain and in 1941 had been an MSFU pilot.

All the ASR squadrons were involved in rescues, but mostly guiding HSLs to men in the water rather than direct rescue by Walrus. However, on 5 September, Len Healey, gunner to Flight Sergeant J.L. Barber, made a rescue in the early evening, flying Walrus W3076.

The American Eighth Air Force had mounted a raid (*Circus 214*) with 36 B-17 Flying Fortresses the previous day, to the marshalling yards at Rouen. Spitfires of 64 Squadron, led by Squadron Leader F.A.O. Gaze, were part of the Hornchurch Wing flying a Diversionary Sweep over the Somme Estuary, their task being to divert enemy fighters away from the main attacking formation. In this they succeeded only too well.

The Wing was intercepted by a number of FW 190s, and 340 (Free French) Squadron lost four Spitfires and claimed two '190s in the battle. 64 Squadron were also engaged, losing two themselves. Flight Sergeant George Mason saw his Section Leader and Flight Commander, Flight Lieutenant Chenery Thomas DFC, shoot down a '190, but then saw him heading out to sea, glycol streaming from his Spitfire. Mason, who had been wingman to 'Tommy' for the last 19 Ops, tried to escort him, but he was then 'bounced' by more enemy fighters. George was hit and with a damaged radiator he was soon forced to bale out, landing in the sea just 10 miles off Dieppe. He recalls:

The omens for *Circus 214* were not good as far as the 'Fighting 64th' were concerned. A new CO had recently replaced the old chief – a highly respected leader who had nursed the squadron through the early days of their tour of operations and had led them with such success that their kill-to-loss ratio was the best in the Command; so much so that we had been selected as the first unit to receive the new Spitfire IX. The new CO wanted to introduce new tactics, so for a while we lost our cohesion. So *Circus 214* was flown at a bad time for the squadron.

It started bad for me as that day I missed my breakfast, and then my kite (BR602/SH-G), cherished by a rigger called Lawrence, was in for inspection and I had to fly SH-E (BR980). I had flown her on my previous Op too and decided she was a cow, not in the same class as my 'G for George'. The only ray of sunshine was that I was flying for the eighteenth consecutive time as 'Number Two' to my Flight Commander, Tommy Thomas, whom I trusted and admired, having been in several combats with him.

We were to escort 12 USAAF B-17s to bomb a target near Rouen, a deep penetration for Spitfires in those days when we only carried a 30-gallon drop tank. The Spitfire IX had a second-stage supercharger which cut in above 20,000 feet, and my third misfortune occurred when mine failed to do so. However, after some fiddling with the manual override switch, by which time we had reached 25,000 feet, it was working.

As Rouen was approached, the well-modulated actor's tones of Ronald Adam, the Hornchurch Sector Controller, warned that there were 20-plus 'Huns' over Rouen above 20,000 feet. There was a thin layer of cloud about 26,000 feet and as the 'Huns' were nowhere to be seen, they had to be above the cloud. As the B-17s turned after the bombing, two FW 190s were spotted just below the edge of the cloud. Tommy's section was despatched to deal with them, Tommy taking on the '190 on the left as he ordered me to take the other. Our other pair were to cover us.

We all knew what to expect. The rest of the 'Huns' had to be above the cloud, waiting to pounce, but we all hoped we could get the two '190s and then use our superior climbing performance to clamber up out of trouble. All except me, of course, because my second-stage supercharger cut out when I opened the throttle for the chase. Because of the 'dicky' engine, I was still out of range when Tommy opened fire. The result was spectacular, because Tommy had just had his guns' point harmonized at 300 yards, with a higher than usual proportion of HE as opposed to ball ammo. Tommy naturally wanted to draw attention to the result, which he did, over the RT, at which moment the remainder of the 20-plus FW 190s pounced on us.

Nobody could warn Tommy because he was transmitting. His aircraft was hit immediately. Glycol vapour poured from both radiators and he stopped transmitting. He must have been hit himself, as he carried on straight and level as though nothing had happened. Meanwhile, my target had taken the standard FW 190 evasive action (stick forward with full aileron) which was impossible to follow, and being too close to Tommy's attacker to turn into it, I rolled up to the left to try and come out behind it, but before completing the manoeuvre I was myself attacked. My only hope of escape was downwards, but I could not throw off the '190. My Spitfire sustained several hits and the engine finally gave up the ghost. It was time to leave.

I wound the trim fully forward while holding the stick back. I undid my straps and jettisoned the hood. Bullets were hitting the wings as I released the stick, to be catapulted out of the cockpit by the negative *g*. I delayed pulling the ripcord as long as I dared, in the hope of avoiding being shot up during the descent. A new range of troubles awaited me as I hit the water before I had time to release the parachute. A 30-knot wind dragged me over, under and through some pretty wild waves and I became entangled in the shrouds. Grabbing my knife from my boot top, I began cutting frantically. Free from the 'chute, I was about to inflate the dinghy when a pair of FW 190s flew overhead. My Mae West was keeping my head more above the water than below, so I waited while they circled around. After a while, the sound of their engines died away.

It was now time to inflate the dinghy. Turn the valve on the compressed air bottle – jammed solid – not a bit like dinghy drill in the baths – far too much water about. Think, think . . . think! Clot! – the split-pin, pull out the split-pin – panic over, thar' she blows! Now to get aboard, again not a bit like the pool – sodding great waves – don't fight them, you can't win, use them to help you aboard – that's better – peace at last.

I now found that in my frantic but life-saving knifework, I had cut off the pack containing the first aid kit, rations and, most important, the fluorescene. That was a real blow because I was confident that our second section would have called a Mayday when Tommy was hit, and I thought someone would be out looking for us in an hour or so. But in this sea I was not going to be easy to spot without a trail of fluorescene.

Sure enough, about an hour later, four Spitfires from 122 Squadron flew over me at low level, but despite my frantic waving they failed to see me. They didn't come back either, so I was left to my own devices.

Well, fair stood the wind for England, all 30 knots of it. If it kept up I could be home in a couple of days. I had a bar of chocolate and some Horlick's tablets in my pocket; I could last out the journey on that, but water was a problem. I tried to keep my mind from thirst and took enough exercise to keep the circulation going, then began reciting poetry. Everything that came to mind seemed to be about the sea – *The Ancient Mariner*, *The Revenge*, *The Tempest*, the Agincourt speech . . . so the day wore on.

I was tired by nightfall. Tired of poetry, tired of sloshing about in the waves and just plain tired. I fell asleep, to be awoken by rain, glorious rain. It lasted long enough for me to save a small cupful, which was better than a pint of 'wallop' any day! When the skies cleared I soon realized the wind had changed, veering round to the north-west.

This meant the abandonment of the plan of a cross-channel passage and the best hope was a landfall on the French coast, hopefully not too close to Dieppe. Throughout the night and the next morning I paddled more or less with the wind but across the waves, which were quite steep, about six feet from trough to crest. By noon I had a diving bird for company, swimming round and round the dinghy, just out of reach, and soon afterwards traces of seaweed appeared. Thinking I must be near the shore I began to back-paddle in the hope of delaying my arrival till after it was dark.

Suddenly I heard the sound of engines. Twelve Bostons, with USAAF markings, thundered overhead at low level, followed by escorting fighters, also USAAF. I nearly fell out of my dinghy, waving and yelling, but they took no notice. My alliance with the US came to an abrupt end.

Then a Polish squadron of Spitfires brought up the rear and detached a pair who began circling the dinghy. I could almost hear them calling Mayday! My joy was boundless, but then I looked again at the height of the waves and strong, gusting wind. No one but no one, could put a Walrus down on this sea. So it would have to be a boat, and by the time that arrived I might well be ashore. I knew it was close as I had seen the flak going up as the Bostons coasted in.

Suddenly I heard another aircraft approaching and a Walrus appeared, circled the dinghy and alighted downwind. So steep were the waves that the hull of the Walrus completely disappeared in the troughs, and it seemed to be about to sink. But by skilful handling the pilot kept her positioned so that the dinghy drifted right up to the hatch, and I was hauled aboard by the hands of Len Healey, the Walrus gunner.

Len was bothered because he could not secure the dinghy as well. I was quite glad to see the last of it, but Len was quite right because if the dinghy was sighted again it could have led to an unnecessary rescue sortie being mounted.

By one of those odd coincidences of war, Len and I knew each other quite well, having been in convalescent hospital together the previous year. Len was recovering from an accident in a Defiant and I from an encounter with a minefield at Walmer after a disastrous engagement with a group of Me 109s over St Omer. After making sure I was OK, Len went forward to tell his pilot. The engine roared and there was much buffeting and bashing of the hull as the Walrus gathered speed. But the waves were too much for it and the pilot abandoned the take-off to prevent the aircraft from sinking. Len came back with a long face and told me that they may have to beach. Then the shell-fire began to arrive. No direct hits but close enough. This fortunately coincided with a bit of a lull and the pilot seized the opportunity and took off, but not without ripping large sections from the bottom of the hull.

All this time we had been sitting in the middle of a minefield, a fact well known to the crew as they had narrowly avoided one mine when setting down and had taxied around another en route for my dinghy. So my rescue was a pretty gallant act indeed, alighting in a minefield only three or four miles from the shore, under gunfire, for which the pilot, Flight Sergeant Johnnie Barber, was awarded the DFM.

The flight back to Shoreham from Dieppe was uneventful, but for me it was the best flight ever! When I got back to Hornchurch, I found that my 'G for George' had been shot down over Belgium while I was paddling around in the dinghy.

Flight Sergeant G.A. Mason, No 64 Squadron

Barber and Healey had been on 'Top Line', and had been Scrambled at 5.30 p.m. to pick up Mason, only to find the sea very rough indeed off the French coast. Nevertheless, Barber made a landing and Healey pulled Mason aboard.

We were notified that a Spitfire pilot was down in the sea, slap in the middle of a minefield. Johnny Barber and I flew out. I remember it was a lovely afternoon – the French coast was bathed in sunshine, really beautiful. We circled and circled and finally spotted the man in the water, but right in the middle of three lines of mines. It was then that Johnny said we were going down, but that he wasn't sure how we were going to get off again!

We landed and taxied very carefully down between two lines of mines. By now the pilot, having seen us coming down, had started paddling towards us. We finally got the man in the back and Johnny had now to take off.

He continued down the lane and gingerly opened the throttle, but it was no go. Then coastal gunfire began falling near us so Johnny tried again and away we went. Unfortunately the lanes of mines curved round at the end and Johnny had to leap-frog the Walrus over them in order to get us clear. We finally became airborne and it was then that I recognized our survivor as George Mason, the same pilot with whom I had shared a room at the rehabilitation centre in Chester. 'Is that you, George?' I said. 'Yes, is that you Len?'

I didn't see him again for several years, but we met in Egypt after he war, where we had a few drinks and talked over old times.

Sergeant L.R. Healey, No 277 Squadron

I was told there was a pilot in a dinghy just off the French coast, so I was ordered to Scramble in a Walrus. I flew up and down near the French coast for about 10 minutes until I spotted a Spitfire circling, and then I saw the yellow of the dinghy. I dived down, and although the sea was very rough for landing I decided we'd better risk it as we were so near the coast.

We managed it and dragged the pilot through the roof of the aircraft. The worse job was taking off. The wind was coming straight out of the sun and I had to take off into it, with the light glaring in my eyes. At least we had no interference from enemy aircraft.

After the third attempt to rise, I opened the throttle, hung on like grim death and we bounced off wave after wave for about half a mile until, after much heaving on the control column, the Walrus lifted and we set off home. I must admit I was relieved when we landed.

Flight Sergeant J.L. Barber, No 277 Squadron

George Mason was commissioned about this time, continued to fly with 64 Squadron and later with 222 and 129 Squadrons. He received the DFC and an American DFC, but was shot down again in 1943 to become a prisoner of war. He eventually retired from the RAF as an Air Commodore.

For his part in the rescue, Johnny Barber did indeed receive the DFM before the month was out, and was commissioned. It was one of five DFMs awarded to NCO's of 277 in the autumn of 1942, one going to Rowland 'Sticky' Glew. Glew had flown in Lysanders during the Battle of France, and by this time had been involved in the rescue of 17 men with 277. The other three went to Len Healey, Tommy Fletcher and Johnnie Snell.

By mid-September, 91 and 277 Squadrons had been responsible for about 100 men being saved from the sea. At this stage most had been picked up by HSLs, but the Walrus rescues were now on the increase, and as the skills of the Walrus crews increased, so too did the number of rescues.

Not you again!

October 1942 began with more excitement. On the 2nd, a No 2 Group *Circus* operation (*Circus 221*) over St Omer involved the Spitfires of 616 Squadron, as part of the Tangmere Wing. They were escorting six B-17s against Longavesnes aerodrome, in company with 124 Squadron, while No 1 Squadron, with Spitfire IXs, flew top cover and three squadrons of American P-38 Lightnings flew support.

The bombs were seen clearly over the target, causing a huge pall of smoke to rise 10,000 ft into the air. The bombers were lost for a moment in the turn away but generally were kept in sight. After bombing, 30-plus FW 190s were seen well below and White Section of 616 Squadron sent two Spitfires down on a gaggle of 12 '190s 6,000 feet below, Squadron Leader H.L.I. Brown DFC, leading the squadron, being unable to see them. Pilot Officer R.G. Large and his wingman, Flight Sergeant M.H.F. Cooper, winged over and when about 800 yds away from the '190s, they broke in all directions. Large closed in behind one straggler, opening fire from 500 yds, but he lost sight of the '190 in a turn as he pulled his nose up in order to get in a long-range shot. When next seen, the '190 was diving steeply with one wheel hanging down, pouring brown smoke. Some bright flashes were coming from its engine cowling which later developed into flames.

Now both Spitfires were heavily engaged with the rest of the '190s, Large firing at one fighter which came at him head-on. Then both he and Cooper, who had flown up beside him, made for the coast. They headed out by Cap Gris Nez, being attacked by '190s all the way, and over the coast Large warned Cooper of a fighter below, ordering him to make a break. However, Cooper was hit in the radiator, but did not realize how seriously until Large called to say he was streaming glycol.

Focke-Wulfs were still attacking as the two Spitfires flew out over the Channel, but it was obvious Cooper wasn't going to make England. He finally had to bale out into the Channel. But at least the '190s now began to leave, allowing Large to circle his 'Number Two', giving a Mayday, but then he had to leave when his petrol ran low, subsequently landing at Hawkinge.

With the emergency call relayed to Hawkinge, a Lysander was Scrambled, crewed by Sergeant P.C. Standen and Flight Sergeant J.B. Snell, with a Spitfire escort, but although they searched the mid-Channel area, they saw no sign of anyone in the water. They were joined by Sergeant W.E. Uptigrove and Flight Sergeant L. Johnson in Lysander V9583, who also found nothing; but then, shortly after Standen and Snell had had to return, the second Lysander crew were told to fly to another spot where a Spitfire was orbiting a dinghy. In fact, Pilot Officer Large had refuelled at Hawkinge and knowing exactly where Cooper was, had flown back out to the spot and was circling and radioing his position. Uptigrove arrived and took over the orbit, while back at Hawkinge a Walrus was Scrambled, with Tom Fletcher at the controls and Len Healey and Flight Sergeant T. Roberts in the back.

Fletcher did not see the Lysander until they were 28 miles out from the English coast, but when he did he then saw the dinghy and proceeded to drop a smoke float to keep the man in sight and also to get the wind direction. Cooper was about four miles to the north of Calais and, as Tom Fletcher recalls, not in the best spot!

We went over and found he was in a minefield. The Navy, we heard, refused to go as they had no definite idea where the minefield was although they knew it was somewhere there. The Navy also controlled the HSLs, and wouldn't let them go either. I went up from Shoreham to Hawkinge and was told that the Navy said there was definitely a minefield there and what did I think about it? I decided to go, but was told that if I could not see the minefield, to come back. We went, myself, Len Healey and Roberts, a New Zealander.

We had quite an escort and they had a nice little battle with the 'Jerries' above us while we were below. When we got there we could see three lines – the wash – of mines, just breaking the surface. There were several lines of these little 'vees', about 400 to 500 yards apart. We had a quick look, assessed the situation, then we were going down.

I landed, went straight up to the dinghy, Len hooked it and fed the line down to the rear hatch, just as the shore batteries began firing at us. [On the first attempt, Cooper had been thrown a rope, but he let it slip so Fletcher had to taxi round again.] It was Roberts' first operational trip and he looked towards the shore and I began to hear him on the intercom, saying: 'E . . . A . . . I . . . H . . . I . . .' various letters. I said, 'What's going on, Robbie?' He replied, 'Somebody's signalling from the beach.' Well, what he was seeing – and reading off – was the gun flashes!

All these splashes around us and he hadn't connected these with what was happening over there. The shells landed in one big circle, then another – closer – as they tried for our range. When I lined up the Walrus to pick the 'bod' up, I headed in to keep clear of the mines and we got a near miss. The weather was good and a nice day for getting off quickly – nice little chops – and so that was that. It was on that do that Len lost the first part of one finger.

Sergeant T. Fletcher, No 277 Squadron

Cooper, from Kenya, was brought safely back to England, where he was able to confirm Large's '190 as destroyed. The air fight Tom Fletcher had seen was between four '190s which had come out to see what all the activity was, and Pilot Officer Large. In company with Flight Lieutenant J.S. Fifield of 616, Large had circled Cooper while Fifield had gone off to contact the Lysander. Fifield had been shot down at Dieppe and been rescued by a boat in mid-Channel, so knew all about being in the sea. No sooner had he flown off than the '190s found Large, but he managed to evade them, joined up with Fifield and then both Spitfire pilots headed for Hawkinge.

Fletcher's air cover had been provided by six Spitfire IXs of 402 (RCAF) Squadron and 12 Spitfire VIs of 416 (RCAF) Squadron. While on the water, and under fire from the shore, two more '190s had flown over but had not interfered because of the Spitfires. 91 Squadron were also in evidence and the whole force flew back at dusk, with Cooper safely tucked up in the rear of the Walrus.

For their actions, Tom Fletcher and Len Healey received DFMs, while Roberts received a 'Highly Commended' mention in despatches.

This had not been Cooper's first dunking, for both he and Pilot Officer Large had been shot down by Me 109s back on 30 July, after Large had probably destroyed an FW 190. They had been picked up by HSLs after being located by 277 and 91 Squadron aircraft. Large later received the DFC and left 616 Squadron in January 1943.

Cooper was commissioned at the end of October, and by the following summer was a Flying Officer. On 16 August 1943, during a mission escorting Venturas bombing Tricqueville aerodrome, led by his CO, Jack Charles, Cooper's Spitfire developed engine trouble and he was forced to bale out. This time, however, he landed inland and was taken prisoner.

★   ★   ★   ★   ★

In mid-October 1942, at a conference at Fighter Command concerning Air-Sea Rescue, the question of aircraft types came onto the agenda once again. With the increased activity and, more significantly, the recent enemy air opposition during rescues, not least the actions over the Cooper rescue, it was decided that ASR squadrons should not have to rely solely on other fighter units for escorts, but to have their own. In consequence, it was decided to replace the Defiants with Spitfires in the near future.

This went down very well with the ASR squadrons, for the Spitfires could not only fly escort to the Walrus, but were better able to look after themselves when out searching for downed flyers, especially those close to the enemy coasts. It also released more air gunners to fly in the Walrus crews.

277 Squadron's association with German minefields of late continued on the 31 October, in what was to become one of the most famous of rescues; mainly, but not solely due to the amount of publicity it received. In any event, it was yet another spectacular rescue.

Chapter Five

Minefields and other Hazards

The Van Shaick rescue

As the autumn progressed, both operational aircrew and the men of the Air-Sea Rescue Service were only too aware of the additional hazards for downed pilots and crews with the approach of the war's fourth winter. Unless rescue came quickly, survival in the cold sea was particularly short-lived.

Things had improved over recent months following the early days of ASR; more squadrons were available, Spitfires were now co-operating well with the rescue boys and with experience, the rescue people were becoming even more daring in their rescues. None more so than the crew of a 277 Squadron Walrus, on the last day of October 1942.

The weather at dawn was not good, but perhaps ideal for *Rhubarb* operations. 137 Squadron at Manston thought so, and laid on a sortie of four Westland Whirlwinds, led by their 'B' Flight commander, Flight Lieutenant John Van Shaick DFM, who had previously flown with 609 Squadron. Their targets were to be hutted encampments near Etaples.

They took off at 11 a.m. and headed out across the Channel at low level. *Rhubarbs* were often dangerous operations – very aggressive and fun to do, but very costly of aircrew. This operation was to be no exception and Van Shaick was hit over the target and his Whirlwind (P7064) severely damaged. His wingman, Sergeant P.G. Waldron, in P7109, was also hit and went down, to be reported as missing. Van Shaick headed for the coast, but he was in trouble.

Meantime, the other section, Pilot Officers D. St J Jowitt in P7115 and F.M. Furber in P7102, attacked a similar encampment three miles further inland, but they faired no better. Both Whirlwinds were hit, and Jowitt headed north with smoke streaming from his starboard engine. As they flew over the French coast, Jowitt called Furber and asked him to make a Mayday call, which Furber did, but he then lost sight of Jowitt in the low cloud. Jowitt called to say he was baling out, but whether he did so or not, his wingman could not see. Furber, with a hole in his starboard mainplane, headed for home and landed safely at noon.

Van Shaick, meantime, had struggled to the coast, but he was not going to make the sea crossing. He was a few miles out but too low to bale out, so he would have to ditch. He succeeded in doing so and minutes later he was in his dinghy. The enemy shoreline was just a few miles away and as his aircraft sank, he wondered how long it would be before he was spotted from the shore, or how long it would be before he drifted into captivity.

At nearby Hawkinge, the Spitfires of 91 'Jim Crow' Squadron had again been alerted, and the pilots were kept busy that morning, for not only had three Whirlwinds been reported as missing, a couple of Spitfires were also reported overdue. Warrant Officer Down and Flight Sergeant Eldrid spotted some wreckage in mid-Channel and called out rescue boats to the scene, but no aircrew were found. Meanwhile, Sergeant J.A. Round took off at 2:20 p.m. in Spitfire EP508 to fly a shipping recce to Dieppe, and by chance spotted a pilot in a dinghy, some eight miles west of Cap Gris Nez. He radioed back to base and then circled nearby. He had to fly low, for the Germans were sure to see him.

The 277 Squadron detachment at RAF Hawkinge, which that morning consisted of seven pilots and eight air gunners, with three Lysanders and three Defiants, had been alerted. At 11:45 a.m. all pilots were called to Readiness when word came that three Whirlwinds had failed to return. In the meantime, one of the squadron's Walruses was flown along from Shoreham by Pilot Officer Tod Hilton, with Flight Sergeant Dizzy Seales as gunner.

Rather than just wait, a Lysander was sent off to make a search. Flight Sergeant Doug Hartwell with Sergeant Pete 'Stan' Standen and Flight Sergeant Waddington, flew off and vectored out on a course of 199° for 12 miles. They found nothing – Van Shaick was twice that distance away. They returned and landed at 2:30 p.m., just as Sergeant Round was heading out.

With Round's report of a dinghy, the Walrus (W3076) was Scrambled, Hilton and Seales heading south, this time on a bearing of 167° for 24 miles, escorted by three Spitfires led by the Frenchman, Pilot Officer Jean Maridor, in BL413. They took off at 3:35 p.m., just after two more of 91's Spitfires had taken off to make yet another search for the other missing pilots.

With help on the way, Sergeant Round returned home, and minutes later the Walrus and its escort were over the stricken pilot. Looking down, everyone could see how close inshore the unfortunate pilot was, but what was causing more anxiety was the fact that the dinghy had quite clearly drifted right into the centre of a German minefield!

The deadly mines could be seen quite easily, fixed to the seabed in parallel rows, with the dinghy right in the middle of them. There was no time to wait for their 'customer' to drift out of the minefield, or to think of what else to do. If the Germans hadn't already seen all the activity just off shore, they soon would, and doubtless German fighters would soon be sent out to see what all the excitement was about, possibly even an E-boat or two.

Pilot Officer Hilton quickly made up his mind – he would have to land, but in order to land between the mines he had to come in crosswind, which made it awkward. He got down safely but overshot the dinghy and

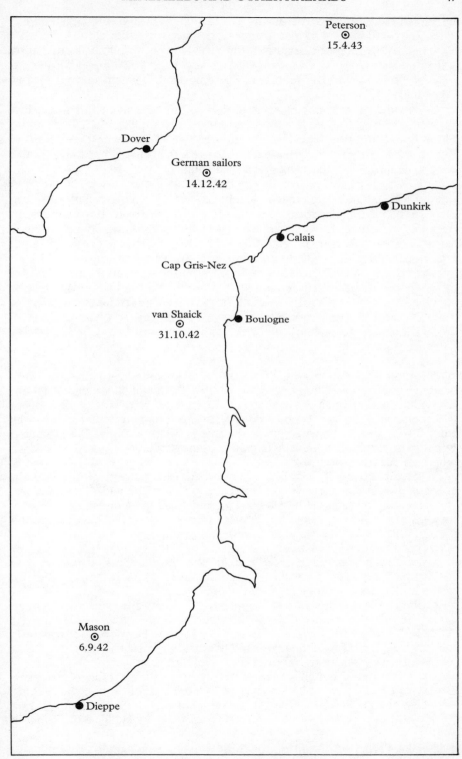

Peterson
⊙
15.4.43

Dover

German sailors
⊙
14.12.42

Dunkirk

Calais

Cap Gris-Nez

van Shaick
⊙
31.10.42

Boulogne

Mason
⊙
6.9.42

Dieppe

had to make a left turn before he could taxi back, passing between the mines as he did so, with just four feet to spare on either side!

Sergeant Seales had scrambled up to the front of the Walrus and threw a line to Van Shaick, who grabbed it, and then together, Hilton and Seales pulled him to the seaplane. Once aboard, it was time to go – and go quickly.

Throttle forward, the Walrus gathered speed amid the mines, but suddenly Hilton spotted a mine dead ahead and only about 15 yds away. Hauling back on the stick, Hilton bounced the Walrus over it and crashed down on the other side; then came six further bounces before he could get the machine off the water and into the air.

The Walrus and Spitfire escort landed safely at Hawkinge at 4:35 p.m., Van Shaick being returned to his squadron the next day, suffering only slightly from exposure. He had been lucky not to have been shot down over France, lucky to have ditched successfully, lucky not to have bumped into a mine with his dinghy, and lucky that Hilton had used every ounce of skill to bring off a landing amidst the mines and take off again without hitting one. Some days its better to be lucky than rich!

However, if he had been taken prisoner, Van Shaick might have survived the Second World War. As it was, he was to die instructing at an OTU later in the war. But that, as the French say, is 'C'est la Guerre'. Tod Hilton, an Australian, died a few years ago, but Dizzy Seales recalls this famous rescue:

We took off from Shoreham, flew along to Hawkinge, refuelled and were briefed again before flying out, covered by Spitfires of 91 Squadron. After we spotted the man in the water we landed, but there was quite a bit of wear because of the swell, and so on. Tod taxied round – we were quite a way from him – and that's when I saw the mines floating about. We managed to get near him and eventually roped him in, got him on board and that's when the real trouble started.

We began taxying down a lane of mines, got our speed up and then, right at the end of the lane, there was a single mine which he hadn't seen before, sort of sealing off the lane! We were now under fire from the shore, not only light gunfire but from shore batteries as well. What would have happened if they'd hit one of the mines, I shudder to think.

Seeing that mine was when the panic started! Tod was yelling back at me to come forward and then we both grabbed hold of the controls, yanked back as hard as we could, feet on the dashboard stuff, and then the suction of the hull suddenly broke and we got off.

We didn't hold the height but fortunately we cleared the mine and dropped down the other side – we did bounce once or twice – and we damaged a float. In fact, when we were coming in to land at Hawkinge, it was only then that we realized the float was full of water because the wing dipped as we lost speed – talk about landing on a wing and a prayer!

We both stayed the night at Hawkinge and the following day, Tod wasn't in a fit state to fly – there had been a bit of a celebration during the evening – so I caught a train up to London and then another down to Shoreham.

Flight Sergeant L. Seales, No 277 Squadron

Tod Hilton received the DFC for this rescue, which gained quite a bit of newspaper publicity, and, in some ways, really began to put ASR in the public eye.

★　★　★　★　★

'Jonah's' rig

Mention of Doug Hartwell in the run-up to this rescue brings the opportunity of mentioning him at this time. Unhappily, when still writing this book, following correspondence with him, Doug died following a long illness; but he left us with some fine recollections of his period with 277 Squadron, and they were not all about flying.

Doug had joined ASR in the early days and one of his stories concerns the inventiveness of the men in overcoming problems. One of these was how a gunner in a Lysander was to direct his pilot in case of air attack. During an operation on 25 October 1941, while the unit was still only a Flight, Me 109s interfered with one search mission where Doug was the pilot and Flight Sergeant Gordon Jones his gunner:

We were attacked by three Me 109s and 'Jonah' made use of the emergency cords that were attached to the straps of the pilot, which then passed through to the gunner's cockpit to his guns. By snatching on either the right or left cord, according to which way he wanted me to turn, I could comply. After the attack, which we survived, and while we were on our way home, the following conversation took place:

Jonah: 'If you had dropped any more than another couple of feet we would have needed floats on this old Lizzie!'

DRH: 'And if you had snatched any harder on those cords I would have sustained a broken neck and you would be swimming back, seeing as how you can't fly this ruddy thing.'

Jonah: 'What are all those holes above your head?'

DRH: 'I think the Air Ministry calls them Air Vents, 'specially to keep the pilots cool. The gunners need to keep cool more than us, that's why they don't cover you in!'

Gordon was a grand chap really. I remember when we first had air gunners assigned to us, when we pilots were told that we were about to be teamed up with gunners for Lysander duty. 'What do we do,' the pilots asked, 'just take our pick?' No indeed, we were told, the gunners will pick the pilots! Never having had the pleasure of gunners' company before, this came as quite a surprise to us, but we were soon sorted out and started immediately to get to know the lad who had made you his choice.

Sergeant Gordon Jones chose me. I noticed that he had the word 'Jonah' painted on the back of his leather flying jacket in large yellow letters. On being asked by me why the word 'Jonah', he replied, 'Well, I have already had two pilots killed while flying with them and I survived both, so the lads called me a "Jonah".' He went on to say that this is where that sequence comes to a halt, so I could rest assured. I must say that a very good partnership was born from that moment.

When we were equipped with Defiants, I had to give the gunner the drill regarding procedure should the electrics fail. In case of trouble, the pilot would inform the gunner over the intercom. However, if the intercom failed, there was a green light in the gunner's turret indicating, when on, all was well. If the pilot pressed the red light, this meant all was not well, and the gunner should bale out. I asked 'Jonah' if this was quite clear and he replied that so far, so good, but what happens if the intercom AND the electrics both fail? I told him I had no answer to this, but promised I would wave to him as I went by his cockpit as I baled out!

'Jonah' and I remained very good friends right to the end. After the war he finished up in a wheelchair due to a crash in 1942 and he died in 1989. The crash occurred when our engine cut on take-off in a Lysander (V9483) on 16 April 1942. I pulled 'Jonah' from the wreck and bandaged his wounds before help came. So this was his last crash, but the jinx was broken. His pilot had survived, but it was the end of his own flying career.

Doug Hartwell also recalls:

When the weather was bad and the aircrew released for the day, with the exception of one Flight of one of the squadrons based on the airfield, the Intelligence Officers organized an Escape Exercise for the rest of us.

We were dressed for flying but were allowed to remove battledress tops, just having sweaters, trousers and flying boots – but carrying nothing else. We were all loaded onto a covered wagon and dropped off individually at about three miles between each man, some 12 miles out from the aerodrome. Our brief was to get back without being caught, while police, Army and our own airfield defence people had all been alerted.

They dropped me off and I noted by the sun's position, which was hardly discernible, that I must be north-west-north of the airfield, so set off on the reciprocal after some travelling across some fields. I then noticed someone else travelling in the same direction, so set off to investigate. It turned out to be my good friend Warrant Officer Dave Waddington, who was in the same Flight as myself.

We decided to team up, and going into a farm outbuilding, found a number of girl's Land Army overalls and hats, and some wellington boots. We donned these, hoping it would make us less conspicuous, but looking at Dave's large RAF moustache made me think otherwise.

Just then, a small open-back van drove into the farmyard, and the driver disappeared into the farmhouse, leaving the van with the engine still running. Waddy and I looked at each other and without a word, dashed as we were to the van, and with Waddy driving, headed off with milk churns rattling in the back.

We soon recognized our position once we were on the Canterbury to Hawkinge Road, and decided to head straight for the airfield main gate, shout 'Milk' and hope we would be allowed through. However, as we approached the gate, the guard immediately lifted the pole for us to proceed into the camp unchallenged, which we did with a wave to the guard, then drove to the Officers' Mess to report in.

We then realized we did not know where the van had come from and were not sure if we could find our way back. But on searching the van, some delivery notes were found with the farmer's name, address and telephone number on them. He was notified by 'phone what had happened and when Waddy and I returned the van to him, he was so grateful that he presented us with some new-laid eggs as well as returning our flying boots.

Another non-flying story was the night we were on flying duty but resting on the beds in the flight dispersal hut. Waddy and I heard pattering of many tiny feet running across the ceiling of the room, and upon investigation the next morning, decided the culprits who had disturbed our slumbers must be rats. Our biggest worry was for our parachutes, not wanting them nibbled to pieces in case we should need to use them.

A very observant airman informed us there were a number of rat holes in the top of the air-raid shelter that ran alongside the hut, so Operation 'Seek and Destroy' was planned. We blocked up all the holes except two, but down which we then poured petrol, then laid a trail of gunpowder to the holes. Men were then stationed by the holes with 12-bore shotguns, baseball bats, etc., to sort out any rats that tried to escape.

Finally, the powder was ignited and did its job magnificently, setting light to the petrol. There was an almighty flash from the escape holes, like a flame from a jet engine, but there were no rats; but there was a loud crumbling noise as the air-raid shelter proceeded to collapse right in front of our eyes. We could not believe it; nor could the Station Commander, who, unknown to us, witnessed the whole episode from his car.

In that nice way Station Commanders have, he told Waddy and I that he was sure it would not be noticed if within the following week, the shelter was restored to its previously immaculate condition. This was achieved, and we reported the fact to the Commander. However, with the experience of how easily it had collapsed, we could not assure him that it would ever be used for its main purpose.

Flight Sergeant D.R. Hartwell, No 277 Squadron

Doug Hartwell's wasn't the only Lysander crash. Pilot Officer J. Dobson with Sergeant Davis, of 276 Squadron, flew a search mission off the coast of Aberystwyth on the evening of 6 November 1942. They had been out for nearly 90 minutes when they were forced to abandon the sortie due to bad weather. An electrical storm sprang up and the compass went u/s. Heading into strong winds, and using a rich petrol mix, their fuel began to run low. They finally had to ditch the 'Lizzie' (V9444) off Stumble Head. Dobson managed to get clear and was later rescued, but Davis was lost. Good sense might have suggested an earlier return, but the rescue crews were never eager to abandon a search. The men in the water deserved every effort of rescue, but sometimes things didn't always turn out well.

Chapter Six

A Variety of Rescues

A tragic accident

On Armistice Day 1942, 131 (Spitfire) Squadron carried out an experiment with new tactics. In the late morning, Flight Lieutenant Ray Harries DFC, led the squadron to a point 15 miles off the Somme Estuary, flying across at sea level, but when 15 to 20 miles off the enemy coast, two Spitfires of Red Section climbed to 16,000 ft as a decoy for German fighters while the rest of the squadron orbited at sea level.

They circled for 15 minutes but nothing of interest occurred, so they turned for home. The Germans had wisely decided to ignore the 'new' tactic. However, on the flight back, the Spitfires were flying in sections in line astern at 4,000 ft. Some 25 miles off Shoreham, the fighters ran into a towering cumulus cloud, which came at them through the sea haze they had been experiencing.

Yellow Section swung away to the left, missing the densest part of the cloud, but Blue Section entered it still in line astern, with about 10 to 15 yds between each aircraft. The air became very bumpy and within a couple of minutes, Pilot Officer Bernard Sheidhauer, a French pilot, saw a tailplane right in front of him. He immediately pushed the stick forward and to the left, but his propeller caught the Spitfire ahead, chopping about 18 in from his blades, although the bumpy conditions actually masked the shock on impact.

The Frenchman decided to dive out of the cloud, which he did at 2,000 ft. He had hit *Blue Two*, Pilot Officer E.A.J. 'Taffy' Williams whose Spitfire began to fall away in a gentle glide. None of the other pilots were as yet aware of the collision.

Then Sheidhauer's engine packed up so it was time to get out. He alerted his Section Leader to his problem, then out he went, and within minutes he was in his dinghy, waving to some of the others who had now descended to circle him. The Spitfires gave a fix, then headed back to Westhampnett. Within 15 minutes of landing, four Spitfires were off again to search for their comrades, but already a Lysander from 277 Squadron was on its way, although the search proved fruitless. The Spitfires arrived and even though they thought they knew where

Sheidhauer had gone in, they couldn't find him either. Finally a Walrus (L2246/'D') from 277 at Shoreham was on its way. At the controls was Flying Officer M.F. Dekyvere, with Sergeant E. Quick and Dizzy Seales.

Tangmere Control had asked for their help, the response being immediate. The Walrus crew searched for well over an hour, finally spotting the dinghy, and within minutes they had the Frenchman safely aboard and were heading for home. The man had been 22 miles off the English coast.

Unfortunately there was no sign of Emrys 'Taffy' Williams. His was a sad loss, made more so because following this operation, he had been due to go home on leave to see his wife and son, who had been born the evening before. Later, Johnny Barber and his crew in another Walrus spotted a man in the water surrounded by his coloured dye but not in a dinghy. They dropped a dinghy and smoke before landing, but the man was dead. Several attempts to hook the body failed, but then an HSL arrived and they got the body aboard.

After a spot of leave to get over his ordeal, Sheidhauer returned to 131 and on 18 November, exactly a week after his sojourn in his dinghy, he flew on a *Rhubarb* sortie. It was the first such operation the squadron had flown for some months. Sheidhauer flew 'Number Two' to Flying Officer de Bordas, taking off for Cherbourg, crossing the French coast at St Aubin-sur-Mer, then hitting the Caen-Cherbourg railway line. Both men attacked trains, light flak being experienced from Carentan and de Bordas lost sight of his wingman, who failed to return. In another *Rhubarb* sortie that afternoon, 131 Squadron lost a second pilot.

Oddly enough, Ray Harries was just about to leave 131 Squadron to take command of 91 Squadron at Hawkinge. He was an exceptional fighter pilot and leader, ending the war with the DSO and bar, DFC and two bars, plus French and Belgian Croix de Guerres.

★ ★ ★ ★ ★

The German seamen

It wasn't always aircrew who were saved, nor was it always men from the Allied side. On 14 December 1942, it was again a 277 Squadron Walrus that had been sent out following a sighting report by the Spitfires of 91 Squadron.

They had reported seeing a rescue buoy out in the Channel, but 277 found that there was no buoy located in the position given. Another search was ordered and this time it turned out to be a raft, with some men on it, drifting in rough seas about seven miles off Dover on a course of 100°. It was now late in the day, and Control warned that rough weather was closing in. The sea was already quite choppy, but at 4:45 p.m., Sergeant Tom Fletcher took off in Walrus X9521, with Sergeants Len Healey and 'Sticky' Glew.

At just on 5 p.m., the raft was sighted, with two Typhoon fighters circling over it. With the sky darkening, there was no time to waste, Fletcher landing on the water five minutes later, despite a heavy swell, and with a good chance of not being able to take off again.

The Typhoons now left them to it, fuel and the dark forcing them to return to their base. Having landed, Fletcher taxied up to the raft which could be seen to have six men on it, five sitting back-to-back, the sixth lying spread-eagled and seemingly already dead. The rough sea caused them to hit the raft, spilling all six men into the icy water. A line was thrown out and one of the men grabbed it, but instead of fastening it to the raft, he wound it round his own wrist. Len Healey pulled the man to the seaplane and hauled him through the rear hatch. In the meantime, the other five had scrambled back onto the raft from where two tried to grab the seaplane's wing, but their frozen hands would not allow them to retain a grip and they fell back into the water. Fletcher again tried to manoeuvre the Walrus beside the raft, but again they hit it – hard. One of the men was killed, caught between the raft and the hull, and the others were once more plunged into the sea. The hook was thrown out again, but they all missed it.

Only one man managed to clamber back onto the raft and by this time it was getting pretty dark and difficult to see the bobbing heads in the water. Fletcher taxied round three or four times, desperately looking for the men, and one was spotted and pulled into the rear hatch, but the rough sea and gloom was beginning to defeat them.

There was still just enough light to see the raft with its single cold and shivering occupant, and they taxied to it and took the man off, 'Sticky' Glew helping him into the seaplane by the front hatch. It then took Tom Fletcher 30 minutes to turn the Walrus round into wind, because of the rough sea which was being whipped up by the increasingly strong gusts. Finally he managed it, opened the throttle and began to crash through the waves for a take-off. As he gathered speed he spotted one of the missing men, but he was almost committed now and as he chopped the throttle he was unable to stop before they had passed him. When they finally pulled round they had lost sight of the man and had to leave without him. Again, getting the Walrus into the wind proved difficult, but he finally managed it and they tried to take off, but it was impossible. The rough sea, the darkness and the extra weight of men and water was too much for the Walrus. Tom Fletcher had no other choice but to try and taxi towards land.

It was now completely dark, and even the two 91 Squadron Spitfires which had escorted them out had had to go home. They tried to head west but the gale-force winds from the south-east forced Fletcher to taxi in a south-west direction, which was no good, so he headed north-west in order to eventually gain the protection of the east coast of Kent. He was then able to turn west and made landfall at North Foreland, then turned west down the coastline, which was illuminated all the way by searchlights whose crews had been alerted of their approach.

Tom thought he was somewhere near Dover when he suddenly saw the coastal defences outside St Margaret's Bay and had quickly to avoid them. Finally, when they reached the vicinity of Dover Harbour, they were guided by a searchlight on a launch. Although reluctant, Tom then had to taxi to a large buoy and 'Sticky' Glew jumped onto it, but in doing so lost the rope end and became stranded. Fletcher could not get back to him. Then a tug came out and led them in with the aid of another searchlight. Tom Fletcher and Len Healey finally tied up their Walrus at 7:30 p.m.

The rescued men were obviously of foreign nationality but the two Flight Sergeants had been unable to decipher their language; and in any event, they had been too far gone to be really coherent. When they got them ashore at Dover, it was found that they were German sailors whose ship had been sunk four days earlier! It was thought they came from an action between Motor Anti-Submarine Boats (MASBs) and German E-boats off the French coast. They had been drifting ever since, were very hungry, exhausted, and with hands and feet frostbitten. However, they had been rescued, even though their three companions had been lost. But for the courage and determination of the three NCO airmen, all six would have soon perished in the wintry sea.

Once on shore at Dover, waiting ambulances whisked the Germans away and everyone else suddenly disappeared, leaving Fletch and Len Healey on a blacked-out dock! Eventually, they found their way to the Watch Office where they were relieved to hear that 'Sticky' had been rescued from the buoy and was already having a meal in the Mess Hall, Tom and Len soon joining him.

Four days later, *HSL 127* from Ramsgate located and rescued two more German seamen from off North Foreland, and the next day this same boat rescued Leutnant Muller, six miles off the Point. Of this rescue, Len Healey recalled:

On 14 December 1942, at 4:45 p.m., we were told to do a search down towards the Goodwin Sands where a raft had been reported, spotted by a Spitfire pilot. With Tom Fletcher and 'Sticky', we proceeded and finally, in very very rough weather and a very high sea, we found the raft.

Tommy decided to go down and have a closer look at it, and on it we could see six men who appeared to be sailors. At that stage the weather was so bad we could hardly tell whether they were English or German. Fletch said they couldn't possibly survive the night and decided to go down and pick them up.

We landed, taxied up to them and finally managed to get one into the back hatch. The sea was so rough, Fletch had to turn and come back a second time to the raft. On this occasion, the aircraft was lifted by a huge wave and crashed down on top of the raft, killing one sailor outright. Fletch then proceeded to turn round again. This time we managed to get another sailor into the front hatch and two more into the back hatch.

By this time there was a foot of water in the Walrus, due to the sea coming over the back hatch and flooding us. The radio began to spark, and then smoke was coming from the damn thing.

After searching the clothing of these chaps, we found they were German sailors, and they were in a terrible state. Their hands were raw down to the bone where they had been hanging onto ropes on their raft. It turned out they had been on the raft for several days.

Fletch said it was impossible to take off because of the weight and high seas, so we notified base that we were going to taxi back and could we please have assistance. Off we went and 'Sticky' and I spent the best part of our time trying to get the water out of the aircraft. By now the windows had all broken in and we were in a sorry state, not believing we were going to get anywhere near the English coast. However, we finally made the coast and reached Dover, from where a boat came out and guided us in.

Having taxied in, we tied up to a huge buoy and transferred our survivors to the Navy, and we were taken off in a launch. The Harbour-Master sent for us and we were torn off a strip for not getting permission to bring our sinking aircraft into his harbour! This was impossible, as our radio had finally packed up and we were almost under water.

However, he cheered up a wee bit and told us to get ourselves a good meal, which turned out to be beans and bacon. What I think really upset him most was that we had taxied through three of his minefields – and nothing had happened!

Flight Sergeant L.R. Healey, No 277 Squadron

Tom Fletcher received a bar to his DFM for this rescue.

★   ★   ★   ★   ★

Akbon 13 is down

At Martlesham, on 27 January 1943, Warrant Officer W. Greenfield and Flight Sergeant W.J. Horan, in 277 Squadron Defiant N3392, were off at 10:45 a.m. after being called to stand-by following a fading radar plot. They flew 50 miles out from Aldeburgh Napes Point and began a 'box' search, then were called closer inshore to begin another.

Then at midday, Ops telephoned the Flight HQ at Martlesham with the startling news that the Defiant – call-sign *Akbon 13* – was going into the sea! Immediately, Flying Officer L.J. Brown and Pilot Officer D.G. Sheppard were off in Walrus X9526, followed closely by Defiant T3948, crewed by Flight Sergeant Boddy and Norman Pickles.

Bill Greenfield had been happily engaged on his 'box' search when he noticed smoke in the cockpit. Checking his instruments, he spotted the engine temperature was rising and oil pressure falling – ominous signs that they would not be flying for too much longer!

Soon the engine began to vibrate and he began to climb, gaining as much height as he could before the engine either stopped or blew up, but he was unable to get above 700 ft. Discussing the options with his gunner, they decided to ditch. Greenfield headed down towards the sea as Horan turned his turret round and eased himself onto the edge, holding on to one side of his head while firmly grasping the dinghy with his other hand.

Having decided to stick to the Defiant, Greenfield had not been able to jettison his hood in case he caused damage to Horan or his turret, but merely slid it back and released his straps and harness. They hit the sea some 28 miles off Aldeburgh, the tail striking first, then the aircraft splashed down at 90 m.p.h. Horan was immediately catapulted onto the nose of the Defiant, Greenfield having fortunately cut the engine just before impact. Horan managed to get onto the mainplane but was then flung into the sea. Looking for Greenfield, he could see no sign of him and so immediately dived under the water to the sinking aircraft, but in the meantime, Greenfield managed to get out and bobbed to the surface. The hood had shut when they hit, and in the 12 or so seconds before the aircraft went under, Greenfield had been desperately trying to reopen it, had done so and was out.

Another problem was that Greenfield's dinghy did not release and had gone down with the aircraft, so both men had to get into Horan's. However, help was on its way, the Walrus having become airborne just

three minutes after the alert call. The Defiant arrived first and dropped
a smoke float in order to help Brown with the wind direction, the seaplane
now being just a short distance away.

Within a few minutes it was over the dinghy and quickly landed nearby,
taxied up and Brown stopped the engine. Greenfield caught hold of the
tailplane and Horan the undercarriage oleo leg, then both men were
being hauled in by both Brown and Sheppard. The engine was restarted,
but Brown was not able to take off immediately owing to the heavy sea
plus a great volume of water having been shipped aboard. So for some
40 minutes the Walrus was slowly taxied towards shore with Sheppard
baling out the water. Later Brown attempted a take-off, was successful,
and soon he had his wet colleagues back at base.

As a postscript to this story, W.J. Horan was later one of the handful
of UK Walrus men to go out to the Far East, to join 292 ASR Squadron.
Horan, who was a New Zealander, became a Warrant Officer, but was
killed in action on 9 January 1945.

The Wintry Sea

In England, the new year of 1943 saw the four main Walrus squadrons still on the alert. Winter weather, of course, curtailed air operations somewhat; but then, if aircrew did come down in the sea, it was even more imperative to get to them quickly.

No 276 Squadron lost a Defiant on 22 January, due to the weather rather than enemy action. Flight Sergeant K. Hall and Flight Sergeant W. Elder took off in T4051 at 1:55 p.m. to search for three men known to be in the water – without a dinghy. So despite the weather, both knew they had to find them and drop a dinghy before the three men died of cold. Bill Elder recalls:

We searched for 50 minutes off the south coast and finally sighted the three aircrew in Mae Wests. We dropped them a large dinghy but by now the weather was deteriorating rapidly so we had to head back.

On nearing our home base, cloud came down to the 200 feet level, and as we were also running short of fuel my pilot ordered me to bale out when we were at around 1,500 feet. I landed on the white chalk of Cerne Abbas Giant, north of Dorchester.

After roaming around in thick fog and drizzle, minus flying boots which had come off in the bale-out, I was arrested by a zealous Home Guard officer, who took me to Godmanstone Police Station. My captor was a Mr Best, who lived at Manor Farm, Godmanstone, but once my identity had been established, I was well and truly entertained.

For many years I kept in touch with him and once paid him a visit with my family, but discovered he died in 1989.

Flight Sergeant W. Elder, No 276 Squadron

Flight Sergeant Hall also baled out successfully. Meantime, another Defiant (N3430), with Warrant Officer K. Bird and Flight Sergeant G. Galloway, had flown out, found another man in the water, and then helped guide launches to all the men.

In the south-east of England, 277 Squadron still held the prime position, 'A' Flight being at Martlesham, 'B' Flight at Hawkinge and 'C' Flight at

Shoreham. Martlesham opened the year's account on 20 February.

A Hampden torpedo bomber of 415 (RCAF) Squadron had come down 40 miles out to sea. They had attacked a convoy and been hit by flak, which shot out an engine. Martlesham was alerted and Flying Officers Lionel Brown, Douggie Sheppard and Tom Rance made a spectacular rescue, along with a second Walrus crew – Warrant Officers Tom Ormiston and Bill Greenfield and Flight Sergeant Nicholls. Flying Officer P.R. Corillo took off too, in Defiant T3948, at 5:30 p.m. to help in the search.

After searching for some time, Brown and Co spotted the dinghy and landed. Tom Rance takes up the story:

The plane had come down a long way out and we had no escort. We searched for quite a while until I spotted a flashing light which was a mirror catching the rays of the dying sun.

We landed as the sea was calm and soon had the crew on board, and took a long take-off with the extra weight. There was a boat a good way off which it appeared was a German E-boat in pursuit, firing a few red lights off at our rear.

The crew of four had been in their dinghy for 42 hours, and our sortie lasted three hours, 10 minutes.

Flight Sergeant W.A. Rance, No 277 Squadron

Flying Officer Carillo in the Defiant had seen the unidentified vessel too, and saw it firing. However, it later transpired that it was not an E-boat but a British Motor Torpedo Boat (MTB), firing warning shots that both aircraft were in a practice firing area! By the time Brown got back to base it was almost dark and a heavy mist had come up, but he got down safely.

Tom Rance was quite right that they had no escort; it had been recalled due to deteriorating weather soon after they'd taken off! No one had called back the Walrus and they would probably have ignored such a call if it had been made.

The pilot of the Hampden, Flying Officer Alfred Brenner RCAF, later rose to Squadron Leader and won the DFC in September 1943.

Harrowbeer begin 1943 well

A couple of days later, on 23 February, 276 Squadron were quick off the mark and rescued a pilot in the sea in just his Mae West. He was eight miles south-west of the Lizard and Flying Officer F.O. Dimblebee, Pilot Officer R. Hughes and Flight Sergeant R. Davies deposited him at RAF Harrowbeer. They had picked up Sergeant R.J. 'Bob' Gourlay of 602 Squadron. He had been out on a practice flight and flying low over the water when his prop hit the sea, smashing the blades. He just had enough speed to pull up to about 400 ft, where he baled out. His parachute opened just in time, but his dinghy broke away.

No 276 Squadron's total number of rescues was fast approaching 100 lives saved. The total of 94 had been reached at the end of the year and Squadron Leader Hamlyn had received the Air Force Cross in the New Year's Honours List.

It was *Rhubarb* weather, and the Canadians at Kenley sent out two Spitfires of 416 Squadron on 28 February, Pilot Officer B.S. Siddall and Flight Sergeant R.W. Lamont flying off at first light.

Flying low over the Channel, the visibility was poor with mist hanging right on the water. Lamont misjudged his height and hit the sea. One of his oleo legs was ripped off and the Spitfire (AD560) began to leak glycol from a ruptured radiator tank. Moments later he had to ditch. Siddell climbed to give a Mayday call and from Hawkinge, Johnny Spence, Flight Sergeant W. Butler and Sergeant P. Graham were away in Walrus W3024 at 8:15 a.m.

Ops gave the position as 20 miles south of Dungeness and six Spitfires of 91 Squadron went out first to try and spot the man. 416 Squadron also sent out a section, led by their CO, Squadron Leader F.H. Boulton. They also ran into trouble because of the mist, Flight Sergeant G.M. Shouldice hitting the sea, but he managed to stagger back to Shoreham with just a damaged propeller.

Meanwhile, 91 Squadron found Lamont and orbited until the Walrus arrived. Spence dropped a smoke float, and despite the mist (and where it parted there was a difficult, smooth, glassy sea, which was difficult to judge), he landed. He taxied up but his front gunner missed the man. Spence grabbed him as he went by the cockpit, then Graham pulled the dinghy to the rear hatch and moments later they were on their way home.

It had been lucky they had the extra eyes of the Spitfires, for Lamont was not 20 miles out but 55, which was only five miles off the enemy coast! Also, the Walrus crew later found out they had landed in the middle of a minefield, about 100 yds west to the French side edge of the field! John Alexander Spence RCAF received the DFC shortly after this rescue.

Lighter moments, sad moments

Just as it was not always enemy action that put men into the sea, as can be understood from the last rescue, there were often moments of light relief on the squadrons. One such came on 1 March.

There was always room for improvement and practice, and 276 Squadron flew a practice sortie that afternoon. Flying Officer Frank Dimblebee, 'Spike' Hughes, Davies and Sergeant R. Churchill, in Walrus W2784, were Scrambled to find a dinghy which had been dropped some miles off the Cornish coast, while two pinnaces were ordered out from Padstow. The race was on!

Within a few minutes of reaching the centre of the search area, the Walrus crew spotted the dinghy, which had failed to inflate, and soon after they found it, it sank from sight. The boats were now in view, so R/T contact was made with them, and Dimblebee told them to heave to while he landed and taxied up. Throwing a line across, the four aviators went on board for a visit. To their great disappointment, they found the boats did not carry any rum, and that they had no poker dice to while away a few minutes gambling!

In April, the tempo of rescues rose as the tempo of operations rose; but initially it cost the lives of some of the men of 278 Squadron, including the CO. On the 4th, Flight Lieutenant P.R. Smith took off on a night patrol in one of the unit's Ansons (DG809), with Warrant Officer C. Telford, Flights Sergeants C. Hogan and J. Bartlett, and Sergeant D. Forestall. A Spitfire pilot had gone into the sea 70 miles out and it was hoped that his distress flares might be spotted. The Anson failed to return, although Ops did hear a brief distress call from it.

I had already made one search that day in that very Anson, and I was due to make this night Op, but Smith said that he would fly it. All that was heard was a call saying, 'They're shooting at us . . !' And that was that.
Sergeant T.H. Humphrey, No 278 Squadron

Stirling rescue!

Exactly a week later, Bomber Command mounted a raid on Frankfurt, and among the 501 aircraft put up by No 3 Group, 12 were from 75 (RNZAF) Squadron. One of these was Stirling BF455, flown by a Canadian, Flight Sergeant C.A. Rothschild, with a mixed crew of Canadians, New Zealanders and Britons. The Canadians were two twin brothers, Sergeants R.E. and R.D. Tod (air gunner and wireless operator respectively), the New Zealanders being the navigator, Flight Sergeant G.K. Sampson, bomb aimer Sergeant J.L. Richards and rear gunner W.A.M. 'Bill' Hardy. The mid-upper gunner and the engineer were British, Sgts H.E. Moss and E. Grainger.

Over the target the Stirling was hit by anti-aircraft (AA) fire and also chased by fighters, so their fuel tanks were damaged. They ran short of petrol over the English Channel and eventually ditched three miles off Shoreham. They had called the rescue service and so as they staggered towards England, Spitfires had met them just as dawn was breaking. They escorted the crippled bomber from the French coast and by the time they had to ditch, a Walrus was waiting for them.

Dinghy drill went off perfectly after an immaculate sea landing, then the Walrus (W2773), crewed by Pilot Officer N.D. Mackertich and Sergeant H.H. 'Teddy' Teillett, was over them.

I was on Spitfires that morning and we slept in the Shoreham airport buildings in bedrooms upstairs. Mackertich was called out with the Walrus and it was his first rescue. The Stirling crew were all in their dinghy but unfortunately he taxied up too fast.

You normally had two choices. If your engine wouldn't slow you down enough – some ran faster than others – or if you couldn't get into wind or something like that, you might well approach too fast. In that case, you put your wheels down into the water. The other alternative was to put out drogues, but not if there was a chance of 'Jerry' coming out. They were pretty hefty things and it was not a good time to start hauling them in quickly.

Mackertich probably didn't put his wheels down, bumped into the dinghy and knocked them all into the water. One of them grabbed hold of the aircraft and he was dragged along for 200 to 300 yards before he had to let go. The rest of the crew got back into the dinghy but now this 'bod' was on his own.

Mackertich then called up Tangmere, who called up Shoreham, so I grabbed Flying Officer Chamberlain, who was the only gunner around and out we went. Over the spot I could see what had happened, so called up

Mackertich, who was going around in small circles trying to turn into them, but you couldn't do that. Once you'd missed them, you had to go off and have another straight run at it.

I told him what to do and then I landed and picked up this other chap. Chamberlain was in the front, with a boat-hook – we would take the pin out and have a cable fitted to it, fastened to the front bollard and with the right length of cable to go down to the back hatch, so the dinghy would end up alongside the rear hatch. If a chap was in the water, you'd put your wheels down anyway to slow right up, so he wouldn't be dragged along and maybe drowned.

Chamberlain hooked him and then went back inside the fuselage to get him down the back, and the bloke floated past me and said, 'Bloody good show, chum.' and that was that. He reached the rear hatch and the next thing I heard was a yell from Chamberlain for help.

I immediately dashed to the back and the bloke had turned into a raving lunatic! To get him in he had to hit him in the middle to make him double-up, then pushed him in.

This was the sort of thing that killed some people. It wasn't the cold, it wasn't anything to do with the sea, it was delayed shock. When they hit the water, they had something to fight for. They were busy and they could survive that. Immediately they knew they were safe, say a boat comes alongside, then the shock takes over. And it was that which was the killer.

Sergeant T. Fletcher, No 277 Squadron

It had been the Engineer, Eric Grainger who had suffered from shock, but after a period in hospital he returned to the squadron, as did the rest of the crew. Robert Tod received the DFM for his part in calling base and having fixes made on the bomber before it ditched. Sadly, Grainger, Richards and the two Tod boys were killed on a raid to Mannheim on the 23 June, flying with another pilot. Flight Sergeant George Sampson, by strange coincidence, was killed on the same raid but with another crew. It was tragic for the Tod family. Both boys had joined up together, had consecutive service numbers, trained together, went to the same squadron, and the same crew; and they died together.

Bandits!

14 April was a busy day for 277 Squadron at Shoreham. At 3:25 p.m. Walrus W2773 was Scrambled in response to a request by Tangmere to search for a downed aircraft 70 miles to the south – near the French coast. An escort was promised by Tangmere but it never showed.

Pilot Officer Johnny Barber DFM was flying the Walrus, with Len Healey, recently commissioned, in the back. They were about 15 miles off the French coast, having spotted nothing, when they were asked to orbit so that radar could fix their position. Then they were given a new course to fly. They were also informed that 'friends' were just 12 miles ahead, but that there were also bandits to the north-west. Five minutes later, Len spotted 15 aircraft to both sides – Messerschmitts! Len remembered:

We had been asked to fly to the French coast where a dinghy had been spotted and told we'd be escorted by a squadron of Spitfires. We hadn't gone far before we saw a lone Spitfire which we thought was a funny 'squadron'; however, he seemed to have been just a stray, so we flew on until we were about half a mile from the coast.

Shortly afterwards, I noticed about 15 aircraft and reported these to Johnny, who had a look at them, both thinking they must be our escort. However, it wasn't long before we knew they were not, simply because they formed a large circle right round us and then, one at a time, they came in – firing. It was just like a bunch of Red Indians going round a waggon train!

Finally, one attack set the Walrus on fire, and from several hundred feet we simply crashed into the water. The sea all around us was alight with burning petrol and Johnny got out and jumped into the water, but hadn't got a dinghy with him and hadn't even had time to inflate his Mae West.

From the rear hatch I managed to throw out two dinghies, one large bomber-type and a single K-type fighter dinghy. We swam to these and both got in. All the time we were still being shot-up by these '109s, which continued to come down one at a time to have a go at us. I was hit in the finger and our large dinghy was burst open which resulted in us both having to get into the one-man dinghy, which, of course, was then half under water.

Flying Officer Hayes and his crew picked us up and took us back to base, where the doctor at Shoreham removed some shrapnel from my finger – the same finger I'd had damaged some months earlier.

Several years later, whilst visiting an Air Training Corps unit at Eastbourne, I was introduced to a Flight Lieutenant and we got talking. He said he'd been one of the Blackgang controllers (on the Isle of Wight). It turned out he'd been on duty the day we were shot down! He admitted that he had been responsible for telling us that the 15 aircraft were our friends coming to escort us. Nevertheless, we had a good drink over it.

Pilot Officer L.R. Healey, No 277 Squadron

As Johnny Barber recalls:

Having 15 Messerschmitt 109s going round you at about 300 knots, having a good grin, when the Walrus was flat out at about 115 knots, is one thing I shall never forget.

Pilot Officer J.L. Barber, No 277 Squadron

The Messerschmitts were from I/JG27, based at Poix, and it was Oberfeldwebel Reiner Pottgen who claimed the Walrus, one of seven victories Pottgen would gain in the Second World War. On this day Leutnant Paul Rautenberg failed to return and may have been the pilot Len saw heading away trailing smoke. In North Africa, during 1942, Pottgen had been the wingman of the highly successful Hans-Joachim Marseille, who claimed 158 Allied aircraft before his death that September.

Colonel Pete's rescue

Martlesham and Hawkinge co-operated on a rescue on 15 April, to pick up a 'big fish' from the sea. The American 4th Fighter Group at Debden had flown on *Rodeo 204* – a fighter sweep over Belgium. Shortly after 5 p.m., some enemy fighters were encountered over Knocke and then off Ostend; three FW 190s were attacked by the Group CO, Colonel Chesley

Peterson. In the fight which followed, two '190s were claimed, but the Americans lost two P-47 Thunderbolts. Then Peterson's P-47 developed engine trouble and he baled out, 30 miles from the English coast.

With the Mayday call received, Martlesham sent off two Spitfires, flown by Warrant Officer W. Greenfield (P8032) and Sergeant J. Brodie (P7321), followed by a Walrus piloted by 'Kiwi' Saunders with 'Sticky' Glew and Flight Sergeant F. Gash, who flew out from Hawkinge. Peterson was located at 6:16 p.m., and while Greenfield went off to bring in the Walrus, Brodie circled.

The Walrus duly arrived, along with two Spitfires of 91 Squadron, and within minutes, Peterson was safely on board. 'Kiwi' Saunders relates:

The search area was 050 degrees from Hawkinge and a distance of 45 miles. From what I can remember, the sea was a bit choppy and the pilot we rescued was not in good condition. On becoming airborne, we were instructed to continue further out into the North Sea and look for someone else. This did not appeal to our rescued pilot who wanted us to return him immediately to dry land. We ignored him, but after probably 20 minutes, we were told to land back at Martlesham.

We were surprised to find quite a large group of people waiting to welcome us – or rather, our passenger. We were completely unaware of his rank, but when we saw officers gazing down at him on a stretcher and saluting, we realized he was of some importance.

Apparently he was leading a P-47 Group at the time and rumour had it at the time that his parachute had not quite opened when he hit the water. The Americans were gratified because a while after that, they gave one US DFC and three Air Medals to 277 Squadron. A big shindig at Bushey Park was my introduction to rum and Coke.

Warrant Officer A.K. Saunders, No 277 Squadron

A shark problem!

There was quite a different story for 276's 'B' Flight on 15 April. Pilot Officer Ken Butterfield, with the CO, Squadron Leader Ben Bowring, and Sergeants O. Evans and R. Churchill, flew Walrus W3029 on an air test and sea landings. It was late afternoon, and on one landing on the sea, the Walrus hit a submerged object which ripped open the hull, whereupon the aircraft immediately sank. The men had no time to get a dinghy out and after first climbing onto the mainplane, they then had to take to the water in their Mae Wests.

There was just time to get off a quick call for help which was answered by 'C' Flight at Bolt Head, who sent out Flying Officer D. Martin, 'Spike' Hughes and Flight Sergeant G. Paxton in W2875. The Walrus had sunk just half a mile out, so the second Walrus was with them in minutes, and so was a launch. 'Tiny' Martin landed and picked up the four men, Sergeant Churchill being unwell as he was a non-swimmer and had had to be supported by Butterfield and Evans.

McBrien also arrived overhead in a Defiant but the men were by this time out of the water, and then three were transferred to the boat while Churchill was flown to Harrowbeer and taken to hospital. Meanwhile, McBrien had spotted a basking shark in the water, just 500 yds from where the men were. Sergeant G. Dougles in the turret fired at it but they doubted whether they could even claim a 'damaged'. However, they did wonder whether the Walrus had hit this or another basking shark! Ken Butterfield recalls:

I had been booked out to do an air test and sea landings. This Walrus had been blown over in a high wind at Portreath and sent up to Harrowbeer for repairs. I took with me for the ride Sergeants Evans and Churchill, plus Squadron Leader Bowring, our CO.

There was quite a nice sea running and I touched down correctly, but almost immediately Churchill called on the intercom that there was water coming in. I instantly opened the throttle to take off, but it was too late; water was coming in very quickly.

I got the three of them up the front, trying to taxi as near to the shore as possible. I told them to sit on the cockpit cowling and as the water started swilling round my feet, ordered them to jump off, which they did.

Unfortunately, the nose of the aircraft was pushed down and I was under water, still strapped in and connected to the R/T. As can be imagined, I didn't hang around and got over the side of the cockpit and clawed my way upwards, between the wings. There were various wires in the way but I broke surface still between the wings.

I could just reach the trailing-edge of the bottom wing and I pulled myself up and peered over the top. Ben Bowring was quite a way off but the other two not too far, struggling just by the wing-tip. I called to Evans to go to 'Ginger' Churchill, which he did while I crawled over the wing and swam to help. Of course, 'Ginger', the only non-swimmer amongst us, was wearing a Mae West which didn't inflate! Not long afterwards, we were rescued.

When the Walrus nosed over, air was trapped in the tail, and it remained in that position until the air gradually leaked out and it sank. I recall I was wearing a thick woolly, lovingly knitted by my fiancée. Unfortunately, as it got wet, and aided by my movements, about a foot of sodden sleeve eventually slapped around, dangling from each hand; but at least my Mae West inflated.

Pilot Officer K.S. Butterfield, No 276 Squadron

Seven days in a dinghy

Four Spitfires of 602 Squadron had flown a shipping recce on 11 April, from Perranporth. Off Guisseny, they were attacked by half a dozen FW 190s from 8/JG2. In the scrap that followed, Pilot Officer W.W.J. Loud claimed one Focke-Wulf, but Sergeant G.F. Eames was shot down.

Because of the distance, an Anson of 276 Squadron was sent out to search for the downed pilot, but they failed to find him. After several searches over the next couple of days, the missing man was still not found and therefore given up as lost. However, luck was with the young Canadian fighter pilot. He was spotted a week later by another RAF aircraft and another Anson (EG505) went out, crewed by Flying Officer Frank Dimblebee, Flight Lieutenant G. Hastings and Sergeant C. Taylor, at 6:25 p.m.

They spotted a man in a dinghy at 7:40 p.m. and dropped a smoke float and an M-type dinghy, into which they saw the customer climb, but about 20 minutes later he returned to his own dinghy.

Meantime, Dimblebee had climbed to give a fix, which, of course, also gave his position to the Germans, but that was always a risk the ASR boys took. The light was beginning to fade now and although boats had been promised, none arrived. Other aircraft had joined in the vigil and Spitfires, Hurricanes and Beaufighters were now over the area. After just over two hours of circling the dinghy, Dimblebee had to leave, but he knew a Walrus was on the way. This was crewed by Flying Officer D. 'Tiny' Martin and Pilot Officer R. 'Spike' Hughes DFM. 'Spike' Hughes had been in the air force since the mid-1930s, having flown on the North-West Frontier of India between 1937 and 1940, where he'd won the DFM. Unhappily, 'Spike' died recently, but he did give the author his account of the rescue:

Squadron Ops Room was advised that a Lancaster navigator, returning from a raid, had seen a flashing light in the sea and marked its position on his air-plot. He reported this occurrence at debriefing and an Anson of 276 was Scrambled to investigate, at approximtely 06:00 hours, but returned having failed to sight anything. Various aircraft – Ansons, Walruses and possibly Defiants – were utilized in intensive search techniques for the rest of the day, but still found nothing. Finally the air crews stood down at 18:00.

However, Frank Dimblebee was not satisfied and at around 18:00, he decided to take an Anson out and have one more look at the search area, leaving 'Tiny' Martin and myself as the two remaining members of the Flight, in the Mess.

Subsequently, just before 9 p.m., the Controller, Main Ops, rang us to say that 'Dim' had found a dinghy containing a live occupant and was circling overhead, and would remain there as long as his fuel state permitted. 'Tiny' Martin and myself took off at 21:00.

On arrival at the search area, we called 'Dim' on the radio but he was on the way home, but a Beaufighter was still over the dinghy and the pilot switched on his navigation lights and dropped a flare. We could see the dinghy and its occupant quite clearly in the light.

We went down for a rough sea landing and taxied across to the dinghy. The occupant was unable to help himelf but told us he had spent the past seven days sitting in the dinghy, half full of water, after it had capsized, losing everything – rations, water and the survival kit. We eventually got him on board through the front hatch, in excruciating pain but still alive. His condition was so bad that I decided against any interference except to wrap him in blankets and put him on a stretcher at the back.

We now attempted to take off for our return to Portreath, only to discover that the fin and tailplane had been stripped of fabric and rather resembled a mangled Meccano set. 'Tiny' and I discussed the situation, in view of the fact that the sea swell was increasing, a storm was brewing and heavy rain was affecting visibility, but it was imperative we got Sergeant Eames back regardless.

We decided to come home by sea, with 'Tiny' at the controls and myself operating radio for contact with RAF Predannack every 15 minutes to get bearings, in order to prevent being carried out into the Atlantic, past Land's End.

Our strategy worked very well and we eventually came ashore at Mullion Cove, where we watched the dawn break. The last we saw of Gerry Eames was when we handed him over to the medical staff on the beach and heard, with great sadness, he had gangrene of both legs.

As for the Walrus, known to us all as the 'Shagbat', the seas had been breaking over the engine and four cylinders were out of action, maximum revs 500. But despite all this and although she couldn't fly, she got us back safely.

Pilot Officer R. Hughes, No 276 Squadron

★　★　★　★　★

A pair of Typhoons from 197 Squadron were flying a standing patrol on the evening of 11 May, the pilots being Pilot Officer H.M. Pattulo and Sergeant Brooks. It could not have been a pleasant experience at this stage of the war to be called upon to fly Typhoons over the sea, their engines being very prone to giving up the ghost at the slightest provocation.

Pattullo found this when his engine's note changed, and he immediately headed for land. Before long, oil began to spray back over his windscreen and spurt back into the cockpit, covering his instruments. Then his engines seized and it was time to leave. He parachuted down into a calm but cold sea.

His Mayday had been heard and a Defiant of 277 Squadron was quickly sent off:

I was Scrambled with Pilot Officer Walker, my gunner, in a Defiant to a position eight miles south-east of Selsey Bill to search for a dinghy, and located it and was pleased to get a wave from its inmate. We climbed and gave a fix, then covered the dinghy until the Walrus arrived, then escorted it back to base.

277 Squadron was unique at that time in that it had a fighter Flight as well as its Walruses, thus enabling us to do search and escort work without calling for fighter aid. The fighter Flight consisted of Defiants and Spitfires, and these carried a large type dinghy underslung the port wing which could be dropped with great accuracy alongside survivors who required help.

Pilot Officer R. Eccles, No 277 Squadron

The 100th rescue by 277

By the late spring of 1943, 277's total 'bag' of live rescues was nearing 100, which resulted in a bit of a sweepstake being organized. As June came, the total stood at 98, but it wasn't until the 12th that the figure topped the 100 mark.

Martlesham sent out a Walrus and two Spitfires soon after dawn, but the Spits had to turn back due to bad weather. Warrant Officer Greenfield, with Warrant Officer Rance and Flight Sergeant Norman Leighton, continued the search, but all they found was a deflated balloon south-east of Aldeburgh and a broken-down MTB, to which they brought assistance.

Continuing, they were nearing Bawdsey on the way back when they got a Mayday call, Greenfield heading out again and spotting some smoking wreckage and a pilot floating in his Mae West. They landed and picked up Pilot Officer C.R. Abbott, a Typhoon pilot of 198 Squadron, whose engine had let him down. That made No 99.

Soon afterwards, at 6:03 a.m., Ops advised Martlesham that several bombers were overdue from the previous night's raids and a number of Spitfires and Walrus aircraft began to search, but found nothing. Later in the day, a Walrus was again required to search, this time for another American fighter pilot down in the North Sea. As it happened, it was Greenfield and Rance again, this time with Flight Sergeant Stirling as the third man.

At 8:25 p.m. they found their man and soon No 100 was in the bag. It turned out to be First Lieutenant E.D. Beatie, of the 336th Fighter Squadron, 4th Fighter Group, a former 'Eagle' pilot (as Chesley Peterson had been) who had transferred to the USAAF in September 1942. Ernie Beatie remembers:

We were protecting a crippled B-17 coming out and Don Blakeslee and I were warding off two 'Jerries' trying to come at it from above. I noticed one of them firing at me from 90 degrees, I thought. Suddenly my engine literally exploded. Fire blew back over the cockpit and I shut down, and the fire went out.

I tried easing the throttle forward, but when it began to catch, the engine would explode. I finally realized I wasn't going to get anywhere that way, so called my leader and told him I was going down with an idling engine but would try to make it to England.

The CO sent Pat Padget down to protect me as I was dropping out and back of the Group all the time. We were at 23,000 feet and I thought I had an outside chance of nursing my plane home. It soon became apparent I wasn't going to make it, so I began Mayday calls and asked Pat to do so too. I got down to about 4,000 feet and decided to leave it, so rolled the stabilizer all the way forward, flipped it on its back and kicked the stick hard.

I flew out of the cockpit – one hell of a jolt! I immediately lost a pair of brand new boots – my pride and joy. However, life got very busy about then and since there were no practice sessions on this manoeuvre, I had to think hard about just what to do and when to do it. Pat was still giving out Mayday signals while circling me as I floated down. I hit the water and swear I went clear to the bottom of the Channel. However, my Mae West inflated beautifully, then my dinghy exploded and opened. Getting into it was quite a chore but I made it without any trouble.

What a lovely experience it suddenly became. Pat circled and then left for the mainland. It was supposed to be a calm day but every other wave broke over me. I'd hate to be in the Channel on a choppy day! Soon the Air-Sea Rescue seaplane appeared, and what a glorious sight! What intrepid characters they were.

They had to make a couple of passes to set that old seaplane down and then couldn't dare stop it, for it would surely flounder. So they made two passes at me in the water, and on the second one a fellow leaned far out of the rear hatch and grabbed my hair and jerked me over and into the cabin – I was black and blue for days. I was in the water a minute or so less than an hour and the first thing the fellow did was offer me a cigarette. I took it, but my mouth wouldn't close on it, so he held my mouth closed on it as I inhaled.

I have never experienced an airplane ride like that one as he tried to take off. It was hairy! But thanks to the pilot's skill, we finally got airborne. He never got over 20 feet off the surface and flew back to Martlesham, landed in one motion, and there was an ambulance speeding alongside us as we stopped. They literally threw me out of the plane and into the ambulance, and off we went to the hospital.

Later, when I began to thaw out, it felt like a thousand needles were sticking into me. No wonder they gave a fighter pilot about an hour before freezing in the English Channel. But suddenly all was well; my clothes were dried and available and I was ushered to the Officers' Mess and the bar.

Lieutenant E.D. Beatie, 336th Fighter Squadron

Ernie Beatie was back in a P-47 fighter within a few days and on 22 June became the second US fighter pilot operating from England to 'bag' two enemy aircraft in one sortie – an FW 190 and an Me 109 – during a *Ramrod* to Antwerp.

Tom Rance, who was in Greenfield's crew that day, recalls:

The rescue of Pilot Officer Abbott of 198 Squadron: we heard the Mayday and he baled out at 900 feet. We were airborne for two hours 45 mins on that Op. The rescue of Ernie Beatie took place in fairly rough water, with a destroyer not far off. It had launched a rescue boat, but we beat them to it!

Warrant Officer W.A. Rance, No 277 Squadron

Tom had been operating in Lysanders earlier in the war and had been one of the first of the ASR men:

Norman Leighton, ex-26 Squadron, Norm Pickles and myself, ex-2 Squadron, were, I believe, the first of the Air-Sea Rescue boys after returning from France and the BEF, at doing coastal recces. We were formed into a small unit at Martlesham Heath as a detachment of 613 or 614 Squadron and also served at Tangmere, Westhampnett and Merston on rescue duties. It was not until we became 277 Squadron that we began to receive Walruses, Defiants and, later, Spitfires for escort.

Warrant Officer W.A. Rance, No 277 Squadron

Fletcher and Healey, with Sergeant E.G. Green, were to help rescue another 4th Fighter Group pilot on 15 June: Lieutenant Howard 'Deacon' Hively, who at that stage was just an embryo fighter pilot. He would later become a Lieutenant Colonel, DSC, DFC and six clusters, Air Medal and seven clusters, the Purple Heart and over 14 kills.

Hively and the 4th were on withdrawal support for B-17s bombing St Nazaire and he'd either been hit by flak or had an engine problem, for he soon found his Thunderbolt overheating. When it finally stopped, he baled out and was soon in his dinghy. With other P-47s circling around trying to locate him, Hively had some fun trying to hit them with his signal flares, little knowing that in fact, his comrades could not find him – nor did they see any flares!

Fletcher and Co were quickly on their way although it was far too rough to land, but they spotted the dinghy and called up a launch from Portsmouth. Not that Hively immediately appreciated the events, as he later recorded:

I heard an airplane. Could it be German, or was it one of ours? And there it was, coming right toward me . . . a Walrus! Not one of the animals but a Walrus airplane, a British seaplane. Round and round it went, just above me. I thought, 'I know it's rough, but couldn't they even attempt a landing?'

Really, at heart I knew they couldn't, but all of a sudden it levelled off and came right at me. There was a bomb hanging under each lower wing – one of them let loose and came sailing right at me! I hit the drink! When I came up, there it was, six feet away and smoking like a fiend. Down I went again! The next time I came up for air, I realized it was a marker, a smoke bomb. And smoke it did, a thick voluminous, greenish-yellow cloud.

I crawled back into the dinghy and watched the Walrus disappear behind the waves. It was gone, so there must be a boat around here some place.

There was, and after a little searching it located him and then the crew were rubbing him down with towels, followed by warm clothes, blankets and rum. Once Hively perked up, he asked if he could drive the launch back to Portsmouth. He was allowed.

Chapter Eight

Some you win, some you lose . . .

Meter Red Two down

Pilot Officer Ramsey Milne was flying wingman to Flight Lieutenant R.J. McNair, their 254 Squadron being based at Matlaske. They were on patrol on the evening of 14 May 1943, five miles east of Winterton, off the Norfolk coast. At 1,000 ft, the engine of Milne's Hawker Typhoon cut out. There was only one direction to go – down.

Fortunately for him, there was a Walrus already in the air. L2268 was being flown by Flight Lieutenant Trevallion with Bill Land as co-pilot, plus Flying Officer A.E. 'John' Peill and Flight Sergeant C. Rolls in the back.

We had been on patrol 20 minutes or so when my oil pressure gauge suddenly registered zero. With only just enough height to bale out, I was out in no time. My leader flew on quite unconcerned, knowing nothing of my sudden change of fortune, having had no time to call him either.

The sea was cold but I was in my dinghy in short order, with the sail up and trimmed for the nearest land. There was a good wind from the north-east, so I figured I could reach the nearest pub before closing time. I finally noticed McNair buzzing round above me, having eventually missed my company – a good look-out he was keeping, the common name for which was 'finger trouble'.

However, it was a great relief to see the Walrus approaching out of the haze. I do not remember it landing but the sea was choppy, with two- to three-foot waves. As it taxied towards me, it approached to pick me up on the port side although the pilot was finding it difficult to keep on track due to the wind and sea.

As I came alongside, two men were in the well of the after part of the aircraft, leaning over to grab me, then hoist me out of the dinghy and into the Walrus. However, at the critical moment, wind and sea hit the aircraft, causing a miss – by inches.

For me it was despair. I figured I had finally had it and in desperation I grabbed the tail assembly wires, which I soon found was a mistake. I came out of my dinghy and into the freezing North Sea again, and that was a shock; the chill went right through me.

Realizing the futility of holding onto the wires and being dragged through the water, I let go. The pilot taxied around and came alongside in a perfect manoeuvre. Two pairs of hands were waiting and quickly pulled me aboard.

After some now forgotten pleasantries they put a blanket over me and I sat on the bottom of the aircraft, took off my shoes and knew I was back in the land of the living.

Words cannot express my feelings as I sat there shivering, looking at these two fellows who hauled me out of the water. They were apologizing for missing me on the first attempt, and me to them for hanging onto the wires. The pilot, too, stuck his head round, saying sorry for the muck-up, and was I OK? I don't remember thanking him but did so when we were on dry land. I looked him in the eye and nodded; words would not have done it.

Pilot Officer R.H. Milne, No 254 Squadron

This flight was originally planned for training purposes, hence the size of the crew. The intention was to fly along the north Norfolk coast and to practice sea landings, possibly in the Wash. Shortly after take-off in the evening, we were ordered to search for an object 30 miles out to sea from Cromer Knoll. When proceeding to this area, we were diverted to a position five miles east of Winterton.

A Mayday distress call was heard over our radio from a No 254 Squadron Typhoon, call-sign *Meter Red One*. We flew for 16 minutes at 3,000 feet, when we saw an aircraft orbiting an oil patch. On reducing height, we pinpointed a fully-rigged fighter dinghy.

The weather was dull due to fog patches, with visibility four to five miles to the north, deteriorating to half a mile to the south. The sea was ideal for landing and take-off, with a two-foot swell.

Stan Trevallion landed the aircraft close to the dinghy and I went aft to the 'midships hatch to help with the rescue, which proceeded without too much trouble. The rescued pilot was Pilot Officer Milne of 254 Squadron, call-sign *Meter Red Two*, from Coltishall's satellite airfield at Matlaske, south of Cromer. He'd only been in the water for 20 minutes or so, having hardly got his feet wet, and the rescue, for us, had come completely out of the blue.

Flying Officer W.A. Land, No 278 Squadron

Comic relief?

28 May 1943, at Hawkinge, saw 277 Squadron mount a practice rescue sortie in the Thames Estuary. The general idea was for a dinghy to be dropped from a Lysander while a Walrus crew tried to locate it. All started out well, Sergeant Moir flying the 'Lizzie', from which he duly dropped the dinghy. Shortly afterwards, Doug Hartwell and Dave Waddington trundled along in a Walrus, found the dinghy and landed. That was when the fun started.

Waddington, instead of hauling it out of the water, decided to clamber into it and go for a paddle round, whereupon Doug turned the Walrus into the wind and took off, leaving his erstwhile friend stuck in the middle of the Estuary. The escapade became more amusing – afterwards at any rate – when Waddington became very wet, and while waving to the Walrus to come down again, his antics attracted the attention of a Naval launch whose crew thought the man was in trouble. The launch hurried to his 'aid', only to find Waddington adamant that he would only accept rescue from his airborne colleague, which upset the Navy boys somewhat.

Eventually Doug relented, landed and took his friend back on board, plus the dinghy. When the heat of Waddington's language had dried him, they took off and returned to base, leaving the Navy chaps shaking their heads in bemused wonderment.

Rescuer lost and rescued

It was a fighter pilot who opened the June account for 276 Squadron, on the 7th. 412 (RCAF) Squadron was scheduled in a *Rhubarb* operation for the late morning, with Flying Officer H.E. Holbrook and Pilot Officer R.W. Thatcher flying Spitfires EE720 and EE769, respectively. Thatcher in fact was an American, from Rushville, Indiana, who had joined the RCAF before the US came into the war. At the same time a second section, Flight Sergeant E.J. Levesque and Sergeant R.H. MacLean, headed out.

Holbrook and Thatcher made landfall at sea level six miles to the west of Plouescat, found some rail traffic and shot-up trains before they headed further east to attack the engine of a southbound goods train eight miles north of Carhaix. The loco stopped and spewed steam, then a second loco was hit and strafed east of Morlaix.

However, this train had two, possibly three, flak cars and Thatcher was hit by return fire from these guns. Both Spitfires headed for the coast, Holbrook flying alongside to inspect the damage to his companion's aeroplane. He reported seeing three or four holes in its fuselage, but then the two aircraft went into cloud and Holbrook lost sight of his 'Number Two'. Thatcher wasn't going to make it across the Channel and radioed a Mayday before going into the sea north of Les Sept Isles. Thatcher was later to report:

Flak from one of the trains hit me in the engine and the propeller and some went through the perspex of my hood. I headed out to sea, but my engine began to vibrate very badly and the temperature rose. When not far north of Les Sept Isles, I had to bale out. As I floated down on my parachute, I could see the French coast quite clearly, much too clearly in fact. After I was in my dinghy I saw a number of enemy aircraft in the distance, but I don't think any of them spotted me.

Holbrook returned and landed, and just over an hour later, 412 Squadron were taking off to search for their friend, led by the CO, Squadron Leader G.C. Keefer DFC. The problem was that neither of the two NCO pilots had returned either!

After searching, Thatcher was finally spotted in his dinghy at 3:10 p.m., but there was obviously some delay before a rescue was mounted, probably because the dinghy was only a few miles off the French coast. The crew of Walrus L2271 was Pilot Officer K.S. Butterfield and Sergeants George Douglas and R. 'Ginger' Churchill – Butterfield had, until recently, been on Typhoons. His first instruction was to fly out on a course of 186° for 61 miles! Not forgetting some of the gallant rescues in minefields late the previous year, Fighter Command was to rate the coming rescue as one of the most daring yet effected!

A unique feature of this rescue, which had several interesting aspects in any event, was that Ken Butterfield had recently married a WAAF plotter. She was on duty during this rescue and actually helped to plot his course to the dinghy, which gave her some anxious moments as she could see how close the 'customer' was to the French coast. Ken and Mary had in fact married just 18 days earlier, on 20 May. Mary was later to record:

I came on duty just after Ken had taken off. I knew it was him at once, because of his call-sign. I also saw at once that his mission was a dangerous one. Later on, I saw there was hostile activity in the same area, but there was nothing I could do except carry on.

On reaching the search area, which was only about five miles off the French coast, Ken Butterfield found visibility good with some cloud. After a short search, he spotted a dinghy with one occupant being orbited by two Spitfires. The Walrus landed on a very calm sea and the two Sergeants in the back had no difficulty in pulling Thatcher on board. Meanwhile, the covering Spitfires found they had company in the shape of a couple of Focke-Wulfs, but after a half-hearted pass, the '190s broke off. After two attempts to take off, the Walrus finally staggered into the air, landing just as the weather was closing in. Thatcher suffered from shock and cold but otherwise he was unhurt.

Ken Butterfield remembers:

From memory we went straight to the pick-up point. It was a clear day and I could see the Sept Isles from quite a long way off, and the dinghy eventually came in sight. We had Spitfire escort and could hear them talking about 'Jerries' near us. I believe two of the downed pilot's squadron were orbiting him.

There was a light wind blowing up along a glassy swell, but I touched down near the dinghy and taxied up to it. My crew pulled the pilot into the Walrus through the rear hatch and got to work on him.

It was the take-off that was the problem. I could not take off into wind because of the swell, which was quite deep. There was no alternative but to take off along the line of the swell, and fortunately we came unstuck quite nicely.

All the time, and on the way back, we could hear there were 'Jerries' still about, and we were doing our usual 90 knots. It was one of those occasions when it seemed to take a long time before we could see the English coast!

Finally we landed back at Harrowbeer, photos being taken as Thatcher was helped out of our Walrus, wrapped in a blanket. He later returned to Harrowbeer to thank us, which was much appreciated by us and all the squadron.

Pilot Officer K.S. Butterfield, No 276 Squadron

While they were on their way back, two Spitfires of 276 Squadron took off at 6 p.m. – Flying Officer B. Hill in P8565/ AQ-H and Sergeant A.V. Dorman in P8674/AQ-J, the latter a presentation Spitfire IIC, *Afrikaander*. They were to drop supplies to the pilot in the dinghy so he could survive the night, if the Walrus was unable to land and get to him. On reaching the spot, all they could see was an empty dinghy, so Dorman climbed to ask for a fix to check their position.

Hill also saw the dinghy, and when enemy aircraft were reported, he called Dorman to join up so they could fly home but received no reply. Later he received an acknowledgement from Dorman, although the Spits remained out of sight of each other. Hill landed back at 7:35 p.m. but Dorman did not return. It was presumed he had run into the '190s, and indeed, No 10 Group RDF estimated there had been six enemy fighters in the vicinity. Sergeant Vic Dorman was later confirmed as being a prisoner of war at *Stalag 4B*.

In a letter received from him some time later, Dorman said he'd been attacked by a '190 and shot down, ending up in his dinghy just off the Sept Isles. It is ironic that this ASR pilot now found himself in just the sort of position of those he had recently being trying to help. But, unlike many of them, he was not rescued. He drifted in his dinghy for seven days until he finally attracted the attention of two Me 109s with his flares. Later, a German ASR Dornier 18 flying-boat landed and took him on board.

However, the Dornier was damaged in the landing and began taking on water, so a tug had to come out to tow it to Jersey. A couple of days after some repairs, the Dornier tried to take off but crashed, the pilot breaking both legs.

So despite the successful rescue of Pilot Officer Thatcher, the RAF had lost Vic Dorman. It was particularly tragic because Thatcher had already been rescued and the two Spitfires need not have gone out. Added to this, Vic Dorman had only returned from leave that day – one day early – so that the RAF dentist could look at a nagging toothache which had been ruining his break. Not only that, but another pilot asked him to fly on the sortie in his place, as he had a date in Plymouth! Vic Dorman recalls:

To the north I saw six planes approaching, head-on, in line abreast from the direction of England. My immediate impression was that they were Spitfires or Typhoons coming out to join the rescue. This idea was quickly dispelled when they broke off and banked into line astern for an attack. The big black crosses and the unmistakable silhouette of the FW 190 shocked me into action.

I went right down on the sea and flew straight underneath them, heading north. They could not fire down on me as they would have risked flying right into the water themselves. They would also have to do a complete turn and this would also give me time to draw away.

However, the '190 had the reputation of being very quick on the turn, and one was soon on my tail. The first time in my life I heard the shells passing my plane, they sounded like very angry bees. Then cannon shells punched plate-sized holes, first in the starboard wing, then in the port side, but I was still flying and able to control the machine.

As I crouched down in my seat for the protection of the armour plate, a shell came over my head, smashing the gun-sight before my eyes, and carried on into the petrol tank in front of the cockpit. I remember thinking, what a daft place for a fuel tank, then flames started to flicker towards me almost in slow motion.

At my height there was nothing for it but to ditch, something for which there was no rehearsal. The Merlin engine weighs more than half a ton and in the water it has only one direction of travel – straight down! The Spitfire started to sink immediately and I must have been 20 feet down before I was able to struggle out of the cockpit. Shooting to the surface with lungs bursting, I gulped the sweet air and inflated my Mae West.

The '190s had gone, probably suspecting a trap. Why else would a stupid 'Englishe Flieger' be playing 'Magic Roundabout' off the French coast on his lonesome? So I watched the red sun setting slowly over the western horizon, sitting in my dinghy, and wondering, what next?

Sergeant A.V. Dorman, No 276 Squadron

Flying Officer Holbrook of 412 Squadron was reported missing after a shipping recce led by Keefer on the morning of 12 June, after a scrap with six FW 190s. Thatcher, still with 412, was shot down on 11 May 1944 but again survived.

Long after the war, Vic Dorman discovered he had been shot down by Leutnant Friedrich May of 3/JG2. May achieved 27 victories before being killed in action in October 1943.

* * * * *

'Tiffie' down

Sergeant Lionel 'Pop' Ewens of 276 Squadron recorded the rescue of Flying Officer H.A. Cooper of 266 Squadron in his log book on 17 June. Cooper's Typhoon engine had put him into the sea after baling out. Even this wasn't straightforward, for Cooper had been caught up on the wireless aerial and fell 500 ft with the machine before he got free. Then he lost his dinghy. Seeing him in just his Mae West, his leader, Flight Lieutenant H.J.D. Wright, cut away his own dinghy and dropped it to Cooper, but it caught in the 'Tiffie's' tailplane and stayed there. Wright alerted the ASR people as he flew over Cooper – with much difficulty.

I went out as No 2 to Barry Hill, being vectored out from Bolt Head, 20 miles. We located a 266 Squadron pilot, F/O Cooper (Rhodesian), floating near an oil patch with no dinghy. Dinghy dropped by Hill. Shortly afterwards picked up by Walrus and then transferred to *HSL 197*. I later discovered Cooper had been on my Spitfire OTU course with me at Aston Down earlier in the year. A small world!

Sergeant L. Ewens, No 276 Squadron

The crew of Walrus L2271 had been Butterfield, Badger and Churchill, escorted out by McBrien in Spitfire P8565/'H'. Ken Butterfield:

The position of this dinghy was given as approximately 20 miles south of Start Point. We had no difficulty finding it, as it was being tossed about a lot in a rough sea. I thought he should be picked up quickly so landed, and my crew got him aboard.

I could not take off because of the rough sea, so set off to taxi back. Fortunately for the pilot, an ASR launch eventually met us and he was thankfully transferred to the launch, but not without a certain amount of trouble.

The crash of the waves against the metal skin of the Walrus made it sound as though we were in a big drum; it was not surprising that the Typhoon pilot was pleased to leave us. Water started coming in and the radio packed up, so Badger and Churchill had to take it in turns to man the pump.

It seemed no time before it was night and pitch black; all I could do was to steer north. At some point a solitary stationary searchlight appeared dead ahead and it felt as though someone cared.

I had the canopy slightly open, and as one Sergeant finished his spell on the pump he would come and stand behind me. It must have been more than frightening crouching in the pitch darkness with water swilling around and waves crashing against the thin hull of the old Walrus, just inches away from them.

Eventually I could dimly see cliffs and started to worry about hitting rocks. I thought it was Start Point. I turned to starboard to follow the coast along to Salcombe Estuary and was relieved to find an ASR launch with a dim light showing, waiting to guide me along the coast into the estuary. They told me that the naval officer in charge of the boom at Salcombe at first refused to let them out but eventually relented.

There was no accommodation on shore for us so after a mug of tea we had to use bunks on one of their launches, anchored in the estuary. We went to sleep with the sound of water lapping against the side of the launch, next to our heads.

Pilot Officer K.S. Butterfield, No 276 Squadron

★　★　★　★　★

Taxi service?

The Flight at Hawkinge was called to 'Top Line' at first light on 16 June 1943, as a Typhoon pilot had gone into the sea during the night. Sergeant A. Rollo of 277 was off in a Spitfire in company with two 91 Squadron pilots at 5:20 a.m. to make a search.

Sergeant J. Lawrence (EJ970) with Sergeant E.K. Ticklepenny (DN948) of 3 Squadron, had flown off at 3:20 a.m. to make a shipping recce between Calais–Ostend–Gris Nez–Dieppe. At the enemy coast, Lawrence headed east, was caught by searchlights but easily evaded them, continued his patrol and eventually returned having seen nothing. Ticklepenny headed south-west, but when he was off Gris Nez, Control informed him of bandits. He saw nothing until he suddenly spied three German E-boats below. He had come upon them so quickly he was unable to evade their fire and in a turn he was hit fore and aft, his Typhoon being badly damaged.

He tried to gain maximum height, then jettisoned the hood, turned over and baled out, landing safely in the water, and was soon in his rubber dinghy. At first light the Spitfires found him, when he fired off his emergency hand rockets. Johnny Spence with Sergeant J. Humphreys Scrambled in Walrus W3097.

They flew out more than 20 miles, well within sight of the French coast, and found the circling Spitfires. Spence dropped a smoke float and could see the sea was pretty rough, but he still had to land. He got down without damaging the machine, then made for the dinghy. Great difficulty was experienced in getting the man into the Walrus and twice he slipped and fell into the sea. Finally, Spence left the controls to help

Humphrey, grabbing the man from the side window, but then lost him. Humphrey then seized him as he drifted by the rear hatch and with help from Spence, they finally succeeded in getting him on board.

It was far too rough to get off, so Spence began to taxi back. All the hatches were closed to prevent the aircraft from being swamped as the waves were crashing over the seaplane. Fifteen minutes later, another attempt to take off was also unsuccessful. Half-way across the Channel, the Walrus was met by two HSLs from Dover. Due to a cross sea, Spence found it difficult to keep the Walrus on a straight course. In the meantime, 20 FW 190s arrived overhead, but 91 Squadron, still on escort, got stuck in and shot down four of them. The Walrus was not hit. Pilot Officer Seydell of 91 was shot down but he was picked up by one of the HSLs. Sergeant Mitchell was also hit, but his Spitfire dived straight into the sea and he was lost.

Finally, at about 8 a.m., the Walrus was finally taxied into Dover Harbour where the Navy took charge of Ticklepenny, although both wing-tips of the Walrus were damaged in the process. It was only then that Spence was told of the air battle that had raged above them!

For this rescue, John Alexander Spence RCAF, received the DFC. Sadly, Sergeant Ticklepenny did not long survive his rescue. Just 11 days later, he was one of four Typhoon pilots on a night *Roadsted* in company with six Typhoons from 609 Squadron. Nothing was seen of the supposed shipping they were after, so they returned. It was very dark and Ernest Ticklepenny crashed into a balloon over Dover and went into the sea. His body was recovered and buried at sea by a Naval unit almost a month later.

There is a sequl to this story which concerned Peter Standen, who joined 277 after a brief spell on night-fighters with 29 Squadron at West Malling. On the squadron had been Guy Gibson, who later won the VC for his leadership in the famous Dams' Raid in May 1943. Peter had already been on 277 for some months, flying both Defiants and Spitfires, as well as the Walrus:

Johnny Spence asked me to go down to Dover and bring back a Walrus he had left there, anchored to a buoy right in the middle of the harbour. There were barrage balloons all the way round, and the engine was white with caked salt where the sea had splashed over it. One of my gunners got up and wound her up on the inertia starter, and then we taxied round and round to try and get some kind of temperature in the engine.

I'd arranged for one of the balloons to be taken down, upwind, so I could get over the harbour wall, which was jolly high by then as the tide was out. I opened up the throttle as quick as I could, aimed into wind – which was towards the land, unfortunately – and just as I was picking up forward speed, a tanker of some sort came out of the inner harbour, belching black smoke, which drifted straight down at me. So I just hoped for the best and just scraped over the wall and through the gap in the balloons. I reckoned I deserved a medal for getting out of Dover Harbour in one piece!

We called Johnny Spence a star in those days, for they used a picture of him looking out from a Lysander's cockpit in an ASR film they made, and he appeared in a wartime ASR booklet. We therefore took the mickey out of him because he was a film star!

I had joined the squadron at Stapleford Tawney in Essex, which was the training place for all 277 people. I converted onto Lysanders and then went to Hawkinge. Then we went onto the dreaded Defiant – Johnny Snell was usually my gunner. With the Defiants we had a dinghy lashed under one wing in a nacelle thing and two or three smoke floats under the other wing. We travelled about at 20 m.p.h. below its designed speed and with a radiator needle which, on a hot day, would just go up and up!

At Dieppe my temperature went right off the clock and I was sweating blood coming home! Fortunately we lost the Defiants after a while and went onto Spitfires, which made life a lot more congenial.

Sergeant P.C. Standen, No 277 Squadron

Halifax crew

Bill Land helped with the rescue of the seven-man crew of a Halifax of 35 Squadron on 22 June, but it took two Walrus crews to do the job:

We proceeded to position H.1525, near the Cross Sands lightship, where we saw an Anson, flown by Flight Sergeant Peskett, orbiting a dinghy. Nearby on the water was a Walrus, pilot Warrant Officer 'Fred' Perry, who had taken seven men from the dinghy. I landed in a three-foot swell at 09:10 hrs.

We transferred four men from Fred's Walrus and I was taxying for take-off when my engine stalled. Paul Roy climbed on the wing and using a starting handle managed to restart it. This was no easy task in view of the swell and the fact that the Pegasus engine required plenty of brawn to turn it over.

Both our aircraft managed to take off at around 09:30, and headed for base. Our customers were all in good shape and spirits, and I was photographed with my four back at Coltishall.

Flying Officer W.A. Land, No 278 Squadron

The Halifax crew had been on a raid to Krefeld the previous night, six of the 19 aircraft being lost. The pilot, Sergeant D. H. Milne, was an Australian, and having just come from 77 Squadron, this was his first trip with 35 Squadron, within No 8 Pathfinder Group. Their bomber (BB368/'H') had been hit in the starboard outer engine by flak 40 minutes inside the Dutch border, but they had flown on to the target. On the way home the port inner engine had failed just after recrossing the Dutch coast and they had just failed to reach the English coast, coming down off Cromer.

Sadly, they failed to return from a raid on Cologne on the night of 3/4 July 1943, in Halifax HR673/'B'.

The other Walrus had been flown by Warrant Officer F.C. Perry and his crewman, Sergeant D.R. 'Danny' Swindell. These latter two had a rough day on the 26 June, landing to pick up a US pilot just a mile off the coast. The American, from the 56th Fighter Group, came down off Scratby, after abandoning his machine when only one wheel would come down after an escort mission to France. On landing, the strength of the sea and current was much stronger than anticipated and the Walrus could not be turned downwind. Perry tried to steer for the beach but the current then carried the Walrus in rapidly and it was washed ashore. It eventually had to be towed off by the Caister lifeboat and towed into Yarmouth by an HSL.

Chapter Nine

Off the
Dutch Coast

Jim Renvoize's first rescue

Following a *Circus* against Maupertus aerodrome on 24 June 1943, 276 Squadron completed a busy week with their third rescue of a fighter pilot. The raid was by 12 Venturas, 504 Squadron being part of the escort.

Over France, Sergeant C.S. Wright's Spitfire (EE621) had been hit by flak and headed out to sea. He gradually lost height and when down to 5,000 ft it was clear he was not going to make England, so he baled out, south of the Needles. In his bale-out his dinghy was ripped, so he was left in the water with just his Mae West; but at least some of his squadron's Spitfires were circling him.

Flight Lieutenant J.V. Renvoise, 276's 'A' Flight commander at Warmwell, was Scrambled in Walrus L2335 and flew out with two of the Flight's Spitfires as escort. By this time a dinghy had been dropped to the Sergeant. Renvoise's crew consisted of Tom Vacquier and Sergeant J.Frisby. The sea conditions were not good and this was James Renvoise's first rescue attempt. He almost crashed on trying to get down but managed to get off again and came round for another try, which was successful.

The position was 30 to 40 miles south of Bournemouth and when we arrived in the area we could see at once a Beaufighter circling above. I understand that a section of 504 Squadron had stayed with Sergerant Wright until relieved by the 'Beau'. Exactly how it should be done? Looking back, I am surprised that the circling Beaufighter did not attract a swarm of Me 109s as he must have been going round and round for some time; it took us an hour to get to him.

On coming down to sea level to weigh things up, I was dismayed to see an enormous swell of about 15 feet and the tops about 40 yards apart, so I knew we wouldn't be able to take off again as there was absolutely no wind. We deliberated for a minute or two and then decided that we would have to try to land just to get the fellow aboard and then start to taxi north.

My first attempt to land had to be aborted as I bounced so high from one swell top that we were in danger of stalling from about 60 feet, so I decided to go round again and have another go. That was the most frightening moment.

We had to land at a fair speed as there was no wind and we bounced from one swell top to the next about three times, before settling down. Fortunately nothing got broken, although it sounded as though the aircraft was breaking in half!

As we taxied towards the dinghy he kept disappearing in the swell, so Flying Officer Vacquier had to stand up with his head through the roof to guide me. Then he went to the front hatch to catch the dinghy and pay it slowly along the hull, down to Sergeant Frisby at the rear hatch, then Vacquier went aft to help Frisby get the man in. I believe they had a hell of a job as he was a dead weight, semi-conscious and delirious. After they got him aboard and settled down on the floor, wrapped in blankets, we started to taxi on a northerly bearing, and after about a quarter of an hour an ASR launch from the Isle of Wight appeared on the scene.

We decided it was too dangerous, as well as very difficult, to transfer Sergeant Wright, so taxied along behind the launch for four hours, 10 minutes, until we got to Yarmouth, Isle of Wight, where he was taken ashore. We then took off from there to go back to Warmwell – mighty relieved to be back.

It had been an horrendous journey, with the Walrus slewing from side to side and first one and then the other wing float crashing into the swell as we had to use quite a lot of throttle to get the aircraft to answer to the rudder, and I had visions of us having to abandon ship. It was also one of those blinding summer days with not a cloud in the sky and the sun reflecting off the smooth water. All the time we were expecting a flock of Me 109s to arrive and blast us and the boat out of the water.

We received a very grateful letter from Sergeant Wright, in the Military Hospital at Totland Bay, a few days later. I could not help thinking that we might have done him a favour if we had arrived about half an hour later; then he would have been picked up by the launch and had a much more comfortable ride home.

Flight Lieutenant J. V. Renvoize, No 276 Squadron

Once clear of the Dorset coast, the sea conditions, with their white caps, looked decidedly uninviting. After about 50 minutes' flying on a set course for the estimated position of our customer, we were spared the normal endless searching (so often heartbreakingly fruitless) by an aircraft orbiting a dinghy.

I would rate the weather conditions as near Gale Force 7 to 8, with sea conditions marginal for sea landing. Anyway, we pressed on and Jimmy managed to put the old 'Shagbat' down close to the dinghy without bending it. The seas were fairly ginormous and there was no way we were going to be able to stop the engine for a gentle pick-up – it had to be a retrieval whilst underway!

Frisby positioned himself in the forward hatch with a boat-hook, getting smothered in spray, while I opened up the rear hatch and with the pusher propeller 'breathing' down my neck, stood ready to do the 'Charles Atlas heaving aboard' bit! After a slightly more than hectic bit of manoeuvring, Jimmy managed to close onto the dinghy so that it would pass between the port side of our hull and the port float, but within reach of Frisby and his boat-hook. He would then be able to hook onto the dinghy and sweep it back to me at the rear hatch.

We missed him on the first pass, the man being very nearly clobbered by the port float. At the second pass, Frisby managed to hook on and the dinghy careered back to me. I grabbed the chap in one almighty panic-stations movement, as the dinghy swept away from under him. I concentrated on heaving him aboard through the essentially one-person hatch, water-logged and semi-conscious. He had injured his head as he jettisoned the hood of his Spitfire. Once inside, I removed some of his soaking flying gear and other clothing, dried him off as much as possible, then wrapped him up in blankets.

Meanwhile, Jimmy had given up the idea of trying to take off as the old 'Shagbat' was fond of digging its nose in, with quite unpleasant consequences. He now decided to head back to the nearest landfall, the Isle of Wight. So with several hours of taxying ahead of us, plus the ever present threat of Luftwaffe intervention, we were grateful for air cover by Spitfires from our man's own squadron.

Jimmy agreed that I should see if I could get some medical help for our 'guest', rather than wait the several hours before we would reach land. With water everywhere in the Walrus, each time I used the Morse key I got a shock, so although I finally got a message through, it was a bit of a 'shocker'!

After a couple of hours or so, a Naval pinnace arrived, but it was still too rough to transfer Sergeant Wright to it, so we took advantage of the smooth wake behind the pinnace and got back to the island after four hours. We saw him off in an ambulance, but not before he had said, 'Thank you for saving me.' We heard later that Sergeant Wright bagged an FW 190 about a month later.

Flying Officer T. Vacquier, No 276 Squadron

To: OC No 276 ASR Squadron.
From: Sgt Pilot C.S. Wright, 504 Sqdn, Ibsley.

Sir,
I have the honour and great pleasure of thanking you very sincerely for the speed and efficiency with which your squadron effected my rescue last Thursday. I should like to stress on two things, the fine skill and daring with which the pilot landed on the heavy swell that was running, and the care and great consideration that was shown to me by the crew.

I should like to thank all those who took part in the rescue, the crew, ground staff, and radio operators from the bottom of my heart for undoubtedly saving my life.

I remain, Sir, Your obedient servant,
Colin S. Wright.

* * * * *

Off the Dutch coast

On the afternoon of 22 June, after several searches for missing B-17s, a message was received from Ops, informing Jack Brown at Martlesham that a dinghy had been spotted perilously close to the Dutch coast. As it was virtually unknown for any of the Walrus squadrons to even consider a rescue to be beyond them, Jack Brown was soon devising a plan of action.

While Ops sought and received Group's approval, Brown briefed his crews. Two Walruses would fly out for 55 minutes and be met and escorted by Typhoons of Martlesham's 198 Squadron, who would take off 27 minutes after the seaplanes. They would be followed by four of 277's Spitfires who would relieve the Typhoons, who in turn would be relieved by more Typhoons of 198 later. The first section of Typhoons, once rendezvous had been made, would escort the Walruses to the dinghy. Greenfield, Horan and Leighton took off in X9526, while Tom Ormiston, Errington and Mann flew the second Walrus, X9563. They were airborne at 6:37 p.m.

The men in the dinghy were from 102 Squadron from Pocklington. On the previous night they had been part of a raid on Krefeld, but on the way out, they had been hit by AA fire near Oberflakkee (an unfortunate name in the circumstances!), and their Halifax (JD206/'T') was crippled. They lost three engines, leaving the pilot, Sergeant G.S.B. Honey, just the starboard outer to play with. The bombs were jettisoned and the Halifax turned and reached the North Sea coast, but soon had to ditch. They were unable to give a distress call as the trailing aerial could not be reeled out and the range of the fixed aerial was insufficient for reception. They also found that once opened, they could not close the bomb doors.

In spite of having just one engine and hanging bomb doors, Honey made a good landing on the sea, but with the bomb bay open the water quickly entered the Halifax. Nevertheless, everyone was out before the machine went down. The dinghy had operated and was the right way up, and it was soon launched into the night. All seven of the crew were successful in getting into the dinghy but they knew they were not far off the enemy coast, so put out the dinghy's drogue to try and stop them drifting ashore.

The men were sighted by a Mustang as early as 6:35 a.m. the next morning and again by Typhoons in the afternoon. As they had not been grabbed by the Germans, and appeared not to be drifting further inshore, it was decided to try and rescue them. There was always the danger, of course, when it seemed obvious the Germans knew there were Allied airmen just off the coast, that the enemy were setting a trap for any would-be rescuers.

The bomber crew finally saw the two seaplanes coming towards them and fired off a distress flare. Bill Greenfield and Ormiston both landed, Greenfield taking on board the Halifax pilot, the engineer and a gunner, while Ormiston took on the navigator, bomb aimer, wireless operator and the other air gunner. With a heavy sea running and the extra weight of the rescued men, the seaplanes were unable to take off so taxied west in the hope of finding better conditions. In any event, they were getting away from the hostile coast. Norman Leighton, in Greenfield's crew, recalls:

As the pick-up 'fix' was near the Dutch coast, it was decided that we should have a fighter escort in the area. We were to take off, flying out at our 90-knot speed, and the fighters would follow and catch us up near the hostile coast.

We found the dinghy and, despite very rough seas, both Walruses landed and picked up the seven men. The sea was very bad and the waves were frequently washing over our aircraft, so we taxied back for about 30 minutes. We were getting really buffetted about so our pilot decided to try to get airborne. I was sitting in the second pilot's seat (the Walrus had dual controls) and Greenfield told me to hang on to the joystick, and when he gave the word I was to also pull back on the stick.

We opened up to full throttle and started porpoising very badly. We also saw a massive wave approaching and Greenfield yelled 'Push'! We just managed to skim the top of the wave and we were airborne!

The windscreen cockpit windows were covered in sea spray and when we had climbed to about 200 feet, two fighter aircraft in an unusual greenish-blue camouflage flew past us at a distance of about 50 yards. I gave them the two-fingered victory sign and I am sure that one of the fighter pilots responded in similar fashion. I mention this because when we had landed back at Martlesham Heath and were being debriefed, I told the Intelligence Officer this, who said that they were not our Spitfires, but he thought Manston might have also sent out some escort fighters.

We had nearly finished our debrief when two Spitfire pilots came into the room and said they had been in combat with two FW 190s which had an unusual greenish-blue camouflage, and they claimed to have shot one of them down. The pilot was Flying Officer Ray Hesslyn. Needless to say, I took a refresher course on aircraft recognition!

Flight Sergeant G.N. Leighton, No 277 Squadron

The four Spitfires had taken off at 7:32 a.m., to relieve the Typhoons and catch up the Walrus. The four pilots were Flying Officers R.B. Hesslyn DFM & bar, A.J. Boddy, Edmiston and Brodie. Ray Hesslyn, a New Zealander, had recently returned from the fighting over Malta and had shot down a dozen enemy aircraft there. It is not certain what he was doing with 277 at this time, for he was with 501 Squadron, but as 501, like 91, took part in a number of ASR escorts, he was probably available to fly and probably giving his experience to the Spitfire pilots on 277.

As they reached the scene, Hesslyn could see the Walruses heading west and assumed they were unable to get off, but about 15 minutes later, one made another run and became airborne (Greenfield) and Hesslyn detached Edmiston and Brodie to escort it back. Remaining over Ormiston's Walrus, Hesslyn spotted two aircraft, flying low down, 40 minutes later, coming from the west out of the setting sun. From that direction he thought it must be the relief Typhoons and turned to meet them, only to identify them as FW 190s at 600 yds.

Both Hesslyn and the '190 pilot opened fire at the same time, the German's shells passing over his port wing as he saw his cannon shells striking the Focke-Wulf's engine and around the cockpit. A large puff of black smoke blew back from it, and Hesslyn continued firing until the '190 dived beneath him. Turning quickly, he got in another burst before the '190 was out of range.

On the water, Tom Ormiston later saw a tremendous splash in the distance and guessed that the damaged '190 had crashed. After this episode, the Spitfire's fuel was starting to run low, so Hesslyn called for the relief aircraft.

By now, some concern for Ormiston was being felt and Jack Brown took off in another Walrus in company with two more Spitfires and flew out to the taxying seaplane. The sea, however, was too rough to land on, so Brown had to content himself with watching over his men, hoping they wouldn't founder. He called up a Naval MTB he knew was on the way, confirming Ormiston's exact position. MTB *D.16* duly arrived and escorted the Walrus back.

Ormiston found great difficulty in staying on course, and Flight Sergeant Errington's assistance was needed to operate the control column in order to maintain a straight line. Nine- to 10-ft waves did not help and the escorting aircraft were constantly calling to guide Ormiston past minefields and other obstructions. Finally, at 2 a.m., the Walrus ran out of petrol.

The waves were now reaching 10 to 15 ft and *D.16* took some time to get a line to the machine, but they finally managed it and took the Walrus in tow. After an hour, the waves were so high and the sea so rough that the men in the Walrus could no longer see the MTB as it dipped into the troughs. Ormiston now decided he must transfer his passengers and crew to the boat, which was finally accomplished after great difficulty, and the Walrus had then to be cut adrift and abandoned. The MTB reached Felixstow at 6:30 a.m.

Surprisingly, the Walrus stayed afloat and was later reported to have beached itself, and Jack Brown decided to try and salvage it. Tools, petrol and oil were loaded onto a truck and Brown, together with Corporals Mills and Thomas, plus LACs Bignall and Iddon drove to Felixstowe where they went aboard an HSL, fully expecting to be taken to the Walrus where they would refuel it and fly it home.

Leaving Felixstowe, they sighted the destroyer HMS *Mackay* towing the Walrus, which, to their horror, was wallowing and floundering in its wake. The HSL hailed the destroyer and came alongside. Brown went on board and then onto the Walrus, which was pitching and tossing in the rough sea, and found two sailors aboard who were being kept busy trying to keep the water level down inside, as the sea came in through holes and broken windows at every turn.

Taking charge, Brown made the necessary towing adjustments, helped with the baling, and from time to time called orders to the ship from the front hatch. After what seemed an eternity, they reached Harwich from where the Walrus was towed to the sea hangers at Felixstowe and taken inside. It was in a sorry state, fowled by sea water and debris as well as oil, which the destroyer had pumped out in an attempt to smooth out the roughness of the sea beneath the Walrus. The engine was caked in salt and the ground crew set to and did a tremendous job of cleaning off most of the muck and filth, while the Engineering Officer at Felixstowe took steps to treat the aircraft against corrosion.

It had been a long 24 hours for the Halifax crew and a long and arduous period for the Martlesham Flight of 277, but they had got the job done and not lost an aircraft. Warrant Officer Thomas McNeil Ormiston received the DFC for this rescue.

* * * * *

No charge for excess baggage

At the beginning of July 1943, Squadron Leader Linney relinquished command of 277 Squadron upon his promotion to Wing Commander and a posting to Fighter Command HQ. 277 was taken over by Jack Brown, who was promoted to Squadron Leader. Also on the domestic side, Johnny Spence received a bar to his DFC in July and was also posted. He had been with the squadron for two years. Squadron Leader A.D. Grace took over command of the Hawkinge Flight.

In some respects, the Walrus was becoming a victim of its own success. In almost anything above a calmish sea, it became difficult to take off when more than four men had been rescued. The conditions and the weight were always a problem, and for this reason it was rare – in fact very rare – for Walrus aircraft to even consider taking guns on sorties. After all, they were not fighting aircraft, and now that they had Spitfires, any thought of defensive armament came second to the weight consideration of guns and ammunition, in favour of a rescued airman.

Yet the Walrus pilot knew that if he was going out to rescue a crew of a bomber, whether RAF or USAAF, he was likely to have anything from seven to 10 men to take on board, plus his own crew. With these types of rescues, unless circumstances dictated otherwise, the Walrus would often take just one crewman rather than two, in order that they could take on the maximum number of 'customers'. This made it difficult for that one crewman, as often the pilot had to stay at the controls in order to keep the aircraft into wind, into waves, or close to the rescued men, who might or might not be in a dinghy.

The dramatic rescue of the 102 Squadron crew recorded earlier in this chapter illustrates the problem, even with two Walruses.

278 Squadron faced another problem on 17 July. This time it was a Fortress crew of the American 511th Bombardment Squadron, 351st Bomb Group, based at Polebrook. They had been part of a force of B-17s which went for Hannover but were recalled due to weather. Over the Dutch coast, enemy aircraft attacked, and one Fortress had to ditch.

An Anson was sent out to locate survivors, flown by Flight Sergeant H.W. Dixon, who found two dinghies with nine men. On receipt of Dixon's call, a Walrus (L2307) set off, flown by Trevor Humphrey, with Pilot Officer Alfie Dunhill; another (L2238) with Flying Officers V.A. Hester and H.R. Cawker, a Canadian, stood by.

Humphrey arrived on the scene first, landed and took five men into the Walrus, keeping the other four in a dinghy close by until Hester arrived. When he landed, he took on the four, but after two attempts neither of the seaplanes could get off, so they set course to taxi towards Yarmouth. Humphrey asked for HSL assistance and two boats, *RMLs 515* and *'496*, eventually were sighted and all the Americans were transferred by rowing dinghy.

The sea had been rough and now it was rougher still, and the Walruses were unable even now to take off, so once again they headed for the East coast but making no more than six and a half knots. It took them over three and a half hours to get into Yarmouth.

Somebody reported seeing two dinghies and told Ops, who in turn alerted us, and we were told to go and have a look. They gave us a grid reference, we flew out and found the two dinghies and realized at once we were going to be in difficulty getting them all aboard.

We could see nine men, five in one dinghy four in the other. We had just something like that happen just a few weeks before with Trevallion, where he found eight men. We did the obvious and radioed back for another aircraft.

The sea wasn't all that good and we'd had a warning from the Met people that the weather was deteriorating and the wind was getting up a bit, so our best bet would be to taxi to Yarmouth if we could. Hester flew out and between us we picked up all the men. Hester then said he'd like to transfer his party onto an RML but damaged his aircraft's nose, although his passengers eventually got aboard and were taken back. He and I continued taxying and beached eventually inside Yarmouth Harbour, and I stayed the night in the CPOs' Mess there.

Flight Sergeant T. Humphrey, No 278 Squadron

The rest tour

I had joined the squadron in April 1943, from 25 Squadron. I was due to go on rest from Ops and that, in those days, meant going to an OTU and instructing. I didn't fancy that – there were easier ways to kill yourself!

So I rang up a friend of mine who was running an ASR squadron – a chap called P.R. Smith. I asked him if he could use an extra pilot for six months and he said, sure. So I flew over, only to find he'd gone missing the night before.

I found a difficult situation, because what they were doing in those days was filling the Ansons with pilots, navigators and air gunners who weren't quite bad enough to throw out, but weren't highly enough recommended to go to a normal squadron. Some were a sloppy lot, too. When I found they were filling up the Ansons with just people to look into the water, but often were just playing cards and things like that, I got a bit hot under the collar.

The Station Commander supported me and he got rid of them, and we filled up with pilots who'd been on Ops and were having a rest (like me!), and this was a totally different outlook.

We did that fairly quickly and it made a lot of difference because they did look and they did search, and it didn't take long to get them used to the Walrus.

I would also ensure the crews did at least one flight per month over land, as the crews, being over the sea all the time, were losing their navigation and map-reading capabilities, which leads me on to an amusing story.

I always allowed them to take up somebody from the station on these trips (it helped morale), and this one chap took up some delightful WAAF officer. After about three hours, the Flight Sergeant came in and said that this chap was overdue. I wondered where he could be, for if he'd landed somewhere else, they'd have telephoned by now. He must have gone out to sea. We waited for another hour and then got everybody out – the Ansons and the Walruses – broke up a good bit of the North Sea and started a search.

Lo and behold, an Anson spotted him sitting on the water. We landed in a Walrus and when we got near, cut out the engine and shouted across, 'What's the trouble?' He replied he'd dropped the starting handle into the water. Now there's only one reason, I think, why he would have stopped the engine, and that was to take that girl down the back of the aeroplane!

So my gunner got out a dinghy and paddled across with a spare handle. I remember that when he reached the other Walrus, my gunner shouted, 'You sit down, Sir, you must be tired!' Anyway, we wound him up and he was able to take off and fly home. When, of course, we got back, all the WAAF officers were round about and this poor girl was saying nothing happened, and everyone else was nodding, saying 'I bet it hadn't.'

By the summer of 1943, the Americans were beginning to put up hundreds of aircraft in daylight raids and when they came down in the water, there could be up to 10 of them to rescue. The poor old Walrus – we had to shut the windows if we got more than three on board! Very often we located them, picked them up, as we did on 17 July, and then we'd hand them over to a launch.

On this day, the boat came up and began dropping nets over the side, but I called that it was no good doing that, for with the swell, the slightest bump would knock a hole in us. I told them to keep way on, I would come up behind them. However, he insisted we come alongside, so we did, and we banged a hole in his boat! We promptly pulled off and they began the usual Naval emergencies of bunging lumps of rag in the hole, which was just above the water line.

I now did it my way and managed to get my four Americans to the launch, and then in my stupidity I cast away and tried to take off. All I could see was spray until a voice came through on a megaphone: 'You're doing four knots!' I then realized I had far too much water aboard and I'd never take off, so we recommenced to taxi.

We taxied for a long time but one of the floats, which had been bent when we landed, filled with water and my delightful Canadian crewman, who was a very tough young man, went out and sat on the opposite wing, tied himself to an interplane strut and took the sea breaking over him now and again, sitting out there for hours, trying to balance the Walrus so I could taxi in a reasonably straight line.

We eventually taxied into Yarmouth Harbour, where there was a strip of sand just on the right. So I stuck the wheels down in the water and tried to run up onto it. Unfortunately we got stuck as it was a bit muddy – and the weight of the water aboard didn't help. Then after a short while, up along the quay marched about 100 to 150 smart young sailors, with, in a car, a Royal Navy Lieutenant Commander and a regular Naval Captain. I discovered later there was a shore training ship at Yarmouth.

They came and looked at the situation and didn't ask me any questions, but a long piece of rope was produced and the Captain, through a megaphone, started giving instructions. A sailor stripped down to his underpants and swam out to just behind my undercarriage and tied the rope to it. He then swam back, saluted the Captain, and then this Captain, who I later gathered had been on Malta convoys and was no doubt a splendid chap, called out, 'Man the line.' All these sailors got hold of the rope, then he ordered, 'Heave heartily!' – which to an airman, and especially my Canadian, who despite being very wet and cold . . . well, he nearly burst his sides laughing.

So they heaved, then all fell over because this one chap hadn't tied a proper knot. My Canadian then nearly fell into the water laughing! All I could see was this Captain looking straight at him. Then out came the sailor again and this time he tied the rope properly. They then heaved and I used the engine and finally we got out of the water and onto the beach, so it could drain off.

In the meantime, the Lieutenant Commander had also stripped down to his underpants, swam out to my side window and bade me good afternoon, then said: 'When you come ashore, will you come aboard?' I agreed, and he swam away!

I found my hat which, like my uniform, was now covered in fluorescene, which made me look more green than air force blue. I went up, saluted the Captain and thanked him very much. He just looked at my gunner and then at his shoulder flashes and said, 'Oh, he's a Canadian!', which seemed to satisfy him as to his behaviour.

I then discovered that the Commander was the skipper of a mine sweeper and we went on board his ship, and he took us down to the wardroom. We stripped off our wet clothes and he gave us nice warm dressing gowns and asked if we would have whisky or gin? I said gin and he produced a bottle of Plymouth Gin, and my Canadian had whisky. I asked for some water and he stopped and looked at me and said, 'I suppose so,' turned to the steward and called, 'Steward, can you go ashore and get some water!'

They gave us two or three lots of bacon and eggs and I finished the bottle of gin – and passed out. Somebody carried me and put me into a bunk. The next morning I had no hangover, I had no cold, no exposure – it was marvellous treatment. I went to thank him, and for the gin, to which he said, 'not a bit'. He then confided that his was the only ship in the Navy the Germans couldn't sink! I knew it was a joke but asked why and he told me to come with him.

He took me round the ship which seemed to have a vast number of really deep cupboards, almost like walk-in larders, and every one he opened was full of Plymouth Gin. He said the buoyancy of the gin bottles would keep the ship afloat however many holes were put in the vessel. When I asked how he managed to get so much gin, he confided that his father was the owner and maker of Plymouth Gin!

At that moment I was called to the telephone and found myself talking to the Harbour Master, who said that yesterday I had entered the harbour without permission. I explained why, but he said that when on the water, my Walrus was a vessel! He then berated me for giving no signals, not asking for orders or permission to enter. I retorted that I had been in distress, to which he said how did he know that – I hadn't said so! I later learned he was a Commander, and a regular.

Later, he wrote a letter, and the next thing we found was that we had to learn all the Naval Signals, and our Walrus had to carry an anchor and a handbell to ring in the event of fog! So for the next couple of days we used to fly round and round his office, with our anchor hanging down and ringing the bell – after all, in the air we were no longer a 'vessel'. That got him over that!

Flying Officer V.A. Hester, No 278 Squadron

Vic Hester also recalls that they had on the squadron a pilot named F.A. Ragbagliati, who had lost an eye on Blenheims earlier in the war. His brother, Wing Commander A.C. Ragbagliati DFC & bar, was the Wing Leader of the Coltishall Wing, following a successful tour on Malta-based fighters. On 6 July 1943, the WingCo went down flying a Typhoon with 56 and 195 Squadrons during a shipping strike. He was hit by flak from the ships, gave a Mayday and when last seen his smoking Typhoon was heading west. All available aircraft flew out to search for him, and the brother went too, but all that was found was some wreckage. It was a lousy trip for 'Rags'.

After his six months' 'rest', Vic Hester returned to more active operations, flying Mosquito aircraft with 613 Squadron within No 2 Group. He received the DFC in April 1944, but in September he was wounded during a sortie over the Arnhem battle area.

Chapter Ten

The Squadron Commanders

Squadron Leader Jack Charles

Flak, fighters or engine trouble could just as easily bring down a senior pilot, as a junior one; and in one week towards the end of July 1943, no fewer than three squadron commanders found themselves thanking the Air-Sea Rescue men for their safety. Coincidentally, all three were Canadians. The first incident occurred on the 25th.

Ramrod 154 took place that day, 611 Squadron being part of the escort Wing to B-25 Mitchells bombing an aircraft factory in Amsterdam. 611's Canadian CO, Squadron Leader E.F.J. Charles DFC – a future Biggin Hill Wing Leader – was leading his men in Spitfire AR610. The Fighter Wing, from Matlaske (Coltishall Wing), was led by Wing Commander P.B. 'Laddie' Lucas DFC, who had seen considerable action over Malta. Jack Charles, by this date, had around a dozen victories and was about to receive a bar to his DFC.

After the Mitchells had bombed, Jack Charles saw several enemy aircraft – Me 109s – behind the formation, reported them to Lucas, then turned to engage. In the air battle which followed, he shot down one FW 190 and damaged an Me 109, before being engaged himself by another '190. He managed to dive away from it, but then found his engine starting to vibrate, and then it cut. He later made out the following report:

As I was gliding down from 10,000 feet, heading west, I called on the R/T and gave my position as 10 miles off the coast. I was alone at the time. I then went on fixer Button 'C' and gave a long transmission. I returned to Button 'B' and heard myself being reported by Rowley Black Section [611]. A Spitfire came alongside and I jettisoned the hood at 5,000 feet and prepared for the jump by taking off my helmet and fixing it under the undercarriage lever. I wound the elevator trim full forward and the rudder full back to make the aircraft skid (this so I could clear both rudder and elevators as I came out). At 1,500 feet I undid the straps, got into a crouching position with my heels on the seat. I eased the aircraft level and when 130 on the ASI, I gave the stick a good push forward, withdrawing my hand so it would not bang the perspex. I came out of the aircraft very cleanly. The last sight I had of it was the passing of the fin underneath me. It seemed to be 10 yards or so away.

I pulled the ripcord and floated down into the sea at about 15:35 hours. I did not release the parachute before hitting the water as there might have been damage to the dinghy as it came out of its case. I inflated the dinghy slowly and climbed in. There was three inches of green fluorescene water in it; evidently the fluorescene was pulled as I got in. This I baled out while I was drifting, a dipper-full to every 20 yards, so that I left a trail of green spots behind me.

I took off my boots to squeeze the water out and opened my jacket to let the sun dry my clothes.

After 1¹/2 hours, my feet began to get cold, and I found that by sitting on something hard – the two paddles – and straightening my knees out, the circulation improved. By this time I had managed to bale out most of the water except at the back of me. The dinghy was leaking at the bottle connection and needed pumping up every 15 minutes. I had closed the bottle after first inflation at the beginning (in case I found a large leak which I could plug and then reinflate).

The wind began to get stiffer, so I buttoned the canvas flaps. After three hours I did not expect to be found and put up the sail. The wind was drifting me south and possibly towards the French coast.

At 19:00 hours (my watch was still going) I heard a low hum in the water and then saw some Spitfires, 1¹/2 miles north of me, on a course east, flying at 1,000 feet. I did not explode the hand smoke flares until they were almost abreast of me. The first smoke flare did not work – the second one did. I later found it was the smoke I was spotted by, not the actual flare. They turned towards me; four circled low down. I saw they were 611 Squadron. Four circled high: one went very high to get a fix; the other three went away to lead the Walrus in. They circled for an hour and 10 minutes, then the Walrus arrived, landed and pulled me out.

It is too little to say how grateful I am to ASR and to the squadron taking part, their persistence and patience in locating and rescueing me.

The rescue squadron was 278, the crew being Vic Hester, Flight Sergeant J.F. Neal and Alfie Dunhill, in L2307. They had taken off at 7:05 p.m.

This was a fairly easy trip as regards technique because his brother Spitfire pilots saw him bale out and found him again in his dinghy. I noted that he was about 16 miles off Ijmuiden – quite close to the Dutch coast – because they started to shell us at one time. The Spitfires were orbiting so we had no difficulty in finding him. The sea was alright, so we landed and got him in.

We had built a device by the rear gun position, on the Scarf ring – just a piece of metal pole, curved at the top – and adapted a parachute harness so that we could slip that under somebody who wasn't very well and winch them up, swing it in and drop them into the hatch. A good many people who are wet can't climb over the side, even if they are reasonably fit.

We got Charles on board and because of the shelling we immediately took off. The usual routine then was to strip the survivor off and we kept long-johns and woollen long-sleeved vests, blankets, etc., to keep them warm. We also had artificial hot water bottles, things you put a couple of tablespoons of hot water into, shook them up and they got really hot and

The sea did not have them

Above *In the beginning . . . The ASR Flight at Hawkinge used ex-4 Sqn Lysanders. The one shown is coded TV:Q, standing with Hurricanes based at this fighter station.* (D. Hartwell)

Right *F/L Chris Deanesly (left) was twice rescued from the English Channel in 1940, before the ASR Service really got going. He later became successful at night-fighting with his gunner, Sgt W.J. Scott.* (C. Deanesly)

Below *Some of the original Hawkinge Flight in 1941 which later became 277 Sqn.* (Left to right): *LAC Whale, Sgt T. Fletcher, Sgt D. Hartwell, P/O J. Spence, P/O A. Hunt, Sgt P. Patterson, Sgt W. Davies and Sgt S.R. Weston.* (D. Hartwell)

Left *Another original pilot of the Hawkinge Flight and 277 Sqn was W/O David Waddington.* (D. Hartwell)

Above *F/S R.S. 'Sticky' Glew and his wife at Hawkinge in 1941. He later won the DFM but was to die tragically in April 1944 when serving in Italy with 293 Sqn.* (D. Hartwell)

Below *Hawkinge Flight aircrew and ground crews. Front row: Sgt T. Fletcher, Sgt D. Hartwell, P/O A. Hunt, P/O J. Spence, Sgts Patterson, 'Taff' Davies and Weston.* (D. Hartwell)

Above *The Lysander was the first ASR aircraft. As can be seen, it carried dinghy packs attached to its undercarriage spats and smoke bombs under the rear fuselage. This example served with 'A' Flight, 277 Sqn.* (via D. Hartwell)

Right *F/O S.A. 'Sammy' Morrison, 'B' Flight, 277 Sqn. He later served in the Middle East and in September 1943 was OC 294 Sqn.* (D. Hartwell)

Below *Smoke bombs being fitted to the underside of a Lysander.* (via D. Hartwell)

Above left *Three more of 277 Sqn's originals: F/Ss W.A. Rance and J.S.G. Arundel and Sgt W.G. Bunn. Arundel and Bunn were shot down and killed on 25 July 1942.* (W.A. Rance)

Above right *CO of 275 and then 276 Sqns was S/L R.F. Hamlyn DFM, a former Battle of Britain fighter pilot. He added the AFC for his ASR work.* (via R.C. Bowyer)

Below *Aircrew of 278 Sqn, at Matlaske, March 1942.* (Front, l to r): *Sgt Knox-Williams, F/S W.A. Land, F/O S.A. Trevallion, F/L P.R. Smith, P/O Jessop and F/S W.F. Simms;* (rear): *Sgt J. Bartless, F/S C. Hogan, F/S Atkinson, Sgt T. Templeton and F/S S. Hurrell. Smith, Hogan and Bartless were lost during a night sortie just over a year later.* (via W.A. Land)

Above *Some of 277 Sqn's aircrew in 1942.* (Standing): *Sgt W. Greenfield, P/O R.A. Morrison, Sgt T. Rance, Sgt V. Errington and F/S Kirby;* (on wing): *Sgt J.S. Horan, F/S Pickles and P/O D.G. Sheppard.* (W.A. Rance)

Below left *P/Os Tony Hunt and Johnny Spence RCAF, 277 Sqn.* (D. Hartwell)

Below right *Johnny Spence and his air gunner, Johnny Snell, discuss a sortie with 277's Intelligence Officer, F/O A.J. Harman.* (via D. Hartwell)

Above *A Lysander of 276 Sqn, with P/O Peter Jupp and air gunner F/S G. Galloway. Note the squadron's unofficial crest.* (C. Ashworth)

Left *F/S Tommy Ormiston and P/O Louie Nault RCAF, 277 Sqn.* (W.A. Rance)

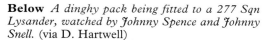

Below *A dinghy pack being fitted to a 277 Sqn Lysander, watched by Johnny Spence and Johnny Snell.* (via D. Hartwell)

Above left *Sgt S.R. Weston and F/S Douggie Hartwell. Note the dinghy pack.* (D. Hartwell)

Above right *Sgt Gordon 'Jonah' Jones, 277 Sqn.* (D. Hartwell)

Below *Standing in front of one of the first Walrus aircraft, members of 277 Sqn in October 1942, Martlesham: Tom Rance, F/S V.H. Jarvis DFM, Hall, Louie Nault, Sgt Allan (on wheel), Tom Ormiston, Errington and Morrison. Jarvis was the first ASR man to receive a DFM.* (W.A. Rance)

Above left *A 276 Sqn Walrus in Salcombe Bay, Bolt Head.* (L. Ewens)

Above right *P/O Tony Egerton-Green, Spitfire pilot with 276 Sqn.* (L. Ewens)

Below *'A' Flight, 276 Sqn at Warmwell, 1943: Bill Elder DFM, Sgt Bud McKay RCAF and F/S A. Scott, with ground crews.* (T. Vacquier)

Above *Some of 276 Sqn, early 1943: F/O R. Hughes DFM, F/O F.O. Dimblebee, S/L R.F. Hamlyn (in mufti), F/O P. Hastings, F/L J.V. Renvoize and one unknown. The three NCOs kneeling have also not been identified.* (R. Hughes)

Below *276 Sqn outside Ravenscroft, the Officers' Mess at Harrowbeer.* (Front row, l to r): *F/L Hastings, F/L Renvoize, F/L McBrien, S/L Hamlyn, F/L Dimblebee, P/O Hoskins, F/L Pushman;* (rear): *W/O Douglas, F/O Brooks (adj), Sgt Kyle, Sgt Badger, F/O Martin, F/S Kirby, W/O Badger, F/O Butterfield, F/S Galloway, W/O Evans and Sgt Dorman.*

Above left *George Mason, 64 Sqn, rescued by Johnny Barber and Len Healey, 6 September 1942. (G.A. Mason)*

Above right *F/L J.E. Van Shaick DFM, 137 Sqn, rescued by Hilton and Seales from a minefield on 31 Octoer 1942. (J.A. Wray)*

Below *A gaggle of 277 Sqn: Bob Holland, Tom Fletcher, 'Dek' Dekyvere, R.F.F. Harris, Norm Peat RCAF, F.D. Hubbard and Johnny Barber. Peat would go missing with 283 Sqn in the Mediterranean in May 1943. (L. Healey)*

Above left *Tod Hilton, 277 Sqn, received the DFC for Van Shaick's rescue.* (W.A. Rance)

Above right *The Frenchman, Bernard Sheidhauer (second from left) with his rescuers, 'Dizzy' Seales, 'Dek' Dekyvere and Eddie Quick (Walrus L2246), 11 November 1942. Sadly, Sheidhauer was taken prisoner exactly one week later and was murdered by the Germans following the Great Escape in March 1944. He was actually shot with Roger Bushell, the man who organized this mass escape.* (L. Seales)

Below left *Ted Karren, rescued on 25 November 1942 by a Naval Walrus.* (E. Karren)

Below right *F/O Doug Sheppard, F/O Jack Brown, 'Kiwi' Horan and Bill Greenfield, following the rescue of Greenfield and Horan on 27 January 1943, when their 277 Sqn Defiant caught fire during a search mission. Horan was killed with 292 Sqn, Burma Front, in January 1945.* (W.A. Rance)

Above *Norman Leighton, 'Taff' Davies and Norm Pickles, 277 Sqn. Pickles was later with 284 Sqn in 1943/44 and won the DFC.* (W.A. Rance)

Below left *S/L Ben Bowring* (far right), *later CO of 278 Sqn, with 'Pop' Ewens* (left), *Ken Butterfield and Ginger Churchill* (front) *of 276 Sqn, April 1943.* (L. Ewens)

Below right *F/L P.C. Smith, CO of 278 Sqn, was lost on a rescue sortie in an Anson on the night of 4 April 1943.* (T. Humphrey)

Above *The 75 (RNZAF) Sqn crew rescued on 11 April 1943 by 277 Sqn. (Back): F/S Sampson, Sgt W. Hardy, the Tod twins with Rothschild between them; (front): Sgt Moss and Sgt Richards. Note the ill-fitting tunics with no brevets, the survivors having been loaned dry clothes following their rescue.* (W. Hardy)

Below left *F/S G.K. Sampson, the navigator, receiving his Goldfish Club badge from P/O J.M. Bailey, 75 (RNZAF) Sqn. George Sampson was killed with another crew on 23 June 1943.* (via W. Hardy)

Below right *Ramsey Milne RCAF, 245 Sqn, rescued by 278 Sqn on 14 May 1943.* (R.H. Milne)

Above *P/O C.R. Abbott* (third from left) *of 198 Sqn was 277 Sqn's 99th live rescue, on 12 June 1943. In the centre is 198's CO, S/L Johnny Baldwin DFC; on the right is F/L Vaughan Fittall RNZAF.* (V. Fittall)

Below left *277 Sqn's 100th live rescue was Lt Ernie Beatie of the 4th Fighter Group, on the same day – 12 June 1943. He was picked up by Bill Greenfield.* (E.D. Beatie)

Below right *W/O Bill Greenfield, 277 Sqn, received the American DFC for his help in rescuing Peterson (see page 109) and Beatie.*

Above left *'Kiwi' Saunders, 277 Sqn, and Becky on their wedding day.* (via L. Healey)

Above right *P/O R.W. Thatcher, an American with 412 (RCAF) Sqn, rescued by Ken Butterfield, 276 Sqn, on 7 June 1943.* (Public Archives of Canada)

Below left *Ken Butterfield in the (opened) cockpit of a Walrus.* (K. Butterfield)

Below right *Although Thatcher was rescued, 276 Sqn lost one of their Spitfire pilots, Sgt Vic Dorman, to FW 190s. He got into his dinghy and was rescued several days later – but by the German ASR service.* (V. Dorman)

Above left *276 Sqn rescued P/O N.V. Borland of 266 Sqn on 21 June 1943. He is seen here being helped from the Walrus by F/S Tony Egerton-Green, and Sgt Archie Kyle, the air gunner who pulled him aboard, and the 'Doc'.* (L. Ewens)

Above right *276 Sqn's 'Doc' helps Borland down; Archie Kyle has done his part. Note Kyle carries a side-arm.* (L. Ewens)

Left *Bill Land, in the cockpit, and Paul Roy with cigarette and Mae West, after their successful rescue of a 35 Sqn crew on 22 June 1943. The ground crew seem pleased, too. Why Bill Land raised two fingers is obscure; he brought back four men!* (W.A. Land)

Below *Bill Land with the four men. The Walrus is K8549/MY:W, Coltishall.* (W.A. Land)

Above left *F/O Don Dring, F/L Jim Renvoize and F/O Tom Vacquier, 276 Sqn. Jim and Tom rescued a pilot on 24 June 1943 and taxied for over four hours to bring him back.* (J. Renvoize)

Above right *Ken Butterfield and Len Badger DFM (left) rescued Holloway on 2 September 1943. W/O N 'Jock' Cameron is on the right.* (K. Butterfield)

Below *Colonel Chesney Peterson, CO of the USAAF's 4th Fighter Group, was rescued on 15 April 1943, having been located by Bill Greenfield in a 277 Sqn Spitfire. Seen here in September 1943 with W/C R.C. Wilkinson DFM, Station Commander Gravesend, Peterson and his wife, and W/C A. Linney OBE, former CO of 277 Sqn, giving a cheque for £100 to the ASR Comfort Fund, and receiving a model of a Walrus in return. Peterson was also rescued from the English Channel during the Dieppe Raid in August 1942.* (via R.C. Bowyer)

Above left *'Pop' Ewens, George Douglas and F/S E.G.A. Sotheron-Estcourt, 276 Sqn, outside Ravenscroft. Ewens and Sotheron-Estcourt were engaged by FW 190s on 31 August during Operation 'Holloway', the latter being shot down and killed.* (L. Ewens)

Above right *Mary Butterfield, Ken's wife, was in the Control Room, listening to her husband during Operation 'Holloway'.* (M. Butterfield)

Below *The moment of rescue. Normally the man at the front would snag the dinghy with a boat-hook, and then let it drift back on a rope to the rear hatch.* (via C. Ashworth)

Above left *'Pop' Ewens, 276 Sqn Spitfire pilot.* (L. Ewens)

Above right *W/C A.D. Grace and . . .* (Mrs Grace)

Below left *. . . F/O F.E. Wilson, 277 Sqn, found and collected four commandos rowing two canoes back from France on 4 August 1943. Despite his rank, Grace was only a flight commander.* (D. Hartwell)

Below right *Three stalwart air gunners of 277 Sqn: Les Seales, Eddie Quick and Cec Walker.*

Above left *Norman Leighton, 277 Sqn, received the American Air Medal in July 1943.* (G.N. Leighton)

Above right *S/L Jack Charles DFC, CO of 611 Squadron, rescued by 278 Sqn on 25 July 1943.* (IWM)

Below *277 Sqn, Martlesham; Walrus X9521. Doug Sheppard in the cockpit, Morrison standing by the engine, Tom Rance and Horan sitting on the nose.* (W.A. Rance)

Above left *F/O Vic Hester, 278 Sqn, who picked up Charles from the sea. They were so close to hostile shore fire they could see the lights of Borkum Island, Germany.* (V. Hester)

Above right *S/L G.C. Keefer DFC, CO of 412 (RCAF) Sqn, rescued by 277 Sqn on 27 July 1943.* (Public Archives of Canada)

Below left *Sgt Jack Mallinson, air gunner on 277 Sqn, who pulled Keefer on board off the Somme Estuary, after two attempts to locate him.* (J. Mallinson)

Below right *S/L R.W. McNair DFC, CO of 421 (RCAF) Sqn, rescued by 277 Sqn on 28 July 1943 – the third Canadian Spitfire CO picked up in four days.* (Public Archives of Canada)

Above *The Walrus boys vied with the High-Speed Launches to rescue men from the sea. Here, HSL 2564, a Vosper-built boat, is put through its paces.*

Below left *W/O George Reeder, 278 Sqn. Along with Bill Land, these two Walrus pilots rescued 10 men from a downed 91st Bomb Group B-17 on 26 July 1943.* (G.B. Reeder)

Below right *P/O C.G. Scott DFM, who was crewman to Bill Land on 26 July 1943. He was no stranger to ASR – 277 Sqn had helped save him when he was shot down in a Boston during the Dieppe Raid in August 1942.* (W.A. Land)

Above *The 91st Bomb Group B-17 crew rescued by George Reeder and Bill Land on 26 July 1943. The photo was taken the following day in their 'survival' attire.* (Front row, l to r): *Carl Smith, Jack Hargis, Capon Simons, Bill Turcotte;* (rear): *Rudy Thigpen, Victor Ciganek, Gerald Tucker, James Bowcock, Jarvis Allen and Albert Di Minnio.* (W.H. Turcotte)

Below *Spitfire II P8375 with Sgt Brodie, 277 Sqn.* (W.A. Rance)

Bottom *Spitfire V AD562/MY:V, 278 Sqn, Martlesham, 1944.* (G.B. Reeder)

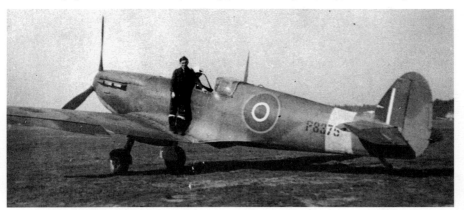

Above left *P/O Taduez Turek, 609 Sqn, rescued by Peter Standen of 277 Sqn, the Walrus being shelled from the French coast.* (T.S. Turek)

Above right *Peter Standen won the Polish Cross of Valour for the rescue of Turek.* (P.C. Standen)

Below left *S/L I.C. Ormston DFC, CO of 411 (RCAF) Sqn, rescued on 26 September 1943 by Peter Standen, Johnny Snell and W/O Jack Rose.* (Public Archives of Canada)

Below right *F/L Marcel Dekyvere RAAF, flight commander with 277 Sqn, won the DFC in 1943.*

Above left *F/S Jimmy Sheddan RNZAF, 486 (RNZAF) Sqn, rescued by Fletcher and Healey of 277 Sqn on 3 October 1943. Jim later rose to command the squadron and won the DFC.* (C.J. Sheddan)

Above right *Len Healey DFC, DFM, 277 Sqn.* (L.R. Healey)

Below *Capt G.E. Preddy, 352nd Fighter Group, USAAF, rescued by Pete Standen on 29 January 1944, poses for a publicity shot with the P-47 pilot who located his dinghy and called up the ASR boys, Lt Fred Yokum.* (USAF)

Above left *Sub-Lt Eric Hall, S/L R.W. 'Wally' Wallens and Sgt Jimmy Cartwright, 277 Sqn, 18 March 1944. They had just rescued the crew of a 320 (Dutch) Sqn Mitchell.*

Above right *Henk Voorspuy, in the cockpit, 320 (Dutch) Sqn. Standing is air gunner Sgt P. de Haan, rescued with his crew by 277 Sqn on 4 May 1944. (H. Voorspuy)*

Below left *Henk Voorspuy and his crew: Cpl Kvan Nouhuis, Voorspuy . . .*

Below right *. . . Sgt Jan Vink and his wife, with Cpl M. Engelsmar at Vink's wedding.*

Above left *John Ot, captain of the second 320 (Dutch) Sqn Mitchell crew rescued on 18 March 1944, by Jack Brown and his crew.* (J. Ot)

Above right *F/O Lockwood and his ASR launch crew, who took Ot and his crew off the Sea Otter after it had taxied for 76 miles* (via J. Ot)

Below *The Sea Otter, which began to equip ASR squadrons in 1944. Very similar to the Walrus, its main visual difference was the fact that the engine pulled rather than pushed.* (R.C. Sturtivant)

Above *Air and ground crews of 278 Sqn, Coltishall, summer 1943. (Front row): P/O Joe Sugg, Trevor Humphrey, P/O Parson (KOAS); (Middle row): P/O Alfie Dunhill, F/O Harrison, F/O Wally Simms, S/L Ben Bowring, F/L Jessop, Bill Land, W/O Fred Perry; (Rear row): P/O C.G. Scott, ?, ?, F/S F.J. Bedford, ?, F/S Wally Hammond, F/S M.J. Peskett, George Reeder, Paul Roy, Sgt Danny Swindell, Paddy Dinneen, ?, F/S Ron Whittaker, W/O Bill Rolls, F/S Cumings. The Walrus in the picture (L2268) had rescued six Polish airmen on 1 December 1942; S/L V. Pheloung, CO of 56 Sqn, on 15 March 1943; Ramsey Milne on 14 May 1943; eight men of a B-17 crew on 16 June 1943; and four Dutch airmen on 20 August 1943. (G.B. Reeder)*

Below *A map showing the locations of rescues by 277 Sqn as at 13 April 1944. The number of rescues close-in to the hostile shore is more than apparent. (RAAF)*

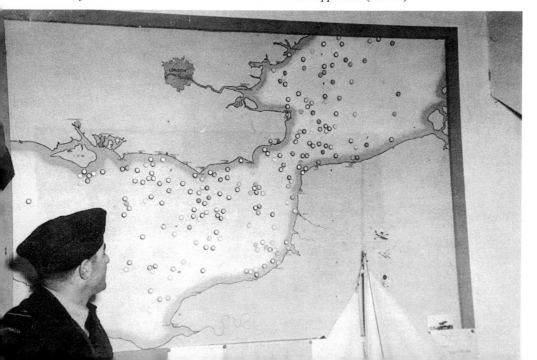

Above *F/O L.J.S. Fittock* (left) *and his navigator, W/O J.W. Hough* (third from left), *of 464 Sqn. 'Kiwi' Saunders rescued Hough on 25 April 1944, but, unfortunately, 'Snow' Fittock died in the crash and was left in the sea.* (J.W. Hough)

Below left *P/O Trevor Humphrey would save 23 lives during his ASR days in both England and the Middle East.* (T. Humphrey)

Below right *F/S Bill Shaw, S/L C.G. Robertson DFC, and Cec Walker, 277 Sqn. Walker, a famous pre-war dirt-track rider, was later killed with Roberston (who had won his DFC as a bomber pilot) during a search mission in March 1945 with 278 Sqn.* (RAAF)

Above left *F/L Tom Slack, 41 Sqn, rescued by 276 Sqn on 18 June 1944.* (T. Slack)

Above right *F/S Ian Dunlop, 263 Sqn, rescued by 276 Sqn on 23 June 1944. He was located in the sea by 'Pop' Ewens in a Spitfire.* (I. Dunlop)

Below *While Sgt Ware (Tom's rescued 'Number Two') waves from the rear hatch, 'Tiny' Martin taxies up to Tom's dinghy in L2335/AQ:V. Note the smoke float for wind direction.* (T. Slack)

Above *WLAC Joyce Millard, who helped pin-point Ross' position in the North Sea.* (J. Smith)

Right *F/O Hugh Ross, 80 Sqn, rescued by 278 Sqn on 14 September 1944.* (H. Ross)

Below *The crew of the 420 Sqn Halifax, rescued on 16 September 1944 by 278 Sqn.* (Rear): *F/L V.G. Motherwell, F/O I.E. McGown, F/O A.J. MacDonald, Sgt J. Porter and Sgt J.A. Wigley;* (front): *F/O L.K. Engomoen, Sgt T.J. Bibby and Sgt J.L. Hickson.*

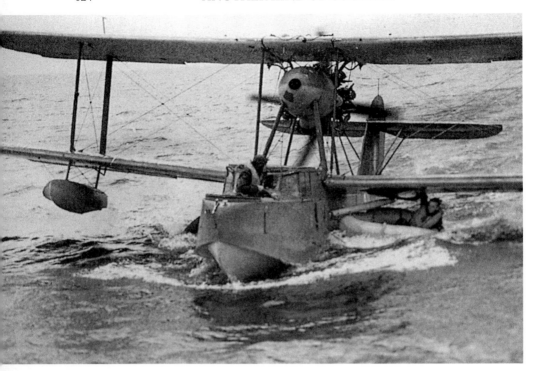

Above *With boat-hook and rope the dinghy is passed back towards the rear hatch, where the 'customer' will be hauled aboard and the dinghy disposed of.*

Below *Walrus P5658, of 276 Sqn, with 88 mm flak damage to one of the elevators, 15 October 1944. The crew were Sgt Shipley, W/O Eddie Lloyd and Sgt Pete Speed.* (T. Vacquier)

stayed so for two to three hours. By the time we'd done this, he was getting as fit as a fiddle, so he came up to the front and asked if he could sit with me, and flew back most of the way in the cockpit.

When we got back, the normal routine was not to go to dispersal, but taxi to the Control Tower where the doctor and ambulance were waiting, because anybody picked up had to go to Sick Quarters anyway. Charles was so fit that I said to him it would save me stopping the engine if he could climb over the front, and he agreed. So I taxied up and he swung his leg over the side to jump down, but, of course, only had these long-john things on, so all his lower region became exposed, just as someone's camera went 'click'. All the WAAF officers said, 'Oh good, he's back!' So it was all a bit difficult. The Station Commander wouldn't give me a copy of the photograph and even ordered the negative to be destroyed!

Charles' father sent the squadron a barrel of apples, I remember, which came over in a convoy; but by the time they arrived, they were all absolutely uneatable. He also wrote to me and said he'd like to do something, would I like to buy a log cabin in Canada? He wasn't allowed to give it under law, but for a couple of hundred pounds, I'd have a cabin, some ground running down to a lake in which there was good fishing, and so on. But £200 I hadn't got. Also, as a young married man, I couldn't see myself going to Canada at some future date, so I wrote back, thanked him, but said no. Later I heard they found uranium on the site!

Flying Officer V.A. Hester, No 278 Squadron

Squadron Leader George Keefer

Hawkinge and 277 got the next Canadian Squadron Leader two days later, the 27th. A *Rodeo* operation in the late afternoon ended with the Spitfire (EN784) of the CO of 412 Squadron, Squadron Leader G.C. Keefer DFC, developing a glycol leak which forced him to bale out way out in the Channel.

The ASR Flight had been put on 'Top Line' at 6 p.m., and 12 minutes later a Walrus was Scrambled to head out on a course of 186° for 46 miles. Three minutes later they were airborne, with an escort of Spitfires from 501 Squadron, but nothing was found and they had to return.

Keefer's position was uncertain, and even the Kenley Wing, returning from another *Ramrod*, were diverted to make a search for him. A call was put through to 412 Squadron to confirm the position and it was given as five miles west of Cayeux. 277 immediately sent off three Spitfires, followed by the Walrus and two Spitfires of 412, plus 501 Squadron as escort. This time they found the dinghy and the Walrus landed.

As happened on quite a few occasions, the prolonged activity in trying to locate a downed airman so near to the French coast caught the attention of the Germans. Just as the Walrus landed, several Me 109s put in an appearance. 501 Squadron engaged them off the mouth of the Somme, and in a brief skirmish, Flying Officer Alfred Grottick shot down one Messerschmitt, and another was claimed as a probable.

Keefer was picked up, found to be very fit and not shocked by his experience. He was soon back leading his squadron, and ended the war as a Wing Commander with the DSO & bar, DFC & bar, and 13 German aircraft to his name. Jack Mallinson was the gunner in the Walrus:

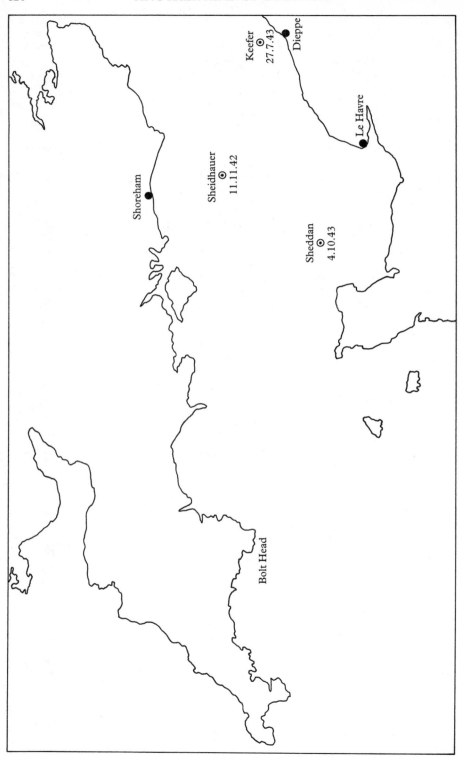

Keefer
⊙
27.7.43

Dieppe

Le Havre

Sheidhauer
⊙
11.11.42

Sheddan
⊙
4.10.43

Shoreham

Bolt Head

Jack Brodie, Lew Butler and myself in Walrus 'D', went to pick up Squadron Leader Keefer who had ditched in the Somme Estuary. We had an escort of Spitfires from his squadron as part of the cover.

We found our 'kipper' in the Estuary mouth which was over a mile wide. The Germans hadn't bothered trying to pick him up, they probably figured he had to come ashore eventually anyway.

When we landed, a certain air of bad feeling entered the game as they opened fire from a shore position. Between operating the old Lewis gun or VGO, or whatever the antideluvian bloody thing was, and trying to drag Keefer in to the back hatch, I didn't have time to worry about much. Canadian voices in the head sets were exhorting us to get our asses out of there as we were going to have company.

We managed to take off and kept low on the shortest course to Dungeness. Some '109s were giving the Spitfires a hard time and there was a bit of a mêlée, but then a 'Tiffie' squadron appeared and Goering's lads headed for the tall timber.

Sergeant J. Mallinson, No 277 Squadron

Squadron Leader Buck McNair

Canadian CO number three was Squadron Leader R.W. McNair DFC & bar, commanding 421 Squadron, based at Kenley, so it was Hawkinge which was again the rescue flight. The date was 28 July 1943.

The Kenley Wing had been part of the escort to B-17s on *Ramrod 165*, to Rotterdam. The operation had been due to start at 9 a.m. but fog prevented take-off, after refuelling at Manston, until 11:45 a.m. A rendezvous was made with the Fortresses although not much happened, but then near the Dutch coast, Buck McNair's Spitfire IX (MA586) developed engine trouble. He immediately broke off and with his 'Number Two' for company – Pilot Officer T. Parks – he headed for England.

Twelve miles off the French coast his engine caught fire and he lost control. He baled out at 5,000 ft, his parachute opening at 2,000! However, in trying to get out of his diving aircraft, he had been badly burned about the face. Once out he had found the flames had burned the release wire of his parachute and damaged the harness. Struggling to get the parachute to function, and hoping the harness would survive the jerk if it did open, was the reason he fell 3,000 ft.

Nearing the water, he then discovered the release box to the 'chute had been fused by the heat and could not be turned. Not wanting to contend with the parachute once in the water, he tore himself loose from the charred harness and fell the last 75 ft into the sea. In the water he found his dinghy had gone.

Meantime, Thurne Parks had been covering him and sending out Mayday calls. As his CO hit the water, and Parks could see he was without his dinghy, he continued to orbit for the next hour, until the Walrus turned up.

This was flown by Squadron Leader Alan Grace, with Lew Butler and Sergeant J. Humphreys. They were Scrambled at 1 p.m., with an escort of four Spitfires from 501 and others from McNair's own squadron who had landed and refuelled at Manston, while other Spitfires from

403 (RCAF) Squadron also went out.

Finding the circling Parks over 40 miles east of North Foreland, they soon had McNair rescued and wrapped in blankets. His limbs were massaged and Gentian violet was immediately applied to his burns. On landing, he was sent to Sick Quarters and then on to Canterbury Hospital.

He was back in action the following month, received a bar to his DFC, ending the war with a double DSO and a second bar to his DFC.

*   *   *   *   *

More taxi rides

While 277 had been busy with those three squadron commanders, 278 had picked up a US crew off the Norfolk coast on 26 July, on their way back from Germany. Flight Sergeant R.C. Whittaker in Anson EG496 found them first and called up the amphibians. George Reeder had been one of the two Walrus pilots involved:

I was Scrambled, together with Flight Sergeant Rolls, to rescue the crew of an American bomber ditched off the Norfolk coast. A second Walrus, piloted by Flying Officer Land, was also Scrambled. A sighting was readily made and we landed to pick up five men, the other five being picked up by Land.

Despite many attempts, we were both unable to take off due to the state of the sea and the additional weight. Finally taxied to within a few miles of the coast and rendezvoused with an HSL and safely transferred the 10 Americans.

Although relieved of the extra weight, neither of us was able to take off because of the worsening sea, until finally, disregarding normal procedure, I headed out of wind, concentrating on riding on top of the sea-swell, and after a few miles, eventually became unstuck and returned to Coltishall.

Poor Bill Land had to suffer the indignity of being towed, arriving at Great Yarmouth in the early hours of the following morning, with a damaged aircraft.

Warrant Officer G.B. Reeder, No 278 Squadron

Flying with Bill Land on this sortie was someone we have met before in this book, but as one of the rescued, not as a member of the rescue side. Clarence G. Scott DFM had been in that 418 Squadron Boston which had gone into the sea during the early stages of the Dieppe Operation in August 1942. He had won his DFM for his efforts in saving his crew, while Fletcher and Healey had guided a launch to the three men. Now Scott was a member of 278 Squadron and flying with Bill Land, who remembers him as a former lumberjack from Moose Jaw, Saskatchewan, complete with a facial scar from his earlier adventure:

I first saw a copy of the RAF Form 540 relating to this sortie on the occasion of the 50th Anniversary reunion of the squadron at RAF Coltishall, in 1991. I consider that the sequence of events and the timing recorded in the account are not accurate regarding myself and I find it very confusing. I think also that this could possibly apply to George Reeder's part in the action. We were never asked to 'proof read' the 540 entries; had we been asked, they would have been rewritten.

We were Scrambled in the evening to an area 20 miles north of Cromer, and on reaching the search position, we were met by one of our Ansons and a Spitfire. The Anson dropped a smoke float and we located two American-type dinghies each containing five men, and a third, circular-shaped dinghy, all tied together. The third was a Lindholme-type which had been dropped with great accuracy by the Anson – in fact it was almost a direct hit!

Visibility was about $1\frac{1}{2}$ miles, with thick haze. The tide was running north to south but the wind was west to east, so I anticipated that a take-off would have to be made running along the top of the swell.

I landed at 6:50 p.m. in a moderate swell which was rapidly rising. I taxied to the dinghies and found the 10 men in good spirits and uninjured. They were eating the contents of the Lindholme containers. We ascertained that they were a Fortress crew returning from Hamburg. With the aid of our boat-hook, Scotty transferred five men to the Walrus and I attempted to take-off along the swell, but due to the weight could not get airborne.

A second Walrus, George Reeder, landed and took on the other five crew members. The swell was getting nasty and after another unsuccessful attempt at take-off, Scotty said he wasn't feeling very good, and he went to the back of the aircraft, I believe to be sick.

I watched George make his first attempt at take-off, along the top of the swell, and it appeared to be a very hair-raising operation. He disappeared in clouds of spray into the haze and I thought he had made it as I didn't catch sight of him again.

I expected another Walrus to arrive to relieve us of some of our load but in the meantime, prepared for another try to get off. The swell had become very heavy and as I turned across it, a wave came over the rear of the aircraft and tore a piece out of the starboard tailplane. It was impossible to assess the damage, so I decided the only thing to do was to get the hell out of it and taxi towards the coast.

Here, I disagree with the squadron account. We attached the two American dinghies to the struts on the wings of the Walrus and these were towed behind us. We did not meet an HSL that night. Had I done so and we had transferred our five men, I would have attempted another take-off, and with reduced weight, would have been successful. I certainly didn't relish the thought of taxying all the way to Yarmouth, with just two of us aboard.

I followed a south-east course on the aircraft compass and plodded on steadily. As it got dark, the swell subsided considerably, and it was about midnight that Scotty reported that the aircraft was taking water, having been taxying now for four hours. He thought our own dinghy pack was floating in the aircraft. I ordered everyone to sit on the wings, three each side, and I opened the cockpit hatch to make a rapid escape should the aircraft capsize. We were also ready to cut the two dinghies loose and occupy them in the event of an emergency.

From time to time, I throttled back to listen for any outside activity. It was a dark, moonless night and on the horizon I could see a line of searchlights dipping from the vertical to a horizontal position, indicating the direction of Yarmouth. We could hear aircraft in the distance also, but as I estimated we must be in the shipping lane and what was known as the notorious 'E-boat Alley', we made no visual signals.

About this time, water must have seeped into the electrical circuits, because suddenly the cockpit and landing lights came on. The landing light shone like a great searchlight out across the darkened sea. Scotty took a fire axe, edged along the wing and chopped it out. All the other lights went out at the same time.

As first light was dawning, at about 3 a.m., we saw a light approaching and we were intercepted by an HSL. The five Americans were transferred to the craft and I accepted a tow. The Pegasus engine had not faltered at any time and was behaving marvellously. The towing proved awkward as the aircraft was moving under its own power. A few miles from the coast, we slipped the tow and following the rear light of the launch, we taxied into the Navy base at Gorleston, where I lowered the wheels and ran up the beach. The time was 4:25 a.m., and I estimated that we had been taxying for eight hours at an average speed of about six knots; a distance of some 50 miles. There was 18 inches of water in the hull.

We were welcomed by the base Commodore and I was presented with an open bottle of whisky, which we both appreciated, being very cold and wet. We were taken to the Mess, where, in addition to our Fortress crew, I think there were two other crews of 20 men that had been picked up by launches the previous day. A merry party followed until a coach came and took all the Americans away, and we were also taken back to Coltishall.

A maintenance party from base later drained the aircraft and made repairs to the tail. Despite a big mag. drop when the engine was run-up, the aircraft was floated and flown back to Colts without mishap. When the engine was stripped down in the hangar, it was found that the insides of the cylinders were thickly coated with dried salt.

Our Fortress crew had been flown back to their own base when we returned to Coltishall, but they had left me with a French 50-franc note (from their escape kit) with their 10 signatures on it, including the skipper, Lieutenant Jack Hargis. They also noted their unit – the 322nd Squadron, 91st Bomb Group, 8th Air Force.

Flying Officer W.A. Land, No 278 Squadron

The full crew list, in fact, was Lts Jack Hargis (pilot), Carl N. Smith (co-pilot), William H. Turcotte (navigator) and Capon R. Simons (bombardier); S/Sgts Rudy Thigpen (ball gunner), James A. Bowcock (tail gunner), Gerald Tucker and Albert Di Minnio (waist gunners); T/Sgts Jarvis Allen (engineer) and Victor Ciganek (radio operator). Bill Turcotte had this to say of the operation, which was his first operational sortie:

As was the usual practice, our new crew was split up to fly their first mission with crews having five or more combat missions. 'Si' Simons and I were assigned to fly with Jack Hargis and his crew. We were in a spare plane to fill in any position aborted by one of our Group planes. We were flying in *Destiny's Tot*, which was somewhat the worse for wear and tear, and reputed to be an oil burner.

Following the Group to the enemy coast, Hargis spotted a vacant slot in another Group which we filled. Going in to the target, there was some 'bogey' action behind us and a heavy flak barrage over the target. However, we got through and felt rather cheerful when we reached the North Sea.

However, we were startled to hear the pilot say 'Prepare for ditching!' soon after we left the coast. At first we thought it was just a drill, but by the time we reached the radio room we could see the wave patterns and realized something was truly amiss; it had not been possible to switch gas tanks and we were running on empty!

There was a jolt as the ball turret hit the water first. The plane bounced up and came down again and thrust us forward, tight against the bulkhead. We quickly climbed out by the gun mount opening above the radio room. The dinghy releases were pulled and the two of them popped out on the wings, as the pilots crawled out through the cockpit windows. We pushed the inflated dinghies to the end of each wing and hopped in, hardly getting our feet wet.

Fortunately the sea was fairly calm and the weather was clear and mild, but the water was cold. Within a few minutes the plane had sunk enough so that the stabilizer was below the water surface, and the weight of the engines at the front and the water weight above the stabilizer at the tail caused the ship to break in two at the mid-section. We heard crunching sounds, then the B-17 sank forward as it broke in the middle.

The radio operator had sent Mayday signals before we ditched, and our dinghy had a hand-cranked SOS sender in it, which one of the crew began working on. Rescue was not long in coming. At first, two Spitfires buzzed us and circled. Then a converted Hudson bomber appeared, dropping a large dinghy which landed close; we paddled to it and tied up. Shortly afterwards, two Walrus single-engined pusher-type amphibians landed and each one taxied up to our dinghies. Five of us got into each Walrus and we prepared for take-off.

The pilot began a take-off run with us sandwiched in the rear compartment, but the old bird was sadly overloaded and despite the most valiant efforts of the RAF pilot, we jolted along but could not get airborne. A second attempt was even more disastrous, for we hit a wave that broke the tail stabilizer, so there was nothing left to do but taxi back toward England – about 40 miles from our position.

Just before dark an ASR launch found us, and with the damaged Walrus taxying behind, we proceeded to port, arriving about midnight. We spent the night in RAF quarters and the next morning returned to Bassingbourne. Soon afterwards, I attended a lecture in the event of being shot down over enemy territory. The instruction proved helpful, for with my crew I was shot down by fighters on a raid to Anklam on 9 October, and spent the remainder of the war as a guest at *Stalag Luft III*.

Lieutenant W.H. Turcotte, 322nd Bomb Squadron, 91st Bomb Group

July ended with the rescue of another B-17 crew, from the 335th Squadron, 95th Bomb Group, piloted by Lieutenant R.B. Jutzi, on the 30th. Their early morning target had been Kassel, hit by over 60 bombers from the 4th Bomb Wing. In fact, three of the Wing's bombers ditched on this day, with the crews rescued by HSLs. Hawkinge were alerted at 8:40 a.m. that a B-17 was in trouble and two minutes later Doug Hartwell, Flying Officer Wilson and Jack Mallinson were off and heading to the west of Deal. Spitfires found the men in the sea, five of them, in a dinghy. Hartwell landed, taxied to the dinghy, and while Wilson in the front hatch threw the men a line, the dinghy was left to drift back to be grabbed by Mallinson at the rear hatch. Wilson then went back and all were brought aboard.

The sea was too glassy for a take-off with eight men aboard (if it wasn't too rough it was too calm!) so Hartwell began to taxi the 11 miles to the coast. When asked where the rest of the crew were, the Americans said they had decided to bale out over Belgium rather than risk the sea crossing in the crippled bomber. Outside Dover, the Walrus was met by a Naval launch which towed them inside.

Due to the extra weight we were unable to take off – even when I attempted to bump her off she would not have it, so I had no alternative but to taxi back to Dover.

The following morning, I returned to Dover with a ground crew to collect the Walrus (X9526) and return to Hawkinge. We were taken out to the Walrus by the Admiral's barge from which we borrowed the Admiral's bucket to quicken the process of emptying the 'Old Gal' of sea water, as the pump was a very slow way, for there was plenty of it!

Having removed what I considered to be sufficient water for us to take off, I told the fitter to return the bucket to the barge with our thanks. Being a true landlubber, our fitter proceeded to return it the same way as it was delivered, but on throwing it, let go of the bucket and the end of the rope at the same time; so the bucket was returned to 'Davey Jones' Locker' instead!

I decided to take off inside the harbour itself and had to request the close hauling of one of the Barrage Balloons off a barge in the harbour, which they were good enough to do, so I took off and made my exit through the harbour entrance and returned to base.

Flight Sergeant D.R. Hartwell, No 277 Squadron

Jack Mallinson was involved in the rescue of a B-24 Liberator crew about this time, and recalls:

Dozens of these fine aircraft had to drop into the Channel or North Sea after a raid. I was on a Walrus pick-up but we lost one of the Americans because he panicked, and despite shouting from everyone, he couldn't unsnag a caught harness and went down with the aircraft. Due to overloading, there was no way we were going to take off, so we had a rough taxi job back to Dover. One American had lost his right eye and I patched him up and gave him morphia. The Doc at Dover said I had done a good job which was very gratifying. The final outcome was that the US crew delivered a packing case of American cigarettes which kept the Flight going for ages!

Sergeant J. Mallinson, No 277 Squadron

★   ★   ★   ★   ★

The commandos

A quite unusual 'rescue' took place on the 4 August, by Alan Grace, Flying Officer F.E. Wilson and Sergeant Humphreys. They were Scambled from Hawkinge at just before noon, and rendezvoused with fighters before heading 30 miles out from Deal. When Grace had been flying for 20 minutes, Spitfires were seen orbiting 'customers' 10 miles north of Gravelines.

As Grace approached, he saw his target was two canoes with two men in each. He dropped a smoke float, then landed. He could not get close to the canoes without shutting down the engine, which he then did, allowing the two craft to be paddled alongside. The four men and their kit were taken aboard, and although the canoes were fired at with machine guns, they would not sink, so they were left to be blasted by the Spitfires.

The engine was restarted and Grace took off. He had picked up four men of No 2 Special Boat Service, who had been on a special job and were paddling back to England, having presumably missed their rendezvous with a rescue ship. The four men, who appeared in good shape, were Captain Livingstone, Lieutenant Sidders and Sergeants Weatherall and Salisbury.

Doug Hartwell, flying a Spitfire, was escorting the Walrus as well as searching for the men, and remembered:

Army Commandos, or so we were told, had been operating in Dieppe Harbour during the night, sorting out shipping with limpet mines, but had been spotted and had escaped by going their own separate ways to the rendezvous point where a submarine had initially dropped them.

They were too late and the sub had gone, so they launched their canoes and proceeded to paddle home. At least, that is what they thought, because if they had carried on with their chosen direction they would have missed Britian altogether.

They were transferred to the Walrus and we were told to destroy the canoes and leave no trace of them, which we did. Grace landed them at Hawkinge where they spent the night.

Flying Officer D.R. Hartwell, No 277 Squadron

The nine and a half hour rescue

Squadron Leader Grace had another rescue on 17 August. Two Walrus aircraft had been called to 'Top Line' at 7:45 p.m., for this was the day of the now famous raid by the 8th Air Force on Schweinfurt and Regensburg. It was to cost them 60 heavy bombers, with many more damaged and written-off. Two B-17s of the 1st Bomb Wing came down in the sea on the way home, and it was one of these that Grace was after.

Escorted by 501 Squadron, he was accompanied by Butler and Rose, plus one of the first Navy pilots who were now arriving on the rescue squadrons, Sub-Lieutenant Ralph Mander, flying the second Walrus. Two Norwegian Spitfire pilots had found the men in the water and were circling when the seaplanes came into view. There were two dinghies, but Grace could observe the sea as fairly rough, so it was not going to be easy.

He told Mander he would land first and take on half the crew, and then he should land and take on the rest. After dropping a smoke float for wind direction, he landed at 8:30 a.m., finding the sea conditions worse than he expected. On the water he could no longer see the dinghies and had to ask the Spitfires to dive in their direction so he could taxi to them. He also warned Mander not to land as it was too rough. The Spitfire pilots were relieved by two from 277 – Kipping and Moore – Grace telling them that he would take on all 10 men and taxi back.

The Spit boys called for HSLs and later they relayed the call that they were on their way. Meantime, Grace had found the dinghies. Butler threw them a line, with his revolver tied to one end for weight, and it landed in one of the dinghies. Soon all 10 men were on board. They were all wet through but none too badly injured. It was discovered they were from the 401st Squadron, 91st Bomb Group, the pilot being First Lieutenant E.M. Lockhart and the co-pilot Second Lieutenant Clive Woodbury.

Eugene Lockhart, who had been slighlty wounded earlier in his tour – in 1942 – was now nearing the end of his 25 sorties, Schweinfurt being raid number 21. It had been a disastrous raid for the 8th Air Force, and Lockhart, leading two inexperienced wingmen, had an engine supercharger fail on one engine when forming up after take-off and could have aborted, but chose to fly the mission. With increased boost on the other three engines, fuel would be critical on the way back, but he knew he must lead his element. In the event, one of his wingmen had to abort and the other was shot down on the way to the target.

Now, reality had come true. They had run out of fuel, having also been badly hit over Germany, and had had to jettison their bombs before reaching the target. But he had made a good ditching and all his crew were safe. He received the DFC for this mission and although offered a release from his difficult tour at 21 missions, carried on and reached the magic 25.

For the moment, however, he and his crew had still to get back from number 21! Grace set course for North Foreland and ordered Mander to return to base. It was now getting dark and Grace had to switch on his lights so the Spitfires – Pete Standen and one other had relieved the other two – could see where they were. Nearing the coast at last, two MASBs came to meet them, which caused a moment of anxiety as they had been expecting the shape of HSLs, not these heavier craft. They had been ordered to take off the Americans. Grace later reported:

After consultation, we decided to inflate the M-type dinghy and attach a length of cord to it, and whilst the Walrus was heading into wind as slowly as possible, float three men in the dinghy from the rear hatch astern of the boats. We completed this successfully with three men, but the MASB crew cut the rope from the Walrus to the dinghy, which left us only one M-type dinghy plus three K-types which each member of crew carried. This transfer, which occurred in the dark before the moon was up and with the aid of searchlights from the boats, appeared to be a very risky undertaking, taking into regard the sea conditions and the exhausted state of the rescued crew. We therefore decided, after consultation with the boats, that it was better to carry on taxying back with the remainder of the crew on board, i.e. seven and three Walrus crew. It was feared that if a dinghy was upset or a man knocked out during transfer, it would be very difficult to find him or to get him aboard.

We then proceeded towards North Foreland on a course of 240 degrees, with the two boats as escort. Very hard work to keep the Walrus heading on 240 as the wind was on 100 degrees and had freshened, with a rough slight cross sea running. I had put the wheels down to taxi to the dinghies, to steady the Walrus and slow taxying down.

I now decided to try to taxi with wheels in the up position, but found it most difficult to stop swinging and had to put them down again.

An Albacore appeared overhead at about 10:30 p.m. and dropped three Calcium Phosphaid flares. It stayed with us for about half an hour and at this time our VHF went dead. At about 1 a.m., we were joined by two naval boats and an HSL. The MASBs then went off and left us with the new escort. The Walrus finally in calm water off North Foreland at about 4:45 a.m. and we were able to increase revs and steer into Ramsgate, arriving 5:30 a.m. and towed into harbour.

The rescue, from take-off to gaining Ramsgate Harbour, had taken nine hours, 40 minutes, but all 10 Americans were safe to complete their combat tour. Squadron Leader Alan Dennistoun Grace received the DFC for his gallant and sustained efforts on this night – not bad for an 'old man' of 37!

Chapter Eleven

Operation 'Holloway'

Dover harbour again

On the last day of August, Tom Fletcher notched up a further success. The previous night saw the first of a series of small raids in which Bomber Command called upon OTU crews to bomb ammo dumps in various forest locations in Northern France. They were marked by PFF aircraft, and one object of these raids was to give OTU crews nearing the end of their training a bit of practical experience before going to their Main Force squadrons.

Recorded as a Special Exercise, 29 OTU put up four Wellingtons, four more coming from 17 OTU and four from 26 OTU. Of the first four, BJ967/'F' was piloted by Sergeant T.A. Wilder, taking off with his five companions at 9:05 p.m., the target being the Foret d'Eperlecques, near St Omer. Two of the twelve 'Wimpies' failed to return, so it was some 'experience'. Wilder and his crew were among the missing.

Flying with Fletcher was Sub-Lieutenant Gardner and Pilot Officer C.G. Walker, in one of the new wooden-hulled Walrus IIs, HD908, built by Saro. The Wellington had been hit over France and crashed off the English coast – only the pilot survived. Fletcher got him, but it was the sequel that Tom Fletcher remembers most:

They had been on a raid and got damaged. I picked him up and taxied into Newhaven, We developed a duff engine – plug trouble. As we went into the harbour, on the left-hand side was a newly laid-down 'hard' (slipway), and I taxied up onto it and a mechanic serviced her, put in new plugs and then we got her back onto the water. It was a wooden Walrus and I put in my Log Book: 'LAC Devich; returned from Newhaven, took off in harbour.' Well, that was one of the diciest things I ever did!

The Navy had a Lieutenant Commander as Harbour Master and I rang up his office and asked if I could take off in the harbour, now we'd become serviceable, because the weather outside wasn't too good. There was a long run in the north-south harbour, but the one snag was there was always a lot of shipping coming in and out. I asked if they could guarantee me a slot where there would be no movement for five minutes, so I could get off. Yes, they'd fix that, and they'd do it right away.

So I went to the aircraft, started it up, taxied down into the water, wheels up, taxied up the river, turned, opened up and away. We'd just got nicely on the step, when God knows how many HSLs came steaming in! I swung her round and pulled her up at an angle – made it, but only just.

When I got home, I rang up the Harbour Master and gave him all the names I could think of, and he said: 'Well I didn't know they were coming in!' 'But you're the Harbour Master, you should know the movements.' He replied: 'But these buggers come in any time they like!'

Sergeant T. Fletcher, No 277 Squadron

Operation 'Holloway'

Down with 276 Squadron, 30/31 August proved a busy two days for the Air-Sea Rescue services, which then extended into the first two days of September. It began on the 30th.

Shortly after 2 p.m., Squadron Leader K.F. Mackie DFC and his 'Number Two', Flight Lieutenant G. Holloway, took off from Exeter in their 16 Squadron Mustangs (AM102 and AP263) to carry out a *Rhubarb*. Flying out over Bolt Head, they crossed the French coast eight miles west of Plouescat. Over France, they attacked two trains which were passing each other just west of Landerneau, turned back and headed for the French coast at Ile Vierge.

A few minutes after heading out to sea, they were attacked by six FW 190s from dead astern. They were seen only at the last moment, coming down from some cloud. The Mustangs broke but each was pursued by two '190s. Mackie called to Holloway to climb for the cloud, but the 'Number Two' had already been hit in the engine and starboard wing. He called Mackie that he was baling out after a head-on attack with another '190, both aircraft scoring hits on each other. Holloway headed down, but with another '190 on his tail he decided not to bale out but to ditch.

Mackie, having reached the cloud, then began to orbit inside it while he gave a Mayday call on Button 'B' for a fix. Then he had to head for home, crossing the English coast at Lyme Regis Bay, landing at Exeter at 3:40 p.m.

Holloway had gotten into his dinghy and at 6 p.m.; Mackie and Flying Officer E. Martin were airborne to search for him, together with Spitfires from 610 Squadron. The latter unit spotted a dinghy and when the two Mustangs arrived, they recognized Holloway. 276 Squadron had sent a section of Spitfires out too, but by the time Holloway had been found, and with the distance involved, it was too late to rescue him before dark.

Shortly before 8 a.m. the next morning, another section of Spitfires from 276 – Flight Sergeant A. Sotheron-Estcourt and Sergeant 'Pop' Ewens – were out to regain contact. They met other Spitfires returning from searches and when they reached the search area began a 'strip search'.

Once again, the prolonged activity attracted the attention of the Germans, who obviously knew they had put a man in the water the previous day, which would bring the British rescue people out. At about 9:25 a.m., the two Spitfires were attacked by four FW 190s. 'Pop' Ewens relates:

Very early on this morning I had an out-of-bed call for me by my colleague, Flight Sergeant Sotheron-Escourt, who had taken the telephone call to Scramble two Spitfires for a search. In usual line abreast, a few hundred yards apart – search formation – all I knew was we were going a long way due south, and I was expecting to see signs of the Brittany coast.

I was not aware then that the 'pinging' sound in the radio was indications of German radar tracking us. Four aircraft coming round behind us, almost from nowhere, and at first I thought they were Typhoons with white-coloured engine cowlings. Rather unusual, I thought, then hesitant and almost reluctant to think they could be Focke-Wulfs, never having met them before. I called out 'Break!' twice to my colleague, but could only agonize, for he did not respond at once. I turned into the attack from two of the '190s on myself and saw their 'headlights' flashing, then saw that my colleague had been clobbered. I heard later at Harrowbeer that my yell of 'Break!' had been heard and acted upon by Spitfires of 610 Squadron, causing much bad language by their CO! I did not know 610 were near and certainly did not see them.

I continued my climbing turn up into a fairly low cloud base and after a short while I hoped to use my own guns, so came down, but the '190s had disappeared. I dropped my dinghy on the oil patch on the sea surface, but realized it was rather a futile gesture. I then had a very lonely return flight to Harrowbeer.

I was surprised on landing to find I had a bullet-punctured tyre and a couple of other bullet holes in my Spitfire. I did not realise I had been hit. At the time, I felt I hadn't done too bad. Only with the passing years I began to think perhaps I might have done better. It all happened in a matter of seconds, but if I had given Sotheron-Estcourt a fraction longer warning, or spelt out to him that enemy aircraft were on his tail, he might have had a better chance of survival. I later had the proper duty of writing to his parents, telling them that I feared and regretted we could hold out no hope for him.

Sergeant L. Ewens, No 276 Squadron

Shortly after midday, Squadron Leader Mackie led six Mustangs out to try and find Holloway again, together with two Mustangs of 169 Squadron, but they found no sign of their missing comrade. Later that afternoon, Mackie was out again with four of 16 and four of 169. They saw three FW 190s and chased them back to the French coast, but they still failed to find Holloway, who, for all they knew, might well have been picked up by the Germans by this time.

With the increased activity, 616 Squadron were sent out, led by Wing Commander Jack Charles, now leader of the Middle Wallop Wing since his own dinghy rescue the previous month. 20 miles off the Ile de Batz, the eight Spitfires were engaged by an equal number of FW 190s, Charles and Flight Sergeant F.W. Rutherford each claiming one destroyed and Flight Lieutenant P.W. Stewart a damaged; but they lost two pilots, one being Charles' wingman.

The Focke-Wulfs were from the same unit which had clobbered Holloway in the morning – JG2. In this scrap with 616 Squadron, they did indeed lose two of their fighters, 'White 9', flown by Unteroffizier Hans Dollakamp of the 8th Staffel, with a second pilot baling out. It was undoubtedly the German sorties flown in order to recover their own man that led to the number of enemy aircraft operating in the vicinity over the following day or so. Things were certainly hotting up over the area, but Holloway's dinghy could still not be located.

Further searches continued till dark, but still the sea appeared empty. On 1 September, low cloud hampered all flying. The frustrated pilots sat around all day waiting for it to clear, but Operation 'Holloway' was 'on hold'. It cleared on the 2nd, and the search aircraft were out at first light. Until a search was officially called off, people would always look and hope.

Their persistence paid off when Mustangs spotted the dinghy. At 7:45 a.m., Mackie was off again to relieve Spitfires of 610 Squadron, who were circling the dinghy. A Walrus was already on its way, and in fact the Mustangs overtook it on their way out. In the Walrus was Ken Butterfield, Badger and Churchill. The dinghy was 64 miles out and when they arrived, they could see a number of aircraft circling.

Butterfield chugged into view, landed and picked up a grateful Holloway, who did not seem to have suffered too greatly from his three days in his dinghy, but who was extremely glad to see the Walrus. After several attempts, Butterfield took off along the swell and they soon had their man back at Exeter. They had had no escort on the way out, but on the flight home they had Spitfires, Mustangs, Typhoons and Beaufighters in attendence – a veritable armada!

Despite all the activity, I see I only recorded the barest details of this sortie in my log-book. Our customer was south-west from Bolt Head and was a fair way out; the trip took us 2 hours, 55 minutes!

We picked up Holloway, and we'd been out twice looking for him on 31 August on the same bearings – 200 and 190 degrees. We lost Sotheron-Estcourt on the first sortie.

Flying Officer K.S. Butterfield, No 276 Squadron

Altogether, over the three days, 177 aircraft had been engaged in this prolonged search and rescue, three of which had been shot down, two from 616 and one from 'B' Flight of 276. Kenneth Stanley Butterfield received the DFC not long afterwards for this and his previous rescues. For Edmund Giles Anson Sotheron-Estcourt there was only a watery grave.

On 3 September, the fourth anniversary of the war, Squadron Leader R.F. Hamlyn AFC DFM relinquished command of 276 Squadron, going to Bomber Command HQ as ASR Officer. His place was taken by Squadron Leader J.M. Littler.

★ ★ ★ ★ ★

Anniversary rescue

The fourth anniversary of the war was celebrated with an attack on the Renault works near Paris by the 8th Air Force, which provided 277 Squadron with a successful rescue.

Spitfire patrols were maintained in anticipation of bombers returning damaged, and when a B-17 was reported down in the Channel, 57 miles out from the coast, three Walrus aircraft were sent off from Shoreham.

The dinghies were easily located, the Walruses being escorted by squadron Spitfires. Each landed in turn, Flight Lieutenant Dekyvere picking up three, 'Kiwi' Saunders four including two injured, and Fletcher, along with Flying Officer Chamberlain, now the Gunnery Leader, and 'Dizzy' Seales, taking on the remaining three.

However, Fletch was unable to take off and had to taxi back, his aircraft running our of petrol 12 miles south of the coast. He had to be towed back, firstly by *HSL 2568* from Newhaven, who took off the Americans, and then by *RML 513*.

I will always remember picking up the remaining three members of a Fortress crew, when the weather had turned very rough. We were in a steel Walrus, guns fore and aft, which we didn't usually carry. The hull was all distorted in trying to bang it off the waves.

We were certainly having trouble in trying to get off and it became quite noisy in the Walrus. The Americans became quite up-tight – they were screaming their heads off, saying: 'Don't you dare, we've had enough flying for one day!' In fact, they said that if we tried to take off they'd get back in their dinghy!

Fletcher insisted on taking off but we couldn't, as it would have broken the aircraft up, it was so rough. So he just taxied back as far as it would go and later we made rendezvous with a boat, much to the relief of our American friends.

As soon as the boat arrived the Yanks wanted to get on it, so we let them. We were then towed into Shoreham Harbour.

Warrant Officer L. Seales, No 277 Squadron

Chapter Twelve

Ditching a
Typhoon – 1

The weather wasn't that good on 20 September 1943. The summer was nearly over and there was a touch of autumn about. 609 (Typhoon) Squadron put up a weather recce which enabled the squadron to mount a four-man *Ranger* sortie at midday. The CO, Squadron Leader Pat Thornton-Brown, led the first section of two, with Pilot Officr A.R. Blanco as his wingman. Flight Lieutenant L.E. Smith and Pilot Officer T.S. Turek (JP745), one of the squadron's Polish pilots, were the second section.

Their target was Chateau Dun but there was too much cloud. 'T-B' and Blanco failed to penetrate it, attracted a lot of ground fire in the gaps and gave up. Meanwhile, Smith and Tadeusz Turek squeezed below the cloud through another gap, finding themselves in a valley; but after flying around the valley they heard 'T-B' call the abort, so headed out. Smith crossed the coast and looking back, saw his wingman's Typhoon streaming a ribbon of smoke and falling behind. Tad recalls:

The weather over the Channel was not too bad. Clouds were low, with reasonable visibility, but it deteriorated on our approach to France. We tried to come down just under the cloud base and although I could just see Flight Lieutenant Smith, the other two had vanished. The clouds became thicker and I had difficulty in seeing Smith. Then suddenly, as we were turning, I saw the trees beside me! Thank God we were in some valley.

Then I heard an instruction that the operation was abandoned and Smith turned for home. I could not continue with him, and told him so, but said I would fly on a parallel course, some distance away. I certainly did not wish to finish up ploughing through the trees!

I climbed to 1,000 feet where some minutes later the cloud became thinner and lighter. Then I found myself under the cloud base and in front of me was the coastline – with a railway line running across my view from my left, into the outskirts of a town. On the line stood eight goods waggons. Instantly, I switched the gun-sight on and was ready to fire, when I noticed that the doors of all waggons were open and there was nothing in them. I looked for another target and to my horror, just to my left, spotted a large army camp bristling with guns – anti-aircraft, of course!

I could see some soldiers zeroing those guns on me, others running to their positions – some machine guns ready to fire; they wanted me to be nearer. I was not in the best positon to make an attack so promptly shot into the clouds, acutely aware that some flak must have been following me there. The comfort of invisibility gives a sense of security – blessed are the clouds. However, I decided to increase my height and alter course, when suddenly, there was a hell of an explosion around me. Dark smoke and the smell of gunpowder in the cockpit. Those guns had got me – by radar – which was some salvo!

I glanced at my wings, which looked like sieves, especially the left one. Looking at my hands and body, I could see no sign of blood, but surely I must have been hit? I checked my legs, but to my surprise I was absolutely untouched. My relief was short-lived, for the engine then gave a cough. I looked at the instruments – the oil temperature was up but the pressure down. The cooling system temperature was rising and the engine coughed again. The picture was getting worse and I could feel some hot oil on my face. On the outside of the cockpit I saw smoke; then the engine stopped.

I now had the decision to bale out or ditch. I was now out of the clouds and I could see Smith to my left, about 400 yards away, but was too low to bale out. I called Smith who told me I was on fire, so I asked him to watch my ditching as I headed down, smoke and oil impairing my view.

I could, however, see how rough the sea was – it was almost white everywhere. To land with, or against, the waves meant instant submersion and death. The only answer was to land on the crest of a wave and hope for a cushioning effect when it sank to become a trough. I aligned the aircraft and saw below me the speeding waves coming closer with every second. There was a sudden and great impact, like hitting a wall. I saw in that moment the ASI reading 150 m.p.h. I hit my head and in that instant all I could see was a red glow of flames – everywhere.

I was knocked out on hitting the sea because someone had removed the head cushion from the armour plate. It did hinder baling out, true, but in a crash-landing it could save life. It caused me some loss of memory.

When I came to, I was up to my neck in water. The front of the Typhoon had vanished and I could not move – I was totally paralyzed and could feel nothing. I was going to drown. The oncoming waves were about to bury me. Then came a moment of sheer genius. I was due to get married in three weeks and that thought was enough. 'Lad, if you don't get out, you'll never get married.'

My fingers grabbed the release harness and I was free. I wasted no time in paddling, and looking back, I saw the tail of my Typhoon just vanishing. Blowing up the Mae West, I then had to release my parachute which was holding my bottom up and head down. This was easier said than done. On the ground it was easy, just turn the release and hit it, but in the water – how? I had already consumed a lot of water; it was time to stop this slow drowning. I took a deep breath, bent double under the water and pressed the release with both hands. Success, but then – NO! – the strap from my Mae West to the dinghy snapped. Deep breath and I dived for the parachute, to which was attached my dinghy. I grabbed it and came to the surface, unclipped the dinghy and the parachute, then sank out of sight.

Meticulously, as at the drill in the swimming baths, I removed the dinghy from its cover, spread it out, and gently, a little at a time, I filled it with gas from the bottle. Job done, I pulled myself, as per instruction, from the

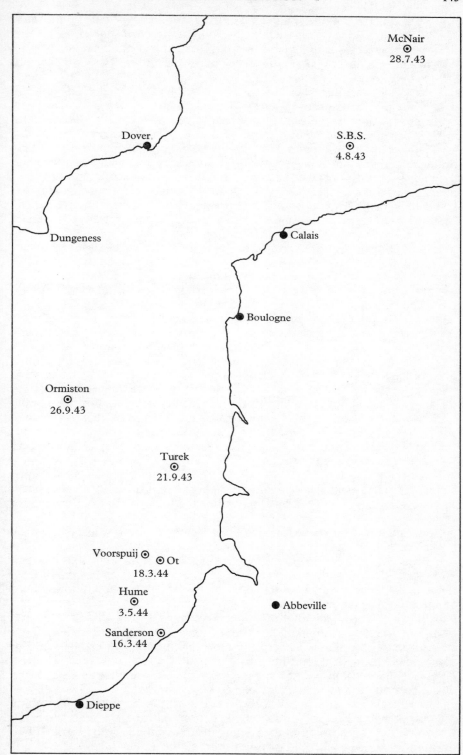

narrow end up to the top. Then I was sitting comfortably, but still in water. Then I felt sick, and was sick. I tried to do it overboard, but, proverbially, the wind blows into one's face. I was now getting rid of all the sea water I had swallowed, and my previous meals, in reverse order. I was sick, on and off, for two hours.

I had ditched at 14:47 by my watch, which had stopped on hitting the water. Then I heard some engines – the boys were searching for me. I saw Spitfires and then Typhoons. Smith had stayed with me till I ditched and must have taken good bearings, but the main difficulty was that I was just a speck in a mountainous sea of waves the height of a house – 30 feet! Many times I vanished under those masses of water, to appear a few seconds later. The Spitfires found me and then lost me. It happened more than once but then one of them dropped a smoke float. To my horror, I saw his aim was so accurate that I was going to be hit by it. I paddled furiously and the missile missed me by two feet! I still had to paddle away for it was oozing heat as well as smoke and likely to damage my dinghy.

Later a Walrus appeared and from the side cabin an arm dropped a Mae West. I paddled to it. Inside was a note which informed me that two Navy trawlers got half-full of water and had to return to port. Landing a Walrus was impossible, so they'll try again tomorrow. The ending read: 'Stick it pal!' Tomorrow looked a hell of a way away to me.

My two Typhoons stayed with me till dusk and an Albacore till nightfall. All the rescue aircraft managed to fly close to me and give me a cheery wave, and I waved back, grateful for their concern – I was not alone.

In the night the weather improved and eventually all the clouds disappeared, so I begun to navigate by the stars. There was a strong wind blowing from the west and realized I was drifting – and fast – to the east. I estimated I was about 20 miles from the French coast, so at this rate I could find myself very close to the enemy. I hated the thought of being a prisoner. Twice I had escaped from them and I was not willing to do it a third time, for this time the chances of escape were slim. I started to paddle west and continued throughout the night.

I was grateful to Jesus for life and I did not want any change – I was happy as I was. In that lengthy conversation I almost felt at times that I could hear the answers to so many questions I raised. My time that night was not wasted.

Something else happened, which I only realized when I was taken out of the rescue aeroplane on to the ambulance – I was never cold thoughout the ditching! The medics tried to cover me up but I told them I was warm. They looked at me rather suspiciously, yet that night, as I sat in the dinghy, there was a frost on land. In those moments of peace, the Germans tried to spoil them twice.

Sometime about midnight a German Me 110 flew almost over me, dropping flares, continuing on a course south to north, dropping more flares from time to time. Later I heard the noise of engines, but on the sea. For some time I thought it could be our Navy and I was almost ready to fire a flare, but realized they would have to cross the German mines first. But in that direction, and at night, they had to be Germans.

After a time the ship came closer, and I saw that the ship was switching a reflector on and off in an easterly direction. Although low in the sea, I realized I had to lay down in the dinghy to reduce the visible height. When the ship came closer, I could distinguish its shape and estimated that it was sailing on the west side of me. I was definitely in the path of the searchlight, and could even hear the voices of the crew. They were damn close. I laid very flat but managed to turn my head to see the sweep of the light. It stopped about 10 metres before me and started about the same distance after me. What luck!

The morning found me observing the French coast, on which I could see some single trees, I was so close. Shortly afterwards, some aircraft appeared some way off to the west, searching for me in the usual pattern. I tried to fire my flare but nothing happened, so in disgust I threw it into the sea where it instantly exploded.

They had not seen me; then two Typhoons joined in and I again tried to help with flares, and this time they worked and I was spotted.

I began to wonder about the rescue Walrus as I was so close to the coast, but it came and produced a landing east to west that made me wonder if there would be more of us in the drink! At that moment I saw a large column of water rising beside me. We were being fired on by coastal batteries – then another column. The Walrus then taxied up to me and a hand with a long stick and a hook on it was passed to me. I grabbed it and soon found myself sliding into the fuselage through the rear hatch. At that instant I saw another column of water. I turned to the Warrant Officer and asked if he saw it? He said no, but I was sure he had. Then just as I was rescued, I saw the Typhoons diving for the batteries and heard some rapid cannon fire. The Germans didn't fire at us again.

Once in the aircraft I needed to take off my trousers since they were absolutely glued with the yellow dye, and then I watched a pile of sandwiches appear from a cupboard – it must have been over a foot tall! It was then that I noticed there were two men up in front. They tried to take off but after a few attempts I was relieved to see that the pilot abandoned the take-off and decided to taxi back home. I returned to my sandwiches, but, realizing they were for all of us, offered some to the crew up front. They nodded politely but refused. They were seasick.

Pilot Officer T.S. Turek, No 609 Squadron

It had been Jack Brown and Wilson who flew out in a Walrus and dropped the parcel of flares and two torches and the message in the Mae West. The Albacore came from 841 Squadron, FAA, but it lost contact with the dinghy. Soon after dawn, 501 Squadron relocated him. At 7:15 a.m., Pete 'Stan' Standen, with Wilson and Bruck-Horst, took off in W3076/'Y', being vectored out 56 miles to the Somme Estuary, with an escort of four Typhoons from 609, led by Thornton-Brown. Peter Standen recalls:

Late on the evening of the 20th, two searching Spitfires of 277 found the pilot in the sea, seven miles west of the mouth of the Somme. As it was too late to rescue him, careful consultations were made with the Naval authorities in Dover, concerning wind and tide in the area during the night.

At first light, more Spitfires took off from Hawkinge, closely followed by me and my Walrus crew. Searching Spits soon located our customer in the sea and I circled, then dropped a smoke float for wind direction. The swell was about eight foot high and a difficult landing was made, closely followed by hauling in the shot down pilot.

Several attempts were then made to take off into wind and along the line of the swell, which seemed more likely to break up the aircraft then get us airborne. Much to the relief of the customer, who said he'd rather get back into his dinghy, these attempts were abandoned and a start was made on the long taxi back across the Channel.

During the rescue, three or four columns of water shot up ahead and to starboard of the Walrus, and it was realized that German coastal guns were firing at us. I reopened the throttle, but the Walrus tried to plough through the next few waves, taking aboard a great deal of water. Taxying was resumed and to everybody's relief, the shelling ceased.

The large intake of water had caused the R/T to fail, but it had been reported there were minefields in the area and a careful watch was maintained from the forward hatch. Nothing was seen but a length of coloured line floating just below the surface of the water, possibly to catch the propellers of surface vessels but which caused no problems for the Walrus. There was some anxiety, however, as a surface vessel, either an ASR or Naval launch, would normally be expected to be visible by the time we had reached mid-Channel, but none were seen.

For much of the day, we made steady progress towards the south coast of England, covered continually by circling Spitfires. When Dungeness lighthouse was just visible on the horizon, a fresh attempt at take-off was made which was successful, and we returned to Hawkinge without further incident.

Pilot Officer P.C. Standen, No 277 Squadron

They finally landed at 1:35 p.m., so they had been out for over six hours; but they had collected their man and brought him safely home. For this rescue, 'Stan' Standen later received the Polish Cross of Valour from the Polish authorities.

In all, over 63 sorties had been flown to effect this rescue, 38 being flown by 609 Squadron. This squadron celebrated Turek's return with a trip to Folkestone during which the CO, sprinting to catch the transport home, ran full tilt into some unseen railings, which caused him to limp for several days. When they got home, another pilot jumped from the transport vehicle while it was still moving at around 15 m.p.h. His feet were seen to flash past the window, but he came up again, his pipe still firmly clenched between his teeth. Not that Tad Turek knew anything about it, for much to his discomfort he was locked up in a hospital room for three days!

★   ★   ★   ★   ★

Almost the 'final' final sortie

A couple of days later, Peter Standen was involved in another rescue, and again it was a Canadian CO. Squadron Leader I.C. Ormiston DFC, had just received his promotion to command 411 Squadron, and on 26 September was flying his last sortie with 401, with whom he'd been a flight commander.

It was a *Ramrod* operation, Mitchells bombing Rouen marshalling yards. On the way back, Ormiston was five miles off the French coast when the engine of his Spitfire packed up and be baled out. Hawkinge were immediately alerted and Standen was Scrambled with Johnny Snell (who was later Standen's best man at his wedding) and Warrant Officer

Rose. Two Spitfires went out moments earlier, Uptigrove and Pilot Officer Kipping locating the Canadian in his dinghy, then orbiting the man. Two more Spitfires of 501 escorted Pete Standen:

I've never known a man so hopping mad. We picked him up off Ramsgate, or somewhere. He'd just been made the CO of some fighter squadron, and he said he'd been briefed for an afternoon show and just had to get back. I tried to explain that I couldn't get airborne – I'd only just managed to get down to pick him up – and the waves were far too high for me to take off again. But he told me I must try, so I demonstrated to him it wasn't on. Shortly afterwards, an HSL came out, really going flat-out, pulled up alongside us, took off the pilot and took us in tow, but then suddenly left us, and we were met by another boat. But I do recall that the Canadian just had to get back!

Pilot Officer P.C. Standen, No 277 Squadron

It was *HSL 2549* which had taken Standen's Walrus in tow, but soon afterwards a call came that another pilot was down in the sea nearby, so they were cast off again, and the launch sped off. Flying Officer Charles Demoulin of 609 Squadron had baled out after experiencing engine trouble, so Ormiston was further delayed while he was picked up. *HSL 149* later came out and towed the Walrus back.

At this time there was another award to 277, Flight Lieutenant Marcel France Dekyvere RAAF, at Shoreham, receiving the DFC.

* * * * *

Lancaster down

It really was 277's autumn, for while the other UK Walrus squadrons were all busy with search and rescue sorties, and directing boats to pick up downed aircrew, it was 277 who had the major pick-ups from the sea.

October began on the 3rd, with a search by 277's Spitfires for a missing Lancaster crew who had failed to return from a night raid on Munich. This was Lancaster ED530, piloted by Pilot Officer K.A. McIver. They had bombed the target without any problem, but on the way back the engineer had reported a rapid loss of petrol for which there was no explanation. It was obvious they were not going to make it back and so they called a Mayday.

They ditched some 25 miles south of Beachy Head at 1:30 a.m., but only one man survived the crash landing – the bomb aimer, Flight Sergeant M.E. McGrath.

Flying Officer J.M. Edmiston and Flight Sergeant Kelly spotted the lone survivor in a dinghy and called base for a Walrus. It just so happened that one of the squadron's Walruses was in the air off Newhaven. Johnny Barber, Teillett, and 'Dizzy' Seales were doing some work with an RAF Film Unit, and they were immediately ordered out to effect the rescue.

The film crew were in a boat and they were taking pictures of us taking off, then flying over and around Newhaven, then landing back on the sea. We were in the air when we received the rescue call and promptly left them, which must have surprised them at first. Johnny soon had us over the spot, which was being covered by two of our Spit boys.

Warrant Officer L. Seales, No 277 Squadron

The afternoon began with the rescue of yet another Typhoon pilot, Flight Sergeant N.E. Frehner of 485 Squadron, by Alan Grace, Rose and Humphreys from Hawkinge. Again it was the cursed Sabre engine which put the New Zealander in peril while on *Ramrod 258*. He baled out of MH351 12 miles south of Dungeness. He was located by Doug Hartwell and Flight Sergerant S. Loader in Spitfires who called Grace to the spot to pick him up. This, however, was just the start of the afternoon's activities. Another Typhoon pilot was about to ditch.

Chapter Thirteen

Ditching a Typhoon – 2

Jimmy's night out!

The Bostons which had mounted the effort on a *Ramrod* against the Transformer Switching Station at Distre, on 3 October 1943, were in trouble. 88 Squadron, led by Wing Commander I.J. Spencer DFC, were reduced from 12 to 10 Bostons IIIs when Spencer developed engine trouble on the way out and returned home with his 'Number Two'. The others carried on but five miles inland from the French coast, Boston BZ316, flown by Flight Sergeant G.G.K. Gray, peeled away and headed back. The rest carried on to bomb, but on the return flight Boston BZ322/'K' began to lag behind, and finally its pilot, Flight Sergeant W.D.D. Davies, was forced to ditch.

Squadron Leader G.C. Knowles had stayed with Davies and was now circling the men in the water, sending out Mayday calls on VHF, until he was relieved by some Typhoons. As if this wasn't enough, 486 (RNZAF) Squadron and 197 Squadron's Typhoons, led by Wing Commander D.J. Scott DFC (until recently, CO of 486), had flown out to pick up the returning Bostons but failed to make rendezvous, and while trying to locate them, Flight Sergeant C. J. Sheddan was forced to ditch. Jimmy Sheddan remembers:

On reaching our allotted position there was no visible sign of the Bostons, so Des Scott called the Boston leader who reported that they had just passed beneath us. They were blending in with the ground cover, so Scotty brought the squadron down to almost ground level so we could pick the Bostons up against the skyline.

This resulted in us being much lower at the French coast than we should have been and well within range of light coastal flak. Just as we crossed out there was a bang, bits and pieces flew around the cockpit and my motor stopped.

I called up and reported my situation, but my impression was that I had not made contact as my Typhoon just seemed to hang in the air as the rest of the squadron flew serenely on. With all the wide Channel stretching out before me there was no fear of overshooting and hitting an obstruction. I was able to come in fast and level off about a foot above the sea, and maintained that height by keeping constant backward pressure on the control column which had the effect of retaining lift as the speed dropped off.

I began to think that landing on the water was going to be a piece of cake. Like waves moving up on a beach on a calm day, the little rivulets of water moved gently along past the fuselage until they reached the trailing-edge of the wings. While this was taking place, I was undoing the safety harness in readiness to leave in a hurry. Then, bang! It was like hitting a concrete wall, and with no straps to restrain my forward progress, I was pitched head first onto the gun sight, and for me the lights went out! By the time I had ditched, managed to get clear, make my way to the surface, inflate the dinghy and clamber in, there was not an aircraft in sight!

Exactly how I got clear of the Typhoon [EK272], I don't recall. My first recollection was of being dragged head first, which was caused by the cord from my headphones which was still securely plugged into its socket in the aircraft. To remove an oxygen mask and flying helmet while under water when both were firmly secured, especially as I was still wearing my thick flying gloves, was no easy task. But I did it and then got sorted out. The dinghy was inflated and without too much trouble I hauled myself in.

As I now sat in my dinghy, I could see in the distance what appeared to be a cloud on the horizon, but that must have been the French coast. For the first hour, all I could do was to try and relax. What the time was or how long I had been there was a matter of guesswork as my watch had been put out of action, but eventually I became aware of Typhoons searching for me in the far distance. At the time I was not aware that I had any means of attracting their attention, and at the distance they were, I might as well have been the Invisible Man.

Flight Sergeant C.J. Sheddan, No 486 Squadron

Flying Officer Allan Smith was part of the 486 formation and recalls:

Just as we crossed the coast, Jimmy was hit by flak and lost flying speed as his engine failed. He did not have sufficient height to bale out and had no alternative than to belly land on the sea – a formidable task in a Typhoon because of the large air scoop at the front of the belly. Luckily, it was a beautiful day and the sea was calm. Jimmy made a good job of it and very shortly afterwards, we saw him in the water with his dinghy, not very far from the French coast.

The rest of the Wing proceeded with the Bostons and I stayed with my 'Number Two', to give a fix on Jimmy's position. I called up on our distress channel to report the ditching and give a fix, but we were approximately 100 miles from England and they could not get an accurate fix, so asked me to gain height and transmit again. This procedure went on for some time and we were above Jimmy at 10,000 feet before they got a satisfactory fix.

I was surprised there was no fighter reaction because we were advertizing our position to the Germans as well and we were very close to Caen and Maupertus airfields – and we were running short of fuel!

The job done, my 'Number Two' and I headed for Tangmere, but meantime, one of the Bostons had also ditched nearer to England and a fix had also been obtained on that aircraft.

After refuelling at Tangmere, I took off with 486 to escort the Walrus from Shoreham that was picking up the Boston crew, while another escorted Walrus flew out to pick up Jimmy.

Flying Officer A.H. Smith, No 486 Squadron

With the initial report of a Typhoon coming down, Tom Fletcher and Len Healey were Scrambled by Tangmere Control at 3:55 p.m. in Walrus W3097:

We got a call-out fairly late in the afternoon to look for this Typhoon pilot, and Tangmere would take me out. They started to vector us and took us on and on and on, until eventually we crossed the French coast! I called them up and said: 'Unless you've got a large field or a lake, I'm going to be in trouble!' Panic broke out and they quickly gave me zero-one-zero, and I turned. Luckily, nobody fired at us or anything – the Germans were probably as surprised as we were.

Coming back, we'd probably got about five miles east of Barfleur when we came across a dinghy. So I called up to say I'd found the 'Babies', to which they questioned, 'Babies?' I confirmed: 'Yes, three.' 'No,' they replied, 'you're looking for one!' I asked them if they wanted me to throw two back!? I went down and we picked up Flight Sergeant Gray and Sergeant R.G. Bickel, who later died, and Sergeant J. Addison.

Sergeant Bickel was the navigator and he'd been in the front, and as the Boston had hit the water, his table had hit him in the stomach. Although he was just alive when we picked him up, he was dead when we got him home.

I started off back and they then sent out Johnny Barber, giving him exactly the same vectors as they'd given me. When I got a reasonable distance away from Barfleur, and could hear Johnny over the radio, I called and warned him that Control had had me over the French coast so don't go near it as by now the Germans were bound to be aware of our activity.

Only a few minutes later, I heard him call to say he'd found the 'Babies' – and again the question, 'How many?' He replied, 'Two.' So another Boston had gone down, but he landed and picked them up. By the time Len and I got back, it was too late to go out again.

Sergeant T. Fletcher, No 277 Squadron

Tom's reference to 'Babies' was how the ASR flyers referred to those whom they were seeking. Initially they would be 'customers', becoming 'babies' or a 'baby' when located. If they were in a dinghy, they were 'babies in a pram'. Len Healey took up the story:

We'd been asked to fly to the French coast to find a dinghy in which a pilot from 486 (New Zealand) Squadron had been seen floating just off the coast. I flew out with Tom, but found a Boston crew instead. Landing, we found two of the crew were alive, but the third died. We managed to get them all into the Walrus and took them back to base. It was now late in the day, but we were warned we would be going out at first light to locate the New Zealand pilot.

Pilot Officer L.R. Healey, No 277 Squadron

Johnny Barber, with Flight Sergeant E Green had picked up Flight

Sergeant Davies, the Boston pilot, and his gunner, Sergeant J. Bateson, in Walrus HD908. The navigator, Flying Officer Robert Christie, from Dunfermline, had gone down with the aircraft.

We collected the Boston crew without any problems, but when the second Walrus returned it had picked up another crew who had ditched in the same area as Jimmy, so Jimmy was still in the 'drink'. By this time it was dusk and too late to make a second attempt that day.

 With hindsight, it would have made more sense for me to escort the Walrus looking for Jimmy, because after flying over him for some time at 10,000 feet, I knew exactly where he was in relation to the shoreline.

 Back at Tangmere, we began to work out how we could rescue Jimmy, and at this point I must give Des Scott full marks. First off, Group refused to authorize any further attempts the next morning, saying it would be suicidal so close to the French coast. Scottie wouldn't give up, and I heard him telling Group that his Wing was continually flying low-level over water and each of his pilots had to know that if they went in the 'drink', that everything humanly possible would be done to get them out! He finally wore Group down, and his next move was to telephone the Navy at Portsmouth and ask them to work from the fix I had obtained and apply the tide and current movements overnight, and tell us where Jimmy's dinghy would be at first light.

 When the Navy advised us the estimated position, we could hardly believe it. They said he would be very close to the French coast, just north of Barfleur, which was a long way from the point at which he had ditched. We had no better idea so first thing in the morning, 486 headed for the position indicated by the Navy.

Flying Officer A.H. Smith, No 486 Squadron

With the coming of night, Jimmy Sheddan was somwhere off the French coast:

The Typhoons I had been watching were from 197 Squadron. Group, in their wisdom, had detailed 197, who had been High Cover and so would not have had a clue where I was, to look for me, while 486, who might have come straight to my position, covered the Walrus aircraft who found one of the Boston crews.

 Darkness comes early in October, and it soon became obvious that if I was to be rescued at all it was not going to be that day. As the light faded the wind started to get up, and with it the sea. Just before dusk, two Spitfires in line abreast appeared from the direction of France, and they were so low that the one which flew directly over me could not have come any lower without hitting the water with his propeller. He was so low, in fact, that I crouched down; had I sat up, I would have been clobbered!

 Then darkness set in, and with it the sea began to perform. Wind and tide had been pushing me steadily towards the shore and from the noise, I could only guess that it was the waves breaking on the shore, and that at any moment I would find myself floating amongst the mines which were liberally scattered along the coast.

 During the night, I gave up trying to empty water from the dinghy, and added to this I had another discomfort. Mae Wests have a packet of dye lightly sewn to them, and the form is for the stranded pilot to detach this and trail it over the side to colour the water so aircraft can spot you. An over-energetic packer had made such a thorough job of attaching the dye container that there was no way that I could detach it. So I spent the night soaking in a concentrated bath of heavily dyed water, and in the morning my skin was so brown I could have passed as a native and my finger nails had turned a brilliant shade of green.

When finally dawn came, after the longest night of my life, I could see I was surrounded by water, with no sign of land. As the morning dragged on, I found I had some signal rockets, and soon afterwards I began thinking that if 486 were coming out to look for me they should be here any time; and as I glanced over my shoulder there were eight white spinners which swept directly over me and started to do a climbing turn.

Flight Sergeant C.J. Sheddan, No 486 Squadron

Desmond Scott and Squadron Leader Holmes, CO of 197, took off at 7:30 a.m., and flew to an estimated position worked out by the Navy at Portsmouth as to where the dinghy might have drifted during the night. The search had begun.

Four more Typhoons took off an hour later to widen the search, and these were followed at 11:35 a.m. by more aircraft of both squadrons who flew in pairs in wide lines abreast, and after 14 minutes they saw a distress flare which Sheddan fired off. Reporting their find back to Control, Scott organized 486 to escort a Walrus out, taking off at 12:35 p.m.

We had about eight Typhoons flying on the deck and spread out in a wide line abreast formation, so that we could cover the maximum area. Meantime, a Walrus was airborne mid-Channel so that it could fly in quickly if we sighted the dinghy.

Although we were hoping for the best, none of us were too optimistic that we would find him, but lo and behold, there he was, right where the Navy said he would be.

The weather had changed overnight – it was a cloudy, dull day, with strong winds and heavy seas. We were very close to the French coast and formed a defensive circle near Jimmy as we called the Walrus in. We went onto low revs and weak mixture to conserve our fuel and extend our flying time.

Flying Officer A.H. Smith, No 486 Squadron

The New Zealand squadron went out the next morning and Des Scott, who I'd known earlier when he was a Sergeant Pilot, led them. They eventually found the dinghy again, too close to the French coast for the Navy to let any boats go out – it was too dangerous! The thought was to send out an International Distress Signal [which would have meant the Germans picking the pilot up – if they felt like it]. Of course, Des Scott was a bit livid about this, so we were asked to go out. They knew where it was, and in fact, as predicted by the Navy, it had almost gone ashore and now drifted out to sea again.

The weather had changed overnight, there was now quite a heavy chop on – four- to five-foot waves – which is not very nice. You could get away with it sometimes but you needed a little bit of luck. I flew down and had a look at the water and Scotty called up, asking one section to point out the dinghy, but they'd lost it. Then they found him again, and where he was was really bad. I called up Tangmere and told them it was pretty rough and if I did get down I didn't think I'd get off again. Scotty then came on the air, asking what the matter was, and I said: 'Scotty, this is Tommy Fletcher!' He was happy to know it was me.

Anyway, I went down and picked him up. I tried to get off, but then decided to taxi, and called up the aircraft and asked them to contact Tangmere to send out an HSL, as I'd not the fuel to make it all the way back.

I got some way when suddenly, for no reason at all in this rough sea – which sometimes happens – there was a calmer patch. Running onto this calm bit, I belted the throttle forward and started to just about lift off, when we hit the other side and smashed the starboard float – and that was that!

Sergeant T. Fletcher, No 277 Squadron

With one of our floats smashed, it would mean the wing dipping into the sea, so I had to get out there and struggle with a big bomber dinghy and tie it under the wing to keep it above the water. Having done this, Tommy told me to get onto the other lower wing, so my weight would help keep the other wing up. Sheddan also came out and sat with me. We began to taxi and finally a boat came towards us. At first we didn't know if it was British or German, but it was British – a MASB – commanded by Captain Browne. He got us all aboard and we wanted to have the Walrus (W3097) towed in. The Captain gave it a try, but it didn't work and finally his gunners sank it. We then headed for Portsmouth.

Pilot Officer L.R. Healey, No 277 Squadron

When the Walrus landed the problem was trying to get aboard her. One moment I was down in a trough with the big machine towering above me, the next the position was reversed, and I had a real fear that I was about to crash down onto it. After a lot of expert manoeuvring, we were both on the same level and close enough for the gunner to reach out with a long pole and snag his hook into the top of my life jacket and drag me in through the hatch. Once safely aboard, my rescuer produced a knife to cut the lanyard by which I was attached to the dinghy and let it drift away.

When the float was torn off, it seemed to me the Gods of War had made up their minds I was going to be their next victim. We counter-balanced the port wing by applying weight to the tip of the starboard wing – the air gunner and myself. We crawled out and he showed me how it was done by grasping the leading-edge in his hands and hooking his toes over the trailing-edge, and thus anchored, he slowly worked his way out to the far end. I would have loved to have stayed in that warm cabin, and having watched the gunner make his precarious journey out along that wildly bucking wing, frankly, I was terrified. They had risked their lives to save me and by now I was part of the show, so there was no way that I could funk it.

We must have been in that position for an hour, both of us knowing that if either of us were swept off, there was no way we would be rescued once in the swirling mass of water. Then the boat appeared. I do not recall how I got off that wing, but I did, and once on the boat I was stripped and wrapped in warm blankets and given a generous tot of spirits, then slept all the way home.

Flight Sergeant C.J. Sheddan, No 486 Squadron

While waiting for the boat to arrive, the old Walrus was beginning to drift towards the French coast, Fletcher watching anxiously as a lighthouse just off shore began to get bigger and bigger. Then the tide turned and the lighthouse began to get smaller. Normally, Tommy Fletcher was a very good sailor, but on this occasion the tension and shock got to him, and to add to his discomfort he very soon had his bottom stuck out over the side!

When the MASB arrived and took them all on board, the Captain had said he'd try and tow the Walrus back, but Tommy warned him that with a float gone, it would quickly turn turtle; but the Captain thought it would be alright. Just as predicted, as soon as they moved off, the cable twisted and over she went.

In point of fact, it was Scott's Typhoon which strafed and sunk the crippled Walrus, after it had been cut adrift, having turned over in the towing attempt. They had had enough time to take off some of the equipment, radio, spare dinghies, rations, etc., plus two machine guns which, for some reason Tommy Fletcher cannot recall, they were carrying that day.

Landing the Walrus in the heavy seas wasn't easy, but the pilot made a first class job of it and after some manoeuvring had Jimmy on board. At this point, tragedy struck – the Walrus damaged a float attempting to get airborne and after several abortive attempts, finally gave up the unequal struggle. We now had a different kind of problem on our hands. After some calls to base, a second Walrus appeared on the scene, but the first Walrus pilot told him it was too dangerous and sent him back to base.

The next move was to bring out a boat which eventually arrived on the scene and picked up Jimmy and the Walrus crew, and the damaged seaplane was sunk by gunfire.

I cannot speak too highly about the ASR teams; they went wherever they were called without regard for their personal safety. My personal flight-time on this show was one hour, 55 minutes – a long time for a Typhoon to be in the air. From the time Jimmy ditched to the time he was rescued, 486 Squadron had flown 46 sorties – add this to the flights made by 197 Squadron and the work of the Walrus aircraft and the boat. A lot of effort to rescue one pilot and probably not good economics, but this kind of action, carried out right under the noses of the Germans, had a fantastic effort on morale right throughout the RAF.

Flying Officer A.H. Smith, No 486 Squadron

Whilst sitting in the crew room one day, a damn great parcel arrived and upon opening it, we found a huge Dundee cake, the biggest I'd ever seen in my life, sent to us by the mother of one of the Boston crew we'd rescued on the 3rd. It went down very well, but it didn't last very long!

Pilot Officer L.R. Healey, No 277 Squadron

The last word shall go to Jimmy Sheddan, who later rose from Sergeant

Pilot to command 486 Squadron and ended the war with a DFC and a modest score of German aircraft and V1 rocket bombs shot down:

Those Air-Sea Rescue boys were the real heroes of World War Two. Out in all sorts of weather and conditions, month after month, nobly did they live up to their motto, 'The Sea Shall Not Have Them'.

Chapter Fourteen

The Winter of 1943/44

Autogyro pilot

The pilots and gunners of 277 Squadron were kept at it during the wintry weather of late 1943 to early 1944. With sea conditions often unfavourable for sea landings, both Walrus and Spitfire searches tended to end with calling and directing launches to pick up those men found in the water.

One of the more unusual pilots rescued during a sea landing was Flight Lieutenant Welch of 529 Squadron, based at Halton. Shoreham had in any event been alerted because of a fighter sweep by the Kenley Wing on *Ramrod 283*, on 24 October, when 'Kiwi' Saunders, Teillett and Bob Birch-Hunt in W2735 were told that an autogyro pilot had crashed into the sea off Worthing. They flew out and found Welch hanging onto the wreckage of the aircraft (V1186), 150 yds off shore.

Flying Officer Ken Creamer and Flying Officer R. Holland had flown to the spot in Spitfires, Holland dropping a dinghy to the man shortly before Saunders arrived:

We picked up Flight Lieutenant Welch who was no more than 200 yards off Worthing Pier. We knew him, for he sometimes flew his autogyro from Shoreham. Some of the remains of it were salvaged and are apparently with the Air Training Corps in Shoreham.

Pilot Officer A.K. Saunders, No 277 Squadron

Just a month later, the squadron lost a pilot. Flying Officer Hugh Chalmers and Sergeant Raymond Powell took off in their Spitfires to fly a patrol for Kenley and off the French coast ran into severe flak near Boulogne. Chalmers had his Spitfire damaged, but Powell was obviously shot down and was never found. The Spitfires did much good work over the following month, directing boats to various airmen in distress, and towards the end of the year, a number of personnel were posted overseas. Among them were 'Dizzy' Seales, Jack Mallinson, Edmiston and Trevor Humphrey. The first three ended up in India and Ceylon, where 292 Squadron were forming, while Trevor

Humphrey left for the Middle East and 284 Squadron.

Little fish, big fish

The following day, 29 November, Hawkinge Scrambled a Walrus piloted by 'Stan' Standen, with Tug Wilson and Humphreys. A Mayday call from a Thunderbolt pilot had started the alert, and two Spitfires flown by Warrant Officer K. Moir and Flight Sergeant Loader were sent off, followed by the Walrus.

The American 352nd Fighter Group were just one of the Groups acting as escort for Fortresses attacking Frankfurt. The Luftwaffe reacted violently to the raid and 29 B-17s and 15 P-47s and P-38s were lost. A number of German fighters were also shot down, but not quite the total claimed – 75 destroyed by the air gunners with another 75 damaged or probably destroyed, and 47 by the fighters with a further 20 probables and damaged! One of the fighter pilots was Captain G.E. Preddy of the 487th Squadron, 352nd Group, who made out the following combat report:

I was leading Crown Prince Yellow Flight and we were escorting two boxes of bombers. The Group leader called for everybody out and I started to join him when my 'Number Two', Whisner, called that the bombers were being attacked. I turned back, coming in behind the bombers and saw an FW 190 below and behind them. Whisner had started a bounce on another enemy aircraft so I went down on this '190. He went into a steep dive and I closed rapidly and saw a few hits and a little smoke before I broke off. I lost the enemy aircraft momentarily but picked him up again on my left at about 4,000 feet. I started after him and he made a steep turn to the left. I turned with him and started firing at 300 yards and 60 degrees deflection. He straightened out and started down at about 45 degrees. I got in a good burst at 300 yards and saw hits all over the ship. The engine was evidently knocked out as I closed very rapidly after that. The last I saw of him, he was at 1,500 feet going down at an increasing angle to the left.

I made a steep climbing turn to the left and saw Whisner. He joined me and we climbed back to 10,000 feet. It was past time to go home so I picked up the heading as we didn't have enough fuel to do anymore fighting. We went below the clouds and came out on the deck, crossing the French coast somewhere north of Calais. A concentrated barrage of flak opened up. I began kicking the ship around but felt hits. She began smoking but did not lose power, so I climbed to 5,000 feet and gave a Mayday. Shortly afterwards, my engine cut out. I baled out at 2,000 feet. A P-47 spotted me and I was picked up out of the drink by a Walrus.

When George Preddy splashed down into the sea, it was cold – very cold – but he was spotted by Lieutenant Frederick Yochim, who circled and radioed fixes for a rescue. Soon afterwards, Standen was on his way.

I remember very little of the actual rescue but Preddy stayed aboard with us until we reached Ramsgate. I recall a couple of Thunderbolts were over him. We tried to take off but I bounced the Walrus off a wave, the port wing dug in and wrote-off the float. 'Tug' had to trot down the starboard mainplane and stand holding one of the struts to keep the port wing up out

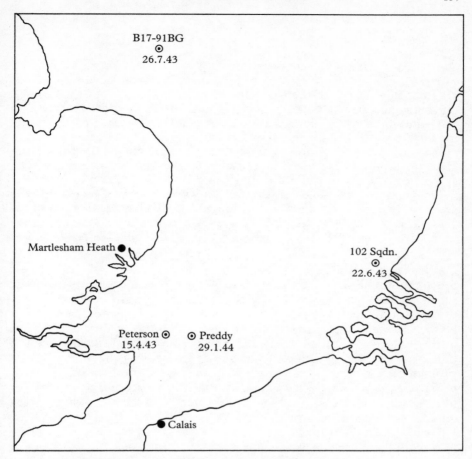

B17-91BG
⊙
26.7.43

Martlesham Heath ●

102 Sqdn.
⊙
22.6.43

Peterson ⊙   ⊙ Preddy
15.4.43   29.1.44

● Calais

of the water, and everytime a wave came, he got fairly wet!

'Tug' and I were both in our best blue uniforms, for we were due off on leave at one o'clock, and wouldn't you know it, the Scramble came about 10 minutes to one!

Pilot Officer P.C. Standen, No 277 Squadron

George Preddy, and even his wingman, Bill Whisner, were still unknown men in the 8th Air Force (little fish), but within a few months both were among the top American fighter aces (big fish).

Preddy received the DSC, Silver Star (and cluster), DFC (and eight clusters), Air Medal (seven clusters) and the Purple Heart. The Focke-Wulf he shot down on the 29th was only his third kill, but he went on to claim a total of 25 before he was killed in action in December 1944 – shot down by American ground fire over Belgium. Bill Whisner ended the war with 18 victories and went on to add five MiGs over Korea.

★ ★ ★ ★ ★

The deadly sea

Every so often, it became a case of 'so near, yet . . .' Bill Land had an agonizing experience on 30 January 1944, flying with 278's CO, Ben Bowring, in Walrus L2268:

We searched an area in very rough weather and we came across a crashed Fortress. There was much wreckage and an empty inflated dinghy was spotted. Low search of the wreckage revealed a floating body and, later, one man, clinging to a floating oxygen bottle. I made three attempts to land but on each occasion the aircraft was tossed 20 to 30 feet into the air by the terrific swell, and I would have certainly crashed had I proceeded.

We circled the man until eventually he was overcome by the cold water. He slipped off and I watched him drown. It was very disturbing and I can still picture the event to this day.

On our return we came across HSL *Seagull 38*, and we directed it to the scene of the crash. We could see the launch's propellers coming out of the water as it plunged into the swell. The HSL retrieved one body.

Flying Officer W.A. Land, No 278 Squadron

Yanks in a minefield

Springing up all over the Pas de Calais during this period were strange ramp-like constructions with a hut or two nearby. In the beginning, only the air commanders knew that these were launching sites, being built by the Germans in preparation for the eventual firing of V1 rocket bombs at England. But the men on the squadrons soon became accustomed to being part of the campaign to attack these sites as the year of 1944 progressed. Later, everyone knew what they were and how important it was to destroy them. They would feature too in producing customers for the Walrus crews, and one of the first batch was the result of an attack on sites on 13 February by the 8th Air Force.

Over 450 B-17s went for 17 rocket sites and lost four to ground fire. A few others made crash-landings at bases in southern England, but at least two of the lost bombers ditched and had crewmen rescued. One of these was from the 385th Bomb Group, another from the 94th.

Squadron Leader R.W. Wallens had recently joined the Flight at Hawkinge, and he was Scrambled at 4:20 p.m. with Rose and Sergeant R Smith in W3042 and vectored out into the Channel, while Shoreham sent off Johnny Barber and Sergeant W. Gregory in L2315, 20 minutes later.

Wallens found aircraft orbiting a spot of water, flew there and found a dinghy with eight men, and nearby, a smaller dinghy with one man. Wallens was warned of a minefield in the vicinity, but he landed and picked up the lone man who was badly injured. The Shoreham Walrus then arrived and landed, collecting the other eight, but could not then take off, so HSLs were called for. Wallens, because of his injured survivor, decided to get the man back to receive medical attention, so took off. In the air, he was asked to help with another rescue, but as his man seemed critical he decided to get him home quickly. This was the crew of the 94th Bomb Group B-17.

Meantime, the Spitfires flown by Flying Officer Kipping and Gooch had found the other dinghy and they directed the boat to them, 18 miles off Dungeness. On the water, Barber's Walrus hit a submerged object and damaged the port float, and after transferring his eight survivors onto the HSL, he was taken in tow.

We found the Fort crew just north of St Valery. As we were near the French coast and in a minefield, I attempted a take-off, but, being overloaded, the Walrus just would not stay airborne. Unfortunately we damaged a float, so had to transfer the survivors to an HSL and were then taken in tow. Poor old Sergeant Gregory had to stand out on the opposite wing to keep the damaged float out of the water, all the way back. It took us seven hours before we were pulled into Dover Harbour.

Flying Officer J.L. Barber, No 277 Squadron

For Wally Wallens, it was his first rescue and first sea landing in a Walrus. In his excellent book, *Flying Made My Arms Ache*, he describes this event as follows:

Needless to say, my first attempt at a sea landing made me look extremely foolish, although I must claim that poor, in fact total, lack of briefing on one important point was to create an astonishing scene.

Vectored from Dungeness for 30 miles in a south-easterly direction, I arrived on the scene where an American Flying Fortress had ditched, and sighted eight men in a large dinghy and, some distance away, one man in the water. My first concern was for the latter, and quickly dropping a smoke flare for wind direction, pulled the Walrus round to land in a calmish sea. So far, so good and I taxied up to the poor chap, as if to the manor born, where the gunner in the front hatch dropped him a line to trail him to the back hatch for hauling aboard.

No one had taken the trouble to tell me that it was essential to switch off the engine at this point and restart later, and the Walrus, even throttled back, was proceeding under steam and the gunners were unable to grab the man. I was apparently towing him down the Channel, clinging desperately to our life-line. I was unsighted to the rear and mistook the yelling of the gunners to be shouts of encouragement, when in fact they were cursing me for not shutting off as they tried to haul on the rope to pull him in.

Fortunately they managed to get him aboard before he had become totally waterlogged. Meanwhile, a Walrus from Shoreham had arrived and picked up the other survivors in the dinghy. They tried to take off but were unsuccessful and had to wait for a high speed rescue launch from Dover to take them in tow.

Not wishing to make any more stupid mistakes that day, I cautiously opened my throttle and got the Walrus airborne for Hawkinge. My 'customer' bore me no animosity and, being little the worse for wear, admitted that it had been, to say the least, quite exciting.

In his book, Wally Wallens also confesses:

Persevering with the Walrus, to which I had become very attached, we carried out searches which extended far down and very close to the French coast, past Dieppe to Fecamp and up the Belgian coast past Ostend, Zeebrugge to Walcheron, hunting for reported sightings of bodies, dinghies and aircraft wreckage. We felt intense disappointment that maybe, after searching for so long without success and returning the long journey home low on fuel, I could have spared another few minutes to look, which might have made all the difference and saved some poor fellow, and I knew I was hooked on air-sea rescue.

★　★　★　★　★

Enter the Sea Otter

On 5 March 1944, 277 squadron were again successful. 'Kiwi' Saunders was Scrambled from Shoreham with Len Healey and Green in Sea Otter JM770, one of the first of this type to arrive on any ASR Squadron.

The Sea Otter had superseded the Walrus by the Supermarine Company, and was in fact the last in a long line of amphibian biplanes designed by them. The prototype had made its first flight way back in 1938, but development had been slow and it was not until 1943 that production by Saunders-Roe, on the Isle of Wight, began. The ASR version – the Sea Otter II – began reaching squadrons in late 1943. It did not look unlike the Walrus, although the main difference in looks was that its engine, an 885 h.p. Bristol Mercury XXX, faced forward rather than being a pusher-type as on the Walrus. It was almost half the weight again of the Walrus, 6,805 lb against 4,900 lb (unloaded). It was a couple of feet longer, had a slightly higher speed, and a metal hull. It did not replace the Walrus, merely adding to the ASR squadrons' stable.

Recently one of the squadron pilots had been severely told off for losing a Walrus in a rough sea when he could have left the rescue to a nearby HSL. However, by this time our squadron's tally was nearing the 500 mark, and we were reluctant to leave anyone for the boats. Although we passed two boats from Littlehampton, on the 5th, on our way out, we were keen to do this one ourselves. With an additional six people in wet flying gear we had quite a load up. One thing I do remember is the long run we took to get unstuck. We weren't quite airborne when we passed the two boats coming out. Losing a new Sea Otter under these circumstances would not have made me popular with the 'powers that be', but all's well that ends well!

Pilot Officer A.K. Saunders, No 277 Squadron

'Kiwi' Saunders had rescued six men from a B-24 of the 704th Squadron, 446th Bomb Group, part of a force of 300 Liberators which had bombed airfields in France. Finding the men 25 miles out from Bognor, the Sea Otter landed and the engine was stopped. Len Healey and Flight Sergeant Green had great difficulty in getting the men into the seaplane as they were unable to help themselves. Three of the Americans had broken limbs, which did not help matters; others had cuts and facial injuries. To get them on board, Len Healey had to get into one of the dinghies and lift each man up to Green who placed them in the best positions given by Saunders, for take-off. The more badly injured man was laid flat on his back with his head beside the navigator's seat, the one with a broken ankle sitting on an M-type dinghy pack where the WOP's seat had been removed. Another with a broken arm was in the Nav's seat while the other three sat between there and Len Healey, who was just forward of the rear hatch.

With Green standing just behind the pilot's seat, having given the men some first aid, the engine was started and off they went. In the air they called Tangmere to have medical services available.

We had been informed that three large dinghies had been seen. When we arrived we flew low to look at them and found them to be the crew of a bomber. On landing, three of them were in good condition, but three had broken limbs. We decided to get two of the chaps who were fitter in with us, so they could help lift the three injured into the back hatch. This took some doing as the hatch was only two feet wide, and with two people trying to pull a third one in, was almost impossible.

We got them in, however, and the others got themselves in, and then we flew back to Tangmere, informing them we required ambulances. During the trip, the Captain of the American crew thanked me and asked how could they ever repay us. I jokingly said that I wouldn't mind a pair of the boots he was wearing.

After landing, the Captain was the first out and on doing so, kicked off his flying boots, and the other uninjured two did the same. We then got the three injured men into the ambulance. A few days later, I received a note from RAF Tangmere – would I please call into RAF sick quarters where a parcel had been left for me. Tommy Fletcher flew me over and I found the parcel contained the other three pairs of boots. So I ended up with six pairs of boots which I promptly sold in the crew room!

Pilot Officer L.R. Healey, No 277 Squadron

In at the deep end
When, on 16 March 1944, Jack Brown located wreckage and three men in the water, 20 miles south of Dungeness, he landed and picked them up but ran into some touble.

Peter Weeden had just arrived at Gravesend, where the Martlesham Flight was now based, 278 now having a Flight stationed at the latter airfield. Being a former Mustang pilot, he had arrived primarily to fly Spitfires, but . . .

On the morning I joined 277, I reported to the CO at Gravesend, Squadron Leader Brown. I arrived there about 11 a.m., and having got the introductions over, we went to the Mess for lunch. I was, of course, dressed in my 'best blue' uniform.

Half-way through lunch, Brownie got a 'phone call to say that a US aircraft had come down in the North Sea near the Dutch coast, and that all available Walrus aircraft were airborne. However, we had a Sea Otter [JM745] at Gravesend which had been in for a major overhaul and he elected to fly this with me as gunner.

We set off and found three US aircrew all as stated, and one at least was wounded; they could not get to us. Also, even with the engine throttled right back, an Otter moves through the water, making it even more difficult. So Brownie switched off the engine and I went over the side and swam the chaps to the aircraft. Then, by ducking under them and pulling up on the rail, with Brownie pulling from the rear hatch, we managed somehow to get them all aboard.

We then tried to restart the engine, but no go. To start the engine one had to stand on the wing and crank a flywheel, and as we were both pretty well flaked out with getting our customers aboard, we could not get enough speed up to start it. So we radioed for a launch which came and we transferred the customers to it. We also borrowed a member of the launch crew to help us start the engine. This was managed but every time Brownie opened the throttle to get some revs up, it cut. However, we could make headway on about quarter throttle, so we taxied back to Dover.

Having taken off from Gravesend at about 2:30, we got into Dover Harbour at about 11 p.m., having gone through all the minefields on the way. One of the Americans died, but the other two were saved. My 'best blue', of course, had been ruined with marker dye, so I now had a 'best green'!

Pilot Officer P.W. Weeden, No 277 Squadron

Too close for comfort!

The Shoreham Flight made three rescues on 16 March, but their initial customer was a Canadian fighter pilot. 412 Squadron had flown on *Ramrod 661* – support for the returning US bombers. They picked up the Liberators near Belleau, France, but Flying Officer T.M. Saunderson was having trouble with the engine of Spitfire MJ149, and had to bale out right over the coast. Flying Officer D.C. Laubman circled over him for a while and gave fixes, but then had to leave him, reporting that he was only about a mile off shore. There was only one crew who would be sent to get him – Fletcher and Healey. They were off in Sea Otter JM796 at 2:30 p.m., escorted by Spitfires. Tom Fletcher had at long last received his commission. He had bucked authority for a long time but whatever they thought of him he knew his job, had been decorated twice and probably knew more about the rescue business than anyone else.

I believe this Canadian had been ashore once. He'd paddled ashore and some Germans were at the top of the beach beckoning, but they wouldn't go down as the beach was mined. Our two escorting Spits then sprayed the beach with cannon shells and the pilot got back into his dinghy and paddled out again.

I went round and had to come over the land to set down, and I was so near the beach that I could see the seaweed breaking the top of the water! By this time the pilot had got about 300 to 400 yards out, and wanting to slow up quickly, we put the wheels down once we'd landed, then whipped them up. Len quickly had the chap and had pulled him in the back.

The shore batteries started to fire at us and the first big 'box' salvo fell, followed by a smaller salvo, then a third, closer and smaller; and if we'd been there when the fourth fell, it would have fallen right on top of us. Len caught a piece of shrapnel which nicked a bit more from the same finger he'd had damaged the previous year.

We gave the pilot dry clothing, which we carried, had his uniform cleaned and returned it to Biggin Hill, and we never even had a thank you from him!

Pilot Officer T. Fletcher, No 277 Squadron

With Pilot Officer Fletcher, as he was now, we headed out to the French coast where a dinghy was reported just a few yards out. We found it but it was so close, Tommy decided to fly over the coast, turn, and come out and land so that we could immediately take off facing the English coast. This we did, amidst gunfire, and picked up the pilot.

Whilst we were landing we came under very heavy shell fire and thought we'd be hit at any moment, or a boat would come out for us. We took off in a hell of a rush and made straight for the English coast, although I was hit again, by a bit of shrapnel, in the same finger that had caught it when Johnny Barber and I were shot down in April 1943!

Our customer was uninjured, hadn't suffered any ill-effects, so we took him straight back to base.

Pilot Officer L.R. Healey, No 277 Squadron

A friend in need . . .
But they were not finished yet for the day:

Having landed back at Tangmere and walked to the office, the I.O. came running out in a bit of a panic while we were hoping for a cup of tea. He asked how much fuel we had left – you've guessed it, another job! He told us one of our own boys was in trouble – in the Somme Estuary.

This was Barry Robinson, a Naval character. He'd taken a wooden Walrus and landed to pick up part of an American Fortress crew. Five had already been picked up by Hawkinge (Wallens) while Robinson had the rest. The Hawkinge aircraft went back, but Robinson said he couldn't get off. It was a nice day but getting a bit late by this time. So I was being asked to go out again and help. So we went.

We found Robinson, and I now had Len and Bill Gregory with me. Bill got a DFM with me later on. I told Robinson to put a dinghy over the side, put some men in it and I'd pick them up. The wooden Walrus was about 600 pounds heavier than the metal ones. He did that and I landed and taxied in and picked them up, told Len to slash the dinghy, then we were away; but Robinson could still not get airborne.

I dropped a smoke float ahead of him to show him the wind direction and told him to try again as I had to go home now, and then he followed. On the way back, Robinson called to say his fuel was low. We were both low for he'd been taxying while I was down at Tangmere, and I had not refuelled. I decided to take him to Friston, at Beachy Head, but if he didn't make it I'd call out a boat from Newhaven.

We pressed on and finally made Friston and I led him in as he didn't know the airfield. Normally, some of the air gunners would help by operating the wheel selector and start pumping them down. They were coming in behind me, me just leading them to the airfield, and coming into land he selected wheels down. But his gunner had already selected them 'down', so instead of them being down, they were now being pumped back up.

So he landed wheels up, but luckily all he did was polish the brass strake on the bottom of the hull. Later we got some air bags and jacked him up and put the wheels down. He didn't even strain the wires on the float – so it was a good landing really!

Pilot Officer T. Fletcher, No 277 Squadron

Chapter Fifteen

400 Up

The flying Dutchmen

No 277's main effort on 18 March 1944 was the rescue of two Dutch B-25 Mitchell crews. 320 Squadron's target was the factory at Gorenflos. The bombers met heavy and accurate flak east of Senarpont, then on the run up to the target, and more when they left. Eight of the 12 aircraft were hit to some degree, and 'M' for Mother (FR177) went into the water on the way back and 'H' (FR180) followed shortly afterwards.

After his rescue effort, Jack Brown, flying Sea Otter JM745 with Rose and Smith, made out this report:

Airborne Hawkinge at 14:25 hours, vectored to a position four miles west of the Somme Estuary. Located dinghy containing four customers, four miles west of the Estuary, alighted 200 yards downwind at 1507, 1/2 mile from a French fishing fleet. Approached the dinghy and Flying Officer Rose threw a rope to occupants who secured dinghy and drifted to the rear hatch. All aboard in one minute, hatches closed and I made an attempt to take off. When hydroplaning at 50 knots the engine cut and would not maintain maximum revs. Two more attempts made and on the third, became airborne, but engine cut out again and I had to alight on the water.

I decided to taxi further out into the Channel before attempting any more take-offs. The R/T was u/s and I could not communicate with the escort [Spitfires]. At approximately 15:20, I started to taxi back on a course of 330, at approx 18 knots. At 16:10 hours, I made two more attempts to take off but could not get more than 2,300 r.p.m., so continued to taxi back at zero boost, 1,900 r.p.m. Kept this up until 17:00 hours when sea became very rough and I had to decrease speed to 12 knots as floating mines were observed on the way out. At about 30 miles south of Dungeness a mine was seen about 200 yards to starboard. At 17:30 a Fortress orbited us for 30 minutes and we expected it to ditch, so we prepared for more customers. About 18:00 hours it made off, steering 330.

Conditions on the sea improved at this period so increased speed which was maintained until five miles south of Dungeness, when two HSLs from Dover arrived. Handed over customers who were still in good shape, having received first aid and hot soup during the trip from the Somme, at average speed of 16 knots.

It then took us nearly 20 minutes to get the Sea Otter started again. At 19:00 hours I tried to take off but had no luck so set course 035 degrees for Dover, in company with one HSL, speed 20 knots. Ten minutes later, sighted Dungeness lighthouse and checked position. At 20:00 hours, requested a course from HSL who asked our destination. He was informed our intention was to make Dover. It was getting dark at this period so reduced speed to 15 knots. Shortly after this I asked the HSL to go ahead and we would follow its lights. Speed reduced to 10 knots. 20:38 hours we sighted Dover. Sea was getting rough now and I could not see the HSL owing to cabin being covered by water. Made our way to the lee side of the harbour entrance and taxied through. Contacted Harbour Master who towed us to an aircraft buoy. At 20:47, aircraft secured and all hatches closed. Distance taxied was 76 miles. Taken ashore by the launch. Names of aircrew rescued were: Sergeant John H. Ot, Sergeant F. Gans, Sergeant J. J.G. Lub and Corporal J.H. Postaumus, 320 Squadron.

Ronald Wallens, with Hall and Sergeant E. Cartwright, flew out 60 miles and picked up the other Mitchell crew which consisted of Flight Lieutenant Hendrick J. Voorspuy, Sergeant J. Vink, and Corporals K. van Nouhuis and M. Engelsma. These nine brought 277 Squadron's total of 'live' rescues to 392! Both Dutch captains recall:

I was flying Number Four in the leading box of six aircraft on our way out when we received two close bursts of heavy flak, the first one near the nose, the second one under the starboard engine. The r.p.m. on that engine went up to 2,700 so I closed my throttle and pitch immediately and tried to feather it, but it proved to be impossible. A lot of oil was lost and when the oil pressure dropped to zero I swiched everything off. My wheels and flaps had come down after our hit and we were losing height which increased when the starboard engine became u/s.

I called Mayday and was told to steer 320 degrees and continued to transmit on Channel B. When we were down to 600 feet I told the Controller I was going to ditch, landing along the swell at about 98 m.p.h.

The tail hit the water first and the aircraft's tailplane broke off. The nose went down. My navigator had opened the hatch at 100 feet and once we came to rest, he pulled the handle for the dinghy release. I got out onto the wing, pulled out the dinghy and inflated it. I then heard van Nouhuis shout for help so got into the dinghy and went to the tail where he was hanging onto the aircraft, saying he had cramp. I got him into the dinghy while Sergeant Vink dived for the emergency packets. He threw a dinghy pack and parachute bag out of the hatch, then followed. We got him into the dinghy as Spitfires appeared overhead. They stayed with us until the ASR Walrus arrived.

After the Walrus taxied up to us, the pilot opened the window and I was greeted with the words: 'Good gracious, Hello Henk!' It is a small world. Wally Wallens and I had been in hospital together earlier and had got to know each other well.

We were flown to Hawkinge. Of course, we had to give our Dutch Naval Air Service 'wings' to the squadron. The MO and his staff had a good laugh as I had kept my pyjamas on after the early call in a cold tent. Later in the evening, Wallens saved me for the second time.

I was issued an RAF uniform, and dressed as an AC2, we went to the Palais de Dance in Folkestone for a little celebration. I met two Dutch sailors from our MTBs in Dover, and on leaving asked them to give my best to their CO, from Lieutenent Voorspuy of 320 Squadron. They looked suspicious at my AC2 outfit and warned the MPs at the door. I was arrested and marched between the two MPs. Just in time, Wallens appeared and saved the situation by declaring that he had fished me out of the water that afternoon.

Flight Lieutenant H.J. Voorspuy, No 320 (Dutch) Squadron

After dropping our bombs we were hit in the port engine which caught fire, so I dived away to the right, away from the formation, pressing the fire extinguisher. The fire went out and I was about to rejoin the formation on one engine when we got a direct hit in the starboard engine. This took the engine completely out of the wing, and about two feet of the wing was standing vertically and about to break off. The perspex in the nose had gone, many of the instruments were smashed and most of the controls were put out of action, except for the elevator. We were going down pretty fast indeed and trying to get some sort of control. I told the crew to bale out, but I could not do so myself as I could not let go of the controls.

My navigator and wireless operator were wounded and when they realized I was unable to go, they all decided to stay and take their chances with me. I was unable to give a Mayday call as Henk Voorspuy was also in trouble and was sending his call. I finally managed a call at about 1,000 feet, but I never knew if it was heard.

As we were going down, the Germans sent up all the flak they could muster, and it was heaven-sent that it did not find us. We hit the water at a speed of 160 knots very close to the French coast, it not being possible to reduce speed with our hydraulics gone. The aircraft went down within two minutes, which seemed like a lifetime. I managed to get the dinghy inflated and as the crew had all been in their ditching positions, all got out and scrambled aboard.

We were about two miles off the enemy coast, in a heavy swell, the dinghy bobbing up and down. We thought we saw a German MTB but it turned out to be a bouy. Spitfires were quickly over us and about two hours later a Sea Otter arrived. A wonderful sight.

While we were waiting, a formation of American B.17s came over, returning from a raid. One decided to jettison three bombs which fell close by us, one exploding just 300 yards away and actually lifting us and the dinghy out of the water.

Once on board the pilot tried three or four times to take off, but with no success, so he decided to taxi, sending out a call for a launch. Four hours or so later, launch *156* arrived under the command of Flight Lieutenant Lockwood. We arrived at Dover at 10 p.m., very cold and wet, but glad to be alive. Unfortunately, Corporal Postaumus was killed later in the war.

Sergeant J.H. Ott, No 320 (Dutch) Squadron

The Dutch squadron later presented 277's Hawkinge Flight with six tankards, duly inscribed with 320's badge. Jack Brown later received the DFC for this and his other recent rescues.

*   *   *   *   *

Magic totals

More rescues followed for 277: Pilot Officer Ormiston rescued an American P-51 Mustang pilot, Second Lieutenant Donald Gerber, 356th Squadron, 356 Fighter Group, on the 24th; Wallens, Hall and Smith saved two survivors from a B-26 Marauder bomber on the 28th – they had been in the sea for four days!; then on the 29th, Martlesham rescued two American fighter pilots, Lieutenants Francis L. Edwards of the 353rd Fighter Group and Glen J. Smart of the 335th Fighter Squadron, 4th Fighter Group.

On the 31st, Flight Sergeants R.A. Dunn and A.T. Bartells were just one pair of successive Spitfires pairs searching for a missing Halifax of 420 Squadron. They found it and directed two HSLs to the spot. This brought the squadron's 'score' to over 400, a figure suitably celebrated.

April 1944 began with the rescue of Captain R.D. Hobart, by Lieutenant A.B. Edgar RNVR with Norman Leighton in Walrus W3072. He had baled out of his P-51 after giving a Mayday, but it took some time to find him. Finally, two 277 Spitfires did, but he was only in his Mae West, not a dinghy. Edgar landed and got him aboard, but he died the next day. He had flown with the 336th Fighter Squadron of the 4th Fighter Group, held the DFC and had two air and three ground kills.

A week later, it was four survivors of a B-17 captained by Second Lieutenant E.M. Kaminsky, 452nd Bomb Group, whom Edgar rescued. 277 may have passed the 400 mark, but individual Flights also reached magic totals. On the 13th, the boys at Martlesham celebrated their 100th live rescue when Flight Lieutenant Mackertich brought back Lieutenant Haws, a P-38 Lightning pilot of the 55th Fighter Group, in company with Flight Lieutenant Sheppard and Sergeant L.J. Mullins.

Into the Scheldt Estuary

Ron Whittaker of 278 Squadron had started flying Ops on the Walrus after a year of operating with Ansons. One of his first Walrus sorties took him right up to the Dutch coast, as he recalls:

With Walrus HD981 on 23 April, I picked up a US fighter pilot just off the Scheldt Estuary, and after abortive attempts to take off, we taxied for four hours, 15 minutes, until taken in tow by an HSL and towed for a further nine hours until we reached Felixstowe in the small hours.

The skipper of the HSL showed me on a chart where we were, putting his finger in the middle of an area marked 'Danger – Minefield'. When I expressed concern about the mines, he said: 'That's alright, we only draw four feet to the propellor tips and the mines are set at six feet below the surface, so we've got 18 inches clearance.'

The fact that the boat was rising and falling about six feet with every wave didn't seem to bother him at all!

Warrant Officer R.C. Whittaker, No 278 Squadron

Anzac Day rescue

On 24 April 1944, 'Kiwi' Saunders was to pick up a fellow New Zealander. It was ANZAC Day, a day very special to Australians and New Zealanders.

Ten Mosquito aircraft of 464 (RAAF) Squadron were assigned to attack a 'constructional target' in Northern France. It was a V1 site, but they had all sorts of names at this stage of the war. They flew out in two sections, one led by Wing Commander R.W. Iredale, the other by Flying Officer L.J.S. Fittock (MM400) whose navigator was Warrant Officer Jim Haugh, who remembers:

Our squadron had moved to Gravesend on 17 April 1944 and we were living under canvas in preparation for the invasion of Europe. ANZAC Day was something special. New Zealanders on an Australian squadron – another ANZAC mission; a London newspaper photographer came down and took photos of a group of us. On the 26th, the photo appeared in (I think) the *Daily Sketch* and Fittock and Haugh were both in the picture.

Preparation and take-off were routine and I recall that we left England at Littlehampton. I recall seeing evidence of invasion preparations; all sorts of military naval and air equipment parked in appropriate places, but not very well concealed.

We flew low over the Channel, came up to 1,000 feet to cross the coast and dived down again to low level to approach our target – a flying bomb site. We dropped our bombs and from observation I thought we had had a strike. Bombs were on 11-second delay so it was difficult to tell. We had the camera on our aircraft to record the result, but that is still at the bottom of the Channel.

We returned to the coast at low level and again climbed to 1,000 feet to cross the coast, and dived down to low level on track back to England. Time was about 3 p.m., flying into a sun low on the horizon. The sea was calm but with a three- to four-foot swell and with a glossy smoothness reflecting the sun's rays.

We had been fired at, of course, but I don't think we had been hit. As we headed out to sea, I was looking back to make sure that no German aircraft were following. Then it happened.

A short time after crossing the coast, the propellers hit the sea. Both props had the tips bent back about six to 12 inches which started the aircraft vibrating. We discussed what to do and 'Snow' Fittock decided we'd have to go into the water.

We had only seconds before we ditched and in those moments I thought about all sorts of things about the drill we had often practised; but also I recalled having been told that no one had survived a Mosquito ditching up to that time. However, I had no thoughts that we would not survive.

The actual ditching was a tremendous thump. The aircraft must have been travelling at over 300 m.p.h. and the deceleration pressed me against my Sutton harness with tremendous force. The aircraft immediately sank and water poured in. I remember swallowing water but do not recollect being thrown against any part of the aircraft and being injured. At the time, to release my harness I had great difficulty in pulling the pin because it had been bent in the deceleration process. As I struggled, I felt the pressure of water getting greater and greater as I went down with the aircraft. Eventually I got free and shot to the surface. I recall that I virtually came completely out of the water! The partly inflated Mae West probably caused this.

On the surface, I found the aircraft had completely disappeared apart from some wood chips, just the aircraft dinghy, fully inflated, and my pilot floating some distance away. I asked him if he was OK and he replied 'Yes'.

I said that because as I was closest to the dinghy I would get in, and he indicated he would follow. At this stage I think I fully inflated my Mae West with the oxygen bottle. I also noted our lead aircraft was circling overhead. When it disappeared, I was overwhelmed by the silence and the utter loneliness.

I got into the dinghy – a difficult job with my parachute harness still on – with my personal dinghy trailing in the water. A swift inspection showed that the aircraft dinghy was fully inflated and the contents were in accordance with specifications.

Fittock got to the dinghy quickly and asked me to help him in. I attempted to do this, but as he was a big man, and with all his gear on, I did not succeed. He fell back into the water several times, and on the final occasion the toggle on his Mae West oxygen bottle punctured the dinghy and we were both in the water without an inflated dinghy.

I then had difficulty in inflating my personal dinghy until I recalled that just a few days earlier, a new safety gadget had been put on the inflation system. When the dinghy was inflated I tried to get in, but by this time I was getting exhausted and very cold. Finally I had no strength to try further and I put my head and shoulders in the dinghy and wound my hands in the side ropes. I then lost consciousness.

I went into the sea at about 3 p.m. and woke up in Friston Air Force hospital at about 8 p.m. I was told that the staff had had much difficulty in keeping me alive and bringing me to consciousness. The hospital, I guess, had been a country residence, and the room I woke up in was large with black ceiling beams with painted white panels. The windows were leaded.

The English Channel had been very cold and to revive me and keep me warm I had been given hot coffee with lots of sugar, whisky and strychnine, and the bed was full of hot water bottles. I was shaking all over and felt uncomfortable, and after three days I was transferred to Eastbourne Public Hospital where I remained for two weeks.

I suffered bruising where the Sutton harness had dug in when we hit the water, I had a broken eardrum and developed pneumonia. I was very grateful to be alive but was very upset that my pilot, 'Snow' Fittock, was missing. We had crewed up together in Canada in July 1943 and had joined 464 Squadron in January 1944. I felt that if I had been able to get him into the dinghy he would have been saved. That still haunts me.

The pilot's seat was very close to the windscreen and 'Snow' was a big man, so his head was always close to perspex canopy. I will never know if he had been injured in the ditching but I think it was likely.

When eventually I returned to the squadron, what most people wanted to know was not how it happened, but how we had managed to ditch in a Mosquito and get out of it. I imagine I was a very rare specimen to have survived a Mosquito ditching.

Warrant Officer J. W. Haugh, No 464 (RAAF) Squadron

I flew out in a Sea Otter, JM798, with Warrant Officer Leighton and Flying Officer Willson. Probably about 25 miles south of Beachy Head, we located what appeared to be a dead body in a Mae West in a calm sea. On getting him on board, one of the air gunners told me he was still alive and we were diverted to Friston where an ambulance was waiting. Because he had a New Zealand flash on his shoulder, I rang Friston later in the day to find out about him. A few years ago, I discovered that he was alive and lived in Wellington, New Zealand.

Pilot Officer A.K. Saunders, No 277 Squadron

Norman Leighton recalls:

Using the Sea Otter, this rescue was a ditched Mosquito crew. We picked up the navigator alright, and I think we also picked up the pilot who was floating face down in the sea. In order for us to be sure of getting off and getting our live man home, we were forced to leave the dead pilot in the water. Unhappily, these things happen and our priority, of course, was with the living.

Warrant Officer G.N. Leighton, No 277 Squadron

Jim Haugh was contacted by 'Kiwi' Saunders in 1984, and when he asked if he had been rescued from the sea in April 1944, Jim confirmed that he had. 'Well, I'm the person who picked you up.' Jim immediately replied: 'Well, there is no one in this world I want to meet more than you!'

★ ★ ★ ★ ★

'Kiwi' makes another friend

'Kiwi' Saunders also met up with another man he had rescued from the sea, just days after picking up Jim Haugh. On this occasion, 3 May 1944, it was Flight Lieutenant W.G.M. Hume, a Canadian fighter pilot.

Mac Hume was flying with 403 (RCAF) Squadron on *Ramrod 827* – dive-bombing a V1 site southwest of Abbeville. All hell had been let loose by ground gunners – the sites were very heavily defended – and his Spitfire IXB was hit. He baled out and Saunders came out for him, but it did not prove such a simple pick-up as with Jim Haugh:

It was my thirteenth operational trip! I climbed away at a considerably higher rate than the rest of the squadron, as was my custom. Unfortunately, I flew directly into a burst of 88 mm flak, doubtless aimed at someone else. All seemed normal for a couple of minutes, but subsequently the oil pressure dropped to zero, the engine overheated, the airscrew went into full fine pitch and it was not possible to shut down the engine. About 10 miles west of Abbeville, it became apparent that the aircraft was not going to be airworthy much longer. I decided, therefore, to bale out, but with the original attempt unsuccessful because of excessive speed, I sat down again, raised the nose, dropped the speed to about 130 m.p.h. and went head-first over the trailing-edge of the port wing.

After a suitable interval, I pulled the rip cord, deploying the parachute. The Spitfire, smoking if not acutally in flames, was seen to go straight into the Channel – spectacular to observe.

During my descent, which was agreeable enough, certain light housekeeping duties were performed: the stem of the Rolex was carefully tightened and my new 25 shilling lambskin gloves were carefully tucked into my socks.

The temperature of the water was said to have been 40 degrees Farenheit. Dusk was approaching and winds were high. Being unfamiliar with proper procedures, I was dragged a considerable distance by the parachute. When, finally, I squeezed the quick-release box, the parachute detached, with the dinghy remaining attached to my harness. It hung suspended under the air-filled parachute, some 20 feet below the surface of the English Channel.

Nightfall approached. Squadron Leader Hartland Finley RCAF, circled to mark my position until his fuel supply became marginal. Despite the parachute remaining afloat, and the fluorescene marker, my exact position had been lost. Meanwhile, ASR Spitfires appeared. Before leaving, Finley dived low over my presumed position, whereupon the ASR Spitfire dropped dinghies, which, alas, I did not see. Nor did I see the Spitfires for that matter! Night fell.

Initially there was no awareness of the extreme cold, either at the time of immersion or for some minutes thereafter. This soon passed, however, as did the subsequent shivering. Although medical school was many months in the future, I sensed that this sequence of events boded ill; a sense reinforced by the development of a tachypnoea that was quite uncontrollable. Spirits were low, very low indeed.

Then, some 75 minutes after immersion, the silhouette of a Sea Otter appeared. It approached slowly and landed with a mighty splash. The pilot, who I later discovered was a New Zealander by the name of 'Kiwi' Saunders, had decided to put himself and his crew at almost unwarranted risk. I was aboard within moments.

The Flight Sergeant undertook to warm me with the heat of his face and of his clothed body, surely an act of great compassion. Attempts at take-off were shudderingly unsuccessful so we started taxying towards Dover in heavy seas. The radio was not serviceable. Hours later, a high-speed launch hove into view. As we transferred to it, the Sea Otter dug in a wing and promptly sank. We arrived at Dover at about 3 a.m. First activity, a steaming bath tub, filled to the brim, and then bed.

I was flown home the next morning in another Sea Otter, where I was well received by my squadron mates, although I noted subsequently that drinks for all had been added to my Mess bill. This was quite standard practice, however. I noted also that two most particular food parcels, put together and sent over at great expense and with considerable care by my loving wife, had somehow vanished completely!

Flight Lieutenant W.G.M. Hume, No 403 (RCAF) Squadron

Again I was in Sea Otter JM798, with Flight Sergeant E.G. Green and Sergeant W. Shaw. About 9 p.m. that day, I was in one of the 'phone boxes downstairs at Shoreham, speaking to my wife of six weeks, when I was rudely interrupted and told to get airborne. Within a couple of minutes we were given a course to somewhere near the Somme area. It took about one hour to get there and by that time it was getting a bit dark. The Spitfires were circling a fellow in a Mae West and had dropped a couple of smoke floats for us.

The sea was decidedly choppy, with quite a few 'white horses' around. The landing must have been awful, though I suppose I was not aware of it at the time. We were completely drenched on impact and the radio was gone. Take-off was out of the question so we headed north. After an hour or two the sky cleared, and in the moonlight we saw a Mosquito circling us. Shortly after this, an HSL appeared out of the gloom and took us on board, and we arrived in Dover Harbour about daybreak. We had apparently travelled about 30 miles before we were picked up.

Pilot Officer A.K. Saunders, No 277 Squadron

Mackenzie Hume went on to finish his tour of Ops, returned home, took up medicine and became a paediatrician. He and 'Kiwi' kept in touch for some years, then lost contact until the early 1980s. They have both visited each other's homes, in New Zealand and New Hampshire.

Chapter Sixteen

Invasion

In May 1944, the greatest seaborne invasion in history was just weeks away. In southern England, the huge build-up of men and war materials was being massed at the seaports in readiness for General Eisenhower's 'Go!'

Britain's Royal Air Force and the American Army Air Force stood ready to support their Navy and Army brothers in the massive assault upon Hitler's Europe. For weeks already they had been pounding target after target in France and the Low Countries, crippling the enemy's railway system, supply dumps, troop camps, panzer parks – the list seemed endless.

Bombers of both Air Forces attacked day and night, not only these targets but targets in Germany too. Fighter Command had two priorities in the late spring: the V1 rocket sites, and German radar stations along the European coast. The latter targets needed to be hit to blind the Germans to the actual invasion force when it set sail, but because of the very nature of these sites, the Germans being able to repair and replace them quite quickly, they had to be attacked again and again.

All this, of course, led to an increase in the activities of the Air-Sea Rescue services, both boats and aircraft, and not least the Walrus and Sea Otter crews, who had already seen a tremendous increase in rescues over the last few months.

277 Squadron still covered the southeast, while 275 had begun to fly from Warmwell – dead opposite the proposed landing beaches in France. 276 continued to cover the southwest, where it would be heavily involved in rescues off the Cherbourg Peninsula and the western end of the Channel. 278 continued to cover the North Sea and had by now a full detachment at Martlesham, now that 277 had finally been concentrated at Hawkinge and Shoreham. The scene was now set.

* * * * *

On 8 May 1944, 'Kiwi' Saunders rescued one of crewmen of an American B-17 from the 547th Bomb Squadron, while Greenfield picked up another. The following day, Saunders was again in evidence. Hugh

Chalmers and Flight Sergeant J.A. 'Jackie' Forrest were out on patrol in Spitfires along with 'Kiwi' in Sea Otter JM770, south of Beachy Head. During the patrol they received a vector to fly to the south of Dungeness where a B-26 Marauder had gone in, leaving a line of parachuting airmen in the sea.

The B-26 was from the 323rd Bomb Group, captained by Major Drukl. Saunders found him in a calm sea, landed and took him aboard. Once in the Sea Otter, Drukl told Gregory and Flying Officer H.J. Archer that more of his crew were strung out over the Channel, so Saunders took off and headed south. Five miles out from the spot, they found Spitfires and an HSL searching, so Saunders returned home. Later, three more of the Marauder's crew were located by HSLs and brought in. Soon afterwards, Alister Keith Saunders received the DFC to add to his American Air Medal.

The Wing Commanders

Squadron Leader Ronald Wallens was also to receive the DFC, following two rescue sorties he made on 10 and 11 May. On the latter date, flying with Butler and Sergeant R N Smith in Walrus L2315, he went out to locate a missing night intruder crew lost the previous night, finding them just three miles off Dieppe. Wallens had been a pilot during the Battle of Britain.

Wing Commander A. Barker RCAF, the CO of 418 (RCAF) Squadron, and his navigator Flight Lieutenant R.J. 'Geordie' Frederick (who had just returned to the squadron after a period in hospital), flew an intruder sortie to Laon-Juvincourt airfield in their Mosquito VI. They were met by flak and searchlights at Juvincourt and the aircraft was hit in the wings and fuselage. Barker flew on to Laon where they were hit again. Flying back to the coast at Bivilie, they had a crack at a gun position on the cliffs, but then the Wing Commander thought he saw an enemy aircraft following him and while looking back his props hit the water. Both engines began to vibrate badly and after staggering to just 200 ft, they knew they would have to ditch.

They came down at 1:42 a.m., both men going out of the bottom of the Mosquito's cockpit when it was ripped off. The machine floated for about one and a half minutes, but both men were quickly in their dinghies which they then lashed together.

Spitfires were out searching at first light but did not find them till 6:15 that evening. Wallens flew out and rescued them at 7.30 p.m., by which time they had drifted to just two miles off the French coast, and the Walrus was chased for a couple of miles by four FW 190s, but they escaped. These two brought 277's score of men saved to 472!

After an X-ray, Fredericks found that he had suffered a broken leg below the knee, so it was back to hospital for him. 418 Squadron sent its Oxford to Hawkinge to pick up its CO, the airfield being 'shot-up' from several directions by three Mosquitos which escorted it.

During May came the announcement of the award of the DFC to Tom Fletcher. With the DFC, DFM and bar, he became the most highly decorated Walrus pilot in the RAF.

The next Wing Commander was saved by Mackertich, Humphreys

and Smith. With a section of Spitfires they went out to Dieppe, finding a pilot just one mile off shore. He landed and picked up Wing Commander Eric Haabjoern DFC, the Norwegian leader of 124 (Typhoon) Wing.

This famous pilot and leader had been taking 247 and 181 Squadrons on a rocket attack on a target near to Dieppe. They met intense heavy flak which hit the Wing Commander's 'Tiffie' (MN542), forcing him to bale out of his burning machine. It was not his first sea rescue, for in July 1942, when flying with 56 Squadron, he had been picked out of the water by *HSL 147*.

Towards 500

On the 23rd, Pete Weeden and Tom Ormiston, in Spitfires, met up with a crippled B-17 and escorted it until the pilot ditched. They then guided a launch to the 10 men, whom the boat picked up.

The sortie on the 23rd May I remember well, but probably not for the rescue itself. At this time, 277 was coming up to its 500th rescue and someone – probably Fighter Command HQ – had organized a 'sweepstake'. The idea was that tickets were sold bearing the squadron pilots' names, and the one that got the 500th won a prize which I think was about £100 – big money in those days. There was also a money prize for the actual pilot or pilots who carried out the rescue.

We had got to somewhere about the 490 mark when Tommy Ormiston suggested to me that if we stood-in for other pilots as often as possible for a couple of days, we could win the money. So this we did, flying Lord knows how many extra sorties. Then on the 23rd, we picked up a damaged B-17 and escorted her until she made her ditching, and directed a launch to pick up her crew. That brought the score to nearly 500. In the event, we were not flying when the total reached 500 – or at least I wasn't – so greed did not pay off.

Other than that, this rescue was just a normal sortie for us. It was just a couple of weeks before D-Day and the Allied bomber force was flying thousands of aircraft every day to soften up the coastal area of Europe, and in particular the USAAF, with their daylight raids, were getting shot down at a rare rate of knots; so we were very busy.

Flying Officer P. Weeden, No 277 Squadron

The 23rd was certainly proving busy. For the second day running, 277 rescued a Wing Commander; this time it was R.E.P. Brooker DFC, leader of 123 (Typhoon) Wing. Flying Typhoon MN143, Pete Brooker, a former Battle of Britain pilot who had also fought at Singapore when Japan joined the war, lost oil pressure during a sortie, and then his engine cut at 3,000 ft over the French coast. He baled out, coming down 40 miles out from the English coast. He was picked up by Lieutenant D.V. Robinson, with Willson and Green, in a Sea Otter – which made 497.

No 498 was Flight Lieutenant J.D. Furneaux of 2 Squadron, flying Mustang FD530. He and Flying Officer L.W. Burt were flying a photo recce sortie, checking on a *Wurzburg* radar station just inland from the French coast which had been attacked but not put out of action. They met heavy ground fire, which smashed into Furneaux's Mustang. Burt told him to fly out to sea and then saw him bale out five miles off Etretat. Gadd and Forrest located him, saw he was only in his Mae West so dropped him a dinghy. Calling for Sea Otter JM770, Flight Lieutenant C.G. Robertson DFC arrived, with Carpenter and Sub-Lieutenant A.W. More, to pick him up.

The magic figure of 500 came on the 27th after three days of no rescues. Shoreham Scrambled Sea Otter JM770 at 1:55 p.m., flown by – you've guessed it – Tommy Ormiston, with Green and Sub-Lieutenant P.F. Mariner. 'Jackie' Forrest and Flying Officer J.I.G. Lloyd were in the searching Spitfires, and they found two men two miles west of Le Treport. They were survivors from a US Boston of the 640th Bomb Squadron, 409th Bomb Group – Captain Nuff and Second Lieutenant Lever – the rest having baled out over France. Ormiston brought them back, creating much excitement, and the lucky winners of the sweepstake found it to be a profitable sortie. It is understood, however, that the celebrations that followed did away with most of the prize money!

Later that day, Hawkinge made it 501 when Mitchell, Hall and Mullins, in a Walrus, rescued Flight Sergeant A.C.H. 'Chalky' White of 127 Squadron, who had baled out of his Spitfire (MK696) seven miles off Le Treport. He had been hit during an attack on a V1 site and had ditched when he found he'd left it too late to bale out, but made it. White had previously flown in the Middle East, would fly on D-Day and complete his tour shortly afterwards.

★   ★   ★   ★   ★

Rescued after six days

Perhaps the most famous rescue of this period for 277 Squadron occurred on 28 May, and involved Len Healey, flying with Flight Lieutenant Robertson and Sub-Lieutenant P.F. Mariner in Sea Otter JM770.

Six days earlier, on the 22nd, 440 (RCAF) Squadron had attacked a radar station at Arromanches, and F/O A.A. Watkins' Typhoon (MN583) had been hit by ground fire, forcing him to bale out five miles off the French coast. He was last seen drifting along in his dinghy, but a Walrus and several Spitfires searched in vain for him until night fell. At first light aircraft were out again, but there was simply no trace of him or his dinghy and it had to be assumed he had been picked up by the Germans.

For many days we were sent out to look for a Typhoon pilot – a Pilot Officer Watkins. We were told to head for the French coast, but all our searches failed to locate him. Other crews also searched, but still nothing was seen. I think I did about four trips over that week, searching the area between other flights, until the last day we did an early morning patrol down the French coast, almost down to the Channel Islands. Finally we asked base for permission to make one final sweep, a ribbon search up the Channel to try and find this pilot. They agreed, but we knew that the search would then be called off, for after seven days there would be very little chance of him being found.

With Flight Lieutenant Robinson, we made a ribbon search up and down and suddenly I spotted something in the 'drink'. We went down for a closer look and found it to be a pilot in a dinghy. This was just north of Fecamp.

We landed, picked up the pilot, slashed his dinghy and pulled the man into the Otter. We started back for base, but Watkins was in a very sorry state and all he had had to eat and drink was the blood and raw flesh of a seagull. This had landed on the side of his dinghy and he had managed to grab and kill it.

On the way back, Mariner and I attended to him. He was covered in sores, following his long exposure to the sun and salt water; his clothes were sticking to him so I took off his Mae West, battledress and shirt, then dressed him in mine, which were warm. I also gave him a few sips of water and a few drops of hot soup. We landed at Tangmere and saw him safely off to hospital. We were told he couldn't have lasted much longer; his eyesight was failing him due to the continual glare of the sun on the dazzling sea. We understood that after a short period in hospital he recovered and went back to Canada.

Flying Officer L.R. Healey, No 277 Squadron

Watkins had been through a terrible ordeal. At dusk on the first evening he had seen rescue planes being fired at by shore batteries, and during that night the tide took him into the Seine Estuary. Dawn found him 10 miles west of Deauville due to a southerly wind. He erected the sail and made his way north and when night came again, he closed the sail and the tide carried him back to the Seine, but nearer to Le Havre. At dawn he was eight miles to the southwest of Le Havre; he erected the sail again and began to paddle, but at night he was carried back once more to the French coast. On the evening of the 26th, he tried to anchor himself to a buoy off Le Havre but missed it. He had now been in something of a tidal stream which was constantly taking him around and around the approaches into Le Havre, and on the evening of the 27th he thought he could hear sirens wailing in the harbour town. Then a Mosquito flew over, but he did not use his last flare in case he was mistaken, and also in case anyone on shore should see him.

Now the dinghy began to drift northeast, towards Fecamp, and he was about eight miles off the coast. He was getting weaker and his vision was becoming distorted, but he did not give up hope of being rescued. At about 10:30 a.m. he saw two Spitfires – Warrant Officers Gadd and A.T. Bartells of 277 – and they directed the Sea Otter to investigate.

★ ★ ★ ★ ★

The Typhoon boys

In spite of the amount of aircraft operating in the first week of June 1944, just prior to and on D-Day itself, there were comparatively few Walrus rescues. The day before the great invasion – the 5th – 275 Squadron picked up two pilots of 245 Squadron in yet another dramatic rescue.

The Typhoons of 245, led by Squadron Leader J.R. Collins DFC, took off soon after breakfast to attack yet another radar station, this one being at Auderville. Flight Lieutenant W. Smith was hit by ground fire and his Typhoon began to stream glycol. Climbing and heading out to sea, he reached 7,000 ft and 30 miles out before he had to take to his parachute and leave. As he got into his dinghy, Flight Lieutenant W.E. Reynolds circled him, but then his engine started to play up and not long afterwards he too was sitting in a dinghy. Collins gave a Mayday which brought Walruses from Warmwell. Flight Lieutenant R. Van Den Honert with Flying Officers T.A. Harper and W.S. Dixon in L2282, collected Smith, Pilot Officer T.F. Murray, Flight Lieutenant S.H. Britton and Pilot Officer D.L. Forster claiming Reynolds in HD908.

On the 7th, the day after D-Day, the Walrus men lost the struggle to save another Typhoon pilot, this time from 181 Squadron. George Rendle, an Australian, had his cursed Sabre engine cut while on his way to France to fly an armed recce around Caen, 275 sending out a Walrus to get him. They found an oil patch and then spotted the man, and quickly landed. He was alive but in poor shape, only just being able to cling to his dinghy as his parachute was entangled about his legs. They got him into the Walrus but he lost consciousness, and despite two hours of artificial respiration on the way back, the Walrus having to be towed in by *HSL 2607*, the man could not be revived.

On this same D-Day plus one, 277 rescued an American Thunderbolt pilot, the Walrus crew being captained by Chief Petty Officer C. Barley, one of several FAA pilots attached to the squadron.

With so many ships around off the coast of Normandy, pilots who were forced to ditch or bale out did so amongst them and so were soon picked up, but the ASR boys were on hand in case of a problem. If they did see anyone in the 'drink' they were soon able to direct some sort of ship or boat to the man in distress.

No 275 Squadron kept two sections of Spitfires and five Walrus crews at Readiness during this period, with two further sections of Spitfires at 30 minutes Available. During June alone, 275 Squadron made 255 sorties, picked up 15 survivors, located a further 12 for launches, spotted seven bodies and searched a number of floating wreckage spots.

Mentioning FAA pilots, another CPO, this time with 275 Squadron, was Les Cox. He joined the squadron on 19 May, and recalls an amusing episode towards the end of June 1944:

We were searching for a dinghy reported down about three miles south of Alderney. We were always monitored by a GCI radar station at Bolt Head, especially during these long sorties. They were extremely accurate and proficient and made a big impression on me as all my previous flying had been done without navigation aids (rule of thumb!).

There was no sign of the dinghy and the weather was perfect: blue sky, bright sunshine and unlimited visibility. Being so near to the island of Alderney, I couldn't resist the urge to go and have a look at it – and it being so peaceful!

This was on 25 June and Alderney was still occupied by the Germans, of course. I was flying along at about 1,000 feet, enjoying the view, when the guns on the fort opened up on me. At the same time, one of the escorting Spitfire pilots called to me, saying: 'Don't look now, but you're being followed!' and shot up into the stratosphere, or wherever they go.

I dived to sea level rapidly. The rear gun was manned at the time and there was a loud chattering noise over the R/T. This I assumed to be my air gunner firing at something, so I threw the Walrus around a bit until it became obvious that it was a defect on the intercom making all the noise!

This event would not normally be worth mentioning, except that mine was probably the last aircraft they had a go at from Alderney. Fancy shooting at a poor old Walrus – the cads!

Chief Petty Officer L.A. Cox, No 275 Squadron

Chapter Seventeen

Final Days
in Europe

As the build up of British and American forces in France slowly escalated, and when finally both RAF and American air force units began using airstrips in the beachhead, it was not long before the number of Walrus rescues began to tail off.

Within a few weeks of D-Day, the pressure was beginning to let up, and although the Walrus squadrons didn't immediately appreciate it, their days were numbered. Aircraft crippled over France and the Low Countries, or returning from raids into Germany itself, now had an alternative to trying to survive a ditching in the Channel or North Sea: they could attempt to reach the occupied areas and crash-land there. In many ways this was more attractive than going into the sea.

But there were still some rescues of note. One very lucky American Mustang pilot was found quite by chance on 24 June, by the Shoreham Flight. It was mid-afternoon as Flight Lieutenant W.B. Dobree, with Pilot Officer R.L. Kennedy and Flight Sergeant E.G. Green patrolled in Sea Otter JM764 off Littlehampton and spotted the dinghy just by luck. Captain L. DeLong Martin had been escorting Liberators and been hit by flak and baled out at 8:30 that morning, without being able to call for help or give a fix.

The ASR boys lost two pilots during this period. Back on 12 May, 278 had lost Warrant Officer D.C. Riddick who crashed and was killed while flying the squadron commander's Tiger Moth to Denham. Then, on 25 June, a Shoreham Spitfire pilot, Flying Officer F.G.D. O'Callaghan, crashed at Sherborne and was killed.

An interesting sideline to the rescue activities came in June 1944, which was also the period of the V1 rocket attacks on England. Patrolling Spitfire pilots saw a number of these flying bombs and a couple were in positions to make an attack – which, of course, they did.

On 29 June, Flight Sergeant A.M. Rollo destroyed one while on an early morning patrol from Hawkinge, and on 4 July, Warrant Officer J.A. Forrest, flying from Shoreham, got another. The following day, Wing Commander Grace bagged two on two patrols; the first dived into the ground at Charing near Ashford, and his second kill dived into the sea off Dungeness. The squadron's fifth V1 kill went to Flight Lieutenant T.G. V Roden on 23 August.

Just along for the ride

Shortly after Jack Forrest's V1 victory on the 4th, Robinson, with Eddie Quick, took an RAF photographer, Flying Officer E.W. Coop, up in Sea Otter JM776 when they were Scrambled. Vectored 45 miles out from Beachy Head, they found their 'customer' being circled by a Spitfire.

Shortly after lunch, a force of 300 Halifax bombers had attacked Rouen and Abbeville, escorted by RAF and American fighters. 66 Squadron was one of the RAF units and over the French coast, Pilot Officer G.T. Emery, in Spitfire PL273, called his leader to report that his radiator temperature was rising and he was heading back. Soon after he crossed out, he called to say he was baling out, but his section leader had lost him in cloud so no fix or exact position was possible.

Search planes went out, and after 66 returned and refuelled, they too sent six Spitfires out, finding Emery in his dinghy 20 miles off St Valery.

When the Otter arrived and landed it was taxied up, and with the help of Coop, Emery was taken aboard. The wind was getting up and sea conditions were worsening every minute. After sinking the dinghy, Robinson attempted to take off, but the engine lost power for some unknown reason and the take-off was abandoned. Another try ended in equal failure so taxying commenced, but a straight course to Newhaven could not be maintained in the conditions without endangering the aircraft. As it was, water was seeping in through the closed hatches and cockpit windows. The Sea Otter was pointed towards Beachy, but at 5:35 p.m., *HSL 190* was contacted, and it arrived to stand by to help.

They continued to move slowly towards Beachy, but finally, at 9:40 p.m., it was decided to transfer Emery to the HSL, this being accomplished by putting him in the crew dinghy. Later, the weather began to settle down, and it looked possible that they might be able to take off. The Sea Otter had shipped much of the Channel despite continuous baling, and it was suspected that the starboard wing, which was dipping seaward, was full of water.

The radio had gone u/s and so had the Aldis lamp, but a signal to take the seaplane in tow was flashed to the HSL by using the navigation lights. Once the tow line was secured there followed the slow process of heading for England, still several miles off. It was way past midnight when they got into the lee of Beachy Head, but now the starboard wing was dangerously low, so Eddie Quick had to crawl out onto the port wing, being relieved by Coop half an hour later. The two men continued this half-hourly routine until 5 a.m., when the Walrus finally got to within striking distance of Newhaven.

To add to the problems, the hand pump had packed up long since, and when not out on the wing, the third man had been baling with a soup tin almost continuously from 7 p.m. to 3 a.m.! Without this constant work by Quick and Coop, the machine would undoubtedly have been lost. The engine was now restarted and Robinson finally taxied into the harbour at 6 a.m. The rescue had thus lasted for 13 hours.

* * * * *

Two for the price of one

Down in the West Country, 276 had a couple of interesting rescues in June, the first one taking place on the 18th. 41 Squadron, flying Spitfire XIIs, were making a shipping recce from St Malo to Ouessant, flown by Flight Lieutenant T.A.H. Slack (MB876) and Flight Sergeant J.P. Ware RAAF (EN231), the latter having just joined the squadron.

They took off at 5:30 a.m., flying out to Lizardrieux and Aberverache. Slack spotted three MTBs and some light flak was encountered from the coast. As he turned for home, Tom Slack's engine cut out, and after giving a Mayday, he baled out. Tom recalls:

There was plenty of flak along the French coast and I heard some of it hitting my aircraft. I noticed the fuel gauge was dropping quickly to zero and within a few minutes the engine spluttered and stopped. I had just time to give a few quick Maydays over the radio before turning the aircraft onto its back to bale out. I shot out, pulled the ripcord and floated down towards the sea near the island of Ushant. I remembered to hit the parachute's safety release the moment my feet touched the water, so that I would surface away from the parachute without becoming entangled in the silk and the cords.

As I came up for air, the small fighter dinghy attached to the parachute harness had inflated automatically and I clambered aboard, sitting there shivering while waiting to be rescued.

Flight Lieutenant T.A.H. Slack, No 41 Squadron

In response to his Mayday calls, a Warwick (HF940) of 276 was diverted from patrol, piloted by Flying Officer H. Gamper. He and the crew sighted a man in the water at 7:30 a.m., and dropped him a dinghy. However, as might be realized, this was not Tom Slack, who was happy, but shivering, in his dinghy. The man in the water, found by the Warwick, was Flight Sergeant Ware!

Having turned for home after giving fixes, Ware was asked by the Controller to return and make certain Slack was in his dinghy, but the Flight Sergeant was unable to find the spot again and after looking for some time had then to return. At 7 a.m. he ran out of petrol and had to bale out, so he too ended up in the 'drink'. Meantime, Tom Slack was waiting for rescue:

Suddenly I saw some stained pound notes floating by which must have fallen out of my pockets as I hit the water. I paddled furiously with my hands to retrieve them, but the ripples from the moving dinghy kept pushing them further from my reach. Anyway, there were more serious problems on my mind, so I sat back, searching the sky in the hope of seeing a British aircraft. My dinghy was first spotted by an Air-Sea Rescue Warwick aircraft which radioed my position back to Portreath and dropped smoke floats to mark the spot clearly. Before long the air was humming with aircraft dropping more smoke floats, until it was difficult to breathe, and then a Sunderland dropped a large dinghy within a few feet of my own. I climbed aboard but tied my small dinghy alongside in case of emergency.

An ASR Walrus arrived and landed in the sea to take me on board, and who should I see waving from the back but Flight Sergeant Ware who had baled out in the middle of the Channel. It was his Mayday calls which had been received because mine were sent too low over the sea. He had then circled around looking for me and had run out of fuel before he could get back to base.

The sea was not rough but there was a large swell and the Walrus couldn't get airborne. Luckily, an RAF Air-Sea Rescue launch appeared and took the two of us on board. The Walrus jettisoned all unnecessary equipment and, with the launch zig-zagging at speed in front of it to help calm the swell, the plane finally managed to take off.

Flight Lieutenant T.A.H. Slack, No 41 Squadron

His rescuers had been Flight Lieutenant 'Tiny' Martin, Flying Officer L. Gayler and Warrant Officer J. Partridge, in Walrus L2335.

Strangely, Tom Slack had had a dream only a night or so before this incident, in which he had been in the sea but was later back in the local pub, drinking. So, in a strange way, his dream told him he would survive a dunking. He had also met a beautiful WAAF officer, with whom he was quite attached. She came on duty in the Portreath Ops Room shortly after Tom was shot down, and discovering it was indeed him, she used all her charm and influence to launch a small armada of aircraft and rescue boats into the area.

Tom had had an interesting war to date. He had learned to fly in the Middle East in 1941 and on one occasion that April, while still at IFTS, piloted an Audax in company with over 50 other training types, above the hostile Iraqi forces in Baghdad. Some days later, the trainee airmen were given their flying badges as it seemed likely they would have to fly on Ops against the Iraqi troops. This was indeed the case and after a bomb raid to Baghdad, his aircraft developed engine trouble which forced him down in the desert.

He was rescued safely, completed his training in South Africa and eventually came to England to fly Spitfires. Then on 18 July 1943, he was shot down over France, but with help from some gallant French people, he succeeded in returning to England via Spain and Gibraltar.

Fate had not finished with him, even after his rescue from the sea, for during a sweep on 23 August 1944, when jettisoning his external fuel tanks, his engine spluttered and stopped. He crash-landed in a field near Hesdin but knocked himself out, and when he came to, two German soldiers ensured that he would not be repeating his evasion route of the previous year.

★ ★ ★ ★ ★

It's not what you know, but who you know!

A Warwick was searching for a missing pilot on 23 June, but failed to find anything other than an oil patch and some wreckage. Spitfires of 276 were also out, Pilot Officer L. 'Pop' Ewens and Flight Sergeant I. Godbolt investigating lights which had been reported 70 miles out, but then a Mayday call was heard, given by a Typhoon pilot.

Flight Sergeant Iain D.M. Dunlop of 263 Squadron was on *Ramrod 144*, an attack on a radar station, but had been hit by light flak and forced to bale out. As the aircraft were out searching anyway, he was only in his dinghy for 30 minutes before the two Spitfire pilots had found him and called up a Walrus. Flight Lieutenant A. Hill, Flying Officer C. Rolls and Pilot Officer A. Kyle, in Walrus W3081, had him aboard in no time.

We had just attacked a radar station at Abbervach, in the vicinity of Roscoff on the north Brittany coast, and were circling round off shore at about 500 feet, in order to have another go. There was a large bang somehwere underneath me and the Typhoon gave a kind of shudder. Quite shortly afterwards the oil pressure started to fluctuate and then began to dip towards zero.

I turned north and started to climb, assuming that I would probably have to jump, ditching being very dodgy in a Typhoon. My suspicion was very soon confirmed as the engine showed every sign that it was about to seize up. I therefore yelled Mayday a few times and jumped. The chap who was flying 'Number Two' to me that day had come up with me, and he hung around as long as his fuel situation allowed and continued the contact with the D/F service.

It was a beautiful, warm summer day and I remember how lovely and peaceful it was floating down towards the calm sea. It seemed to take ages, and then very suddenly I realized that I was about to get very wet. I released the parachute a few feet above the water, as per the recommended procedure, and fell free into the oggin.

I was found very quickly, the Spitfires appearing to fly straight to me without any kind of search. They circled around for a while, dropping smoke floats around me, and then with a waggle of wings, disappeared whence they came.

The next act in the drama concerned a white-painted Warwick which appeared with an airborne lifeboat slung beneath it. They, in turn, dropped more smoke floats, and I remember hoping they were going to drop the boat as I quite fancied the idea of sailing myself into Brixham!

They were, of course, aware that a Walrus was on its way, which I was not, and, sure enough, soon after the Warwick flew off, I heard the drone of the dear old 'Shagbat' as it hove into sight.

It manoeuvred itself into wind and landed straight at me. As it taxied over, one of the crew, standing in the forward hatch, held a pole out to me on which was a removeable clip attached to a rope. He instructed me to fix the clip onto the dinghy and was then able to pay it out as I slid along the side of the fuselage. Another member of the crew hauled me quite easily into the aft hatch, stuck a knife into the dinghy and hauled it in after me as it collapsed.

In no time at all we were roaring across the water, airborne, and landing back at Bolt Head, the very place from which we had departed only a few hours before.

Apart from the obvious skill and coordination of the boys of 276 Squadron and the luck of the perfect weather, there was one other factor in my favour that day. I had, for some time, been very friendly with a WAAF who was a D/F operator in the fixer service. She knew my call-sign, and she told me afterwards that not only did she make sure to get a good bearing on my call, but she alerted her pals in the other triangulation stations to do the same. They obviously obtained a super fix and this enabled the Spits to come straight at me.

Flight Sergeant I.D.M. Dunlop, No 263 Squadron

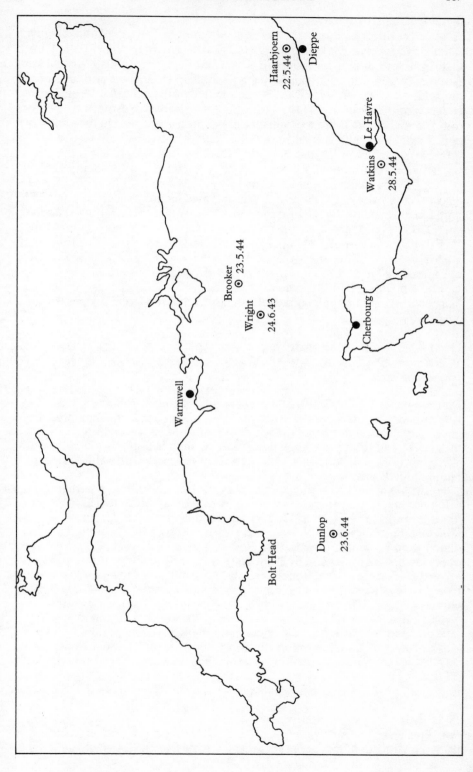

Haarbjoern ⊙
22.5.44

Dieppe ●

Le Havre ●

Watkins ⊙
28.5.44

Brooker ⊙ 23.5.44

Wright ⊙
24.6.43

Cherbourg ●

Warmwell ●

Dunlop ⊙
23.6.44

Bolt Head

The flying doctors?

A slightly different duty was carried out by 278 Squadron on 29 June. Three HSLs had picked up eight US airmen from the 390th Bomb Group, some of whom had been wounded. They were 20 miles west of Alkmaar when one of the launches was shot up by a Ju 88 and four of the crew killed or injured. Sub-Lieutenant J. Robinson and Flying Officer R.A. Green took off in HD918 at 8:20 p.m. to fly two American doctors out to the scene. They accomplished this and transferred the two men but could not then take off, so had to be towed home by one of the HSLs into Yarmouth. While this was going on, the doctors carried out a blood transfusion on one of the wounded boat crewmen, thus saving his life.

Len Healey received the DFC in July and Warrant Officer W.L. Butler also received the DFC, while William Tait Gregory received the DFM and a commission. In 275 Squadron, R. Van Den Honert also received the DFC. Two Canadian pilots with 277, Flying Officers A.E. Gooch W.E Uptigrove, finally became tour-expired and returned to their own country. One other feature of July 1944 was that 277's Spitfires occasionally landed in France to refuel during long search missions.

The Shoreham Flight was taken over by Squadron Leader Ogilvie-Forbes in August as the squadron began to fly Ops from Warmwell, too.

★ ★ ★ ★ ★

On 11 July, a 278 Squadron crew comprising Warrant Officer Ron Whittaker and Flying Officer P.J. Roy, in Walrus HD933, rescued a Liberator crew:

I put down with Paul Roy RCAF, where a US Liberator had ditched. There was only one injured crew member in the dinghy; the rest of the crew were obviously dead, floating on the water. The US Mae Wests seemed to allow the head to go too far back, so that water washed into the nose and mouth. We couldn't get an unconscious man from the water into the Walrus, let alone a dead one.

Again the sea was too rough and we porpoised every time we tried to take off, so we taxied until we were taken in tow by a Naval RML. We had to get the injured man into a 'Neil Robertson' stretcher to get him along the Walrus on our hands and knees, and out of the front hatch, onto the RML, which then took us in tow until we met up with an RAF HSL, which took over our tow. The RML then hot-footed it back to Felixstowe. Again we arrived back in the small hours. Paul Roy was awarded the DFC soon after this. He was actually a wireless operator/air gunner, but we carried no wireless, only VHF, and we had taken the guns and Scarfe rings out to save weight on sea take-offs. He had been involved in other rescues.

If one had ever to restart the engine of a Walrus when down in a rough sea – as a crewman standing up on the wing, winding up a hand-wound inertia starter with the seaplane pitching and rolling all over the place – that deserved a DFC on its own!

Warrant Officer R.C. Whittaker, No 278 Squadron

A U-boat crew

Another slight variation came to 276 Squadron on 19 July. No fewer than 20 dinghies had been spotted 25 miles southeast of Start Point.

276 Squadron sent out a pair of Spitfires, one flown by 'Pop' Ewens, to the position given to see what it was all about:

Our ASR procedure was a square pattern search, i.e. fly to an estimated commencement position, then fly due east for three minutes, then three minutes to the north, turn left, three minutes west, turn right, and so on. We would then continue, so a large area of sea was covered.

On this occasion, the Controller reminded us we were not making much progress towards the west by apparently not making sufficient allowance for the wind, so that we were flying up and down legs, much along the same path.

On correcting this, we were soon able to spot the string of yellow-jacketed 'bods'. In all, we were searching for no more than 10 minutes, or perhaps a quarter of an hour, but the Controller certainly helped us. He later pulled our legs by suggesting he should have ALL the credit for this rescue!
Pilot Officer L. Ewens, No 276 Squadron

Ken Butterfield and Godbolt then went out and circled them, and a Walrus was Scrambled even though there was no possibility of a wholesale rescue; but boats would follow while the Walrus could at least see to any seriously injured men.

Flight Lieutenant McBrien, with Rolls and Perry, landed W3083, only to find the dinghies contained the survivors of a German U-boat! In all, there were 46 men. Initially, the men had been spotted by a Spitfire pilot returning from France. They turned out to be the survivors of *U-672* which had been scuttled the previous night after being damaged by HMS *Balfour*.

McBrien ordered the Captain to come aboard the Walrus, then promised that the rescue of the rest would soon follow. He took off and returned to Harrowbeer where the Wing Commander Flying, 'Birdy' Bird-Wilson DFC & bar, was asked to meet the amphibian. He was there as Oberleutnant Ulf Lawaetz stepped down from the Walrus, and as it was one of 'Birdy's' men who had initially spotted them, he gave the Wing Commander his wrist compass as a souvenir.

Squadron Leader A.F. Sunderland-Cooper was now CO of 276 Squadron. He had previously been with 275 and had commanded 282 Squadron in late 1943. David McBrien DFC was tour-expired in July, his 'B' Flight being taken over by Flight Lieutenant A.B. Hill on the 22nd; but the very next day, Hill was killed when his Spitfire (EN841) crashed into the sea with engine trouble. His body was picked up by a destroyer.

276 squadron approach the 300 mark
July ended for 276 with the rescue of a Liberator VI (EW306) crew from 53 Squadron of Coastal Command. They were engaged on an air-to-air homing exercise. The pilot, Flying Officer J. Osborne, while flying along at 200 ft, had handed over the controls to the second pilot and left his seat. The second pilot failed to maintain height above the calm water and hit the sea. Osborne had returned to find they were just 50 ft off the sea. Ordering his co-pilot to climb, they hit the sea before this could be achieved.

Osborne was seriously injured, the co-pilot and navigator killed, and the three other crewmen also injured. They came down off Trevose Head and Warrant Officer Eddie Lloyd and his crew were Scrambled in L2246 to help. The four injured men were found clinging to a partially inflated dinghy, so Lloyd landed and picked them up. They were later transferred to the Padstow HSL. Being unable to take off, they taxied back to Portreath. This rescue brought 276's score to 298 men saved. However, it would be some months before the total reached 300. This, in the main, was because the squadron, in September, was sent to the Continent. 'C' Flight went to St Denis Westrem, SHQ and 'B' Flight to Amiens Glisy. However, there was little or no need for ASR flights in 2nd TAF.

One of 275's last rescues occurred on 24 July. The 8th Air Force, supporting the US 1st Army in France, bombed the St Lo area. One B-17 from the 613th Bomb Squadron, 401st Bomb Group, was hit by flak and headed back over the Channel. 275 Squadron were alerted for possible casualties and so had aircraft on patrol south of Portland Bill.

Then came the call that, indeed, a B-17 had gone into the water, 25 miles out. In fact, in coming down, the Fortress had exploded while the crew had been taking to their parachutes. Eight men survived but the co-pilot was found to be missing. Flying Officers C.G. Eaton and J.S. Barker and Sergeant S.J. Browning, in Sea Otter JM823, and Pilot Officer T.F. Murray (Australian), Flight Lieutenant S.H. Britton and Flying Officer D.L. Forster, in Walrus R6548, headed for the scene.

Easton landed and picked up seven men, then began to taxi back, guided by another Walrus, flown by Flight Lieutenant V.H. Jaynes. Murray's Walrus arrived and landed amongst the wreckage of the Fortress and found an eighth man, Tech/Sergeant Lindholm, in his Mae West. He was pulled in and flown back to base.

Chapter Eighteen

On to Victory in Europe

Help from the ladies

In August and September 1944, 278 Squadron had a rush of rescues because the land battles were now approaching Northern France and Holland and the Arnhem airborne landings were taking place.

On 29 August Flying Officers M.J. Peskett and E.K. Dinneen, in Walrus W2715, rescued a pilot off Den Helder, damaged a float taking off, but managed to get home. Two weeks later, on 13 September, Peskett and Leading Airman R.H. Westbrook, in Walrus HD912, picked up a man in a Mae West but had to be towed back into Felixstowe.

There was now a Walrus Flight of 278 operating at Martlesham Heath, along with the Warwick aircraft. On the night of 12/13 September, a Walrus crew were themselves rescued. Sub-Lieutenant G.L. Emmette and Pilot Officer L.C. Murray had taken off at 9:05 p.m. on the evening of the 12th when a pilot was reported in the water, but despite lights having been seen, nothing was found, even though the Walrus landed to make certain. However, it could then not get off again as it was damaged by the heavy seas, so *RML 520* was sent out to rescue the two men.

RML 520 was also out, looking for a missing P-38 pilot, and saw the lights of the Walrus, then received the SOS with the message 'Be quick!' flashed by the aircraft's lights. The Walrus was starting to break up in the waves and it did not look as if it would last much longer. The launch crew tried to float a couple of dinghies to the Walrus but the ropes kept snapping, so the craft manoeuvred to enable the two men to leap onto the boat. At 11:40 p.m., Murray jumped, but he misjudged the leap and fell into the water; he was picked up by lifeline and hauled aboard. The pilot got safely across and then the Walrus was cut adrift.

The launch then continued its search for the missing P-38 pilot, and at first light they saw that the Walrus was still afloat, having drifted over 16 miles during the night.

Another Martlesham crew made a rescue on the 14th. Pilot Officer J.E. Meeklah and Sub-Lieutenant J. Felice were Scrambled in Walrus HD830 at 5:20 p.m. and located Spitfires circling a man in the water. The

Spitfires had relieved two Tempests which had previously been above the man. The man in the water was Hugh Ross:

Our Op on this day was called at fairly short notice and involved just two aircraft. Johnny Heap was to lead and I was to be his 'Number Two'. We were to search an area of Holland for signs of any troop movements and carry out ground attacks so that the Germans would not realize the real reason for our mission.

I was in 'B' Flight and, surprisingly, I was allocated the 'A' Flight commander's Tempest (EJ670) which had just been polished from nose to tail with beeswax. It was a beautiful aircraft to fly and the pride and joy of Tony Seager and his groundcrew. I think this was the first time (and last) that anyone other than Tony was to fly it and one of his ground crew jokingly said, 'One scratch and don't bother coming back!' When I eventually got back, there were tears in his eyes when he apologized for bringing me bad luck. We had a marvellous band of ground staff.

We took off, arrived over Holland and started searching the area for troops. When we had completed our search we spotted a long white barge or boat – an ideal target. We attacked and hammered it with our four 20 mm cannon – bits and pieces flew all over the place. As I pulled away I noticed my oil pressure was beginning to drop. It was very soon obvious that I wasn't going to make it back to base. That left me with the choice of a forced landing in Holland and becoming a POW, or flying out to sea and getting as far as I could and hoping that somehow I would be picked up. There was quite a mist on the sea when we flew over but I still felt the sea was the only choice. I told Johnny and he told me to lead and he would cover me. The coastline passed slowly beneath and when we were out to sea the engine gave a great shudder and stopped.

I trimmed the Tempest to glide and decided to bale out at 4,000 feet. It was not recommended to ditch a Tempest because of the large air scoop under the nose. I disconnected my oxygen tube, pulled out my R/T plug, undid my safety straps and pulled the emergency hood and side panel release. I crouched, feet on the seat, and attempted to dive out parallel to the mainplane and was brought up with a jerk, half in and half out of the aircraft. I scrambled back; my R/T lead had snagged on something. I tore my helmet off and dived out. I pulled my ripcord and was relieved to feel the jolt of the parachute opening.

I swung gently and silently towards the sea and watched the Tempest pull up into a stall turn and then dive vertically into the water. When I landed in the 'drink', I inflated my dinghy and clambered aboard. Johnny Heap circled overhead and somehow he managed to keep me in sight whilst flying high enough to keep in R/T contact with base. He stayed overhead, knowing that if he left there would be little chance of me being picked up, until two aircraft from 274 Squadron arrived. Then, desperately short of fuel, he set course for home and arrived with hardly a drop of petrol left.

Sometime later a Walrus arrived and flying towards me, dropped a smoke float from a height of about 50 feet. It then circled, and flying towards me, came down to a perfect landing. It continued towards me until its hull bumped against the dinghy. My dinghy slid along the hull and under the wing root. A crewman standing in an open hatch just behind the wings, caught the dinghy with a boat-hook and held it against the hull until I scrambled aboard. As soon as I was in, the Walrus picked up speed and we were on our way to Martlesham Heath.

A 'blood wagon' was waiting to take me to the station hospital, where two American doctors wired me up to a machine which wouldn't work. They spent ages messing about with this machine, ignoring my pleas for a good meal as I was positively starving!

A day or so later, I was flown back to my squadron to find that my great friend, Pete Godfrey, had been killed along with Spike Mahoney, Bob Hannay and Lofty Haw. The squadron had been sent on an anti-flak duty whilst the Arnhem operation was taking place, and such a mission was bound to take a heavy toll.

Warrant Officer H.F. Ross, No 80 Squadron

It is not generally known that WAAF's on D/F Stations during the Second World War were much involved in the initial stages of Air-Sea Rescue. Many a successful recovery was dependent upon the Walrus or HSL knowing the exact location of the ditched pilot or crew. One such was LACW Joyce Millard (now Joyce Smith), who remembers:

When I joined up in late 1942, WAAFs had only just started being trained as VHF/DF/RT operators. It had become a matter of extreme urgency that ASR facilities should be expanded and improved to cope with the ever-increasing air traffic flying over the waterways. After a two-month course at Cranwell, I spent the next two years on D/F Stations near the coast, in the Kenley and Biggin Hill Sectors, taking bearings on the intercom of the pilots' voices when they were in combat with the Luftwaffe, strafing targets along the coast of Occupied Europe, chasing and shooting down 'Doodlebugs', etc.

The routine work of taking bearings on individual aircraft on a pre-arranged frequency gave the Controller the exact position of his squadrons and enabled him to direct them to intercept the enemy – a vector to target, or give them a 'Homing' – but our main priority was the all too frequent Mayday distress call before a pilot baled out.

We were in constant touch by a direct line with the Triangulator Room at Sector Ops and the Mayday bearing would be passed to them, and simultaneously, two other D/F Stations would do likewise. These would be displayed on a triangulator table and the resulting 'fix' would be the position of the 'ditched' airman. The location on the reference grid would then be immediately passed to the nearest available rescue facility.

Glycol leaks and other mechanical failures of fighter aircraft were as frequent a reason for a pilot having to bale out as being shot down by flak or fighters. As a precautionary measure, fighter aircraft did not generally fly solo over the sea, and it was normal policy to at least fly in pairs during a Mayday incident, as this was the most satisfactory method of getting an accurate position as the other aircraft would circle overhead, continuing the Mayday call while we took frequent bearings, updating any change in the location until the Walrus or HSL arrived.

In the circumstances where a pilot took to the water in an emergency, unseen by another pilot, it could well be that the time it took him to get out of his aircraft and reach the water, depending on weather conditions as well, his actual position could be some distance from the bearing and fixes the D/F Stations got on his Mayday position when he last transmitted from the cockpit.

With the help of the author of this book, I was gratified to find a pilot
that I had had a hand in helping to save in September 1944. I was on
afternoon duty on a D/F Station at Tolleshunt D'Arcy, Essex, that day, and
wrote in my diary: 'Worked for a spell, aircraft in trouble. One baled out
but he got back OK.'

We were only ever given the call-sign of the squadron, never the number
or type of aircraft. Sometimes we were told when our efforts had resulted in
a successful rescue, but no details of the circumstances as to how or why
he had to bale out. I think it quite extraordinary that from that vague diary
clue, I have now discovered who that pilot was on that September day. In
a letter from Hugh Ross, he asked me if he had been one of 'mine'. I am
very pleased to say that he was.

LACW Joyce Millard, D/F Station

Canadian Halifax

On the night of 15/16 September 1944, 420 (RCAF) Squadron was part
of Bomber Command's attack on Kiel. Flight Lieutenant Vic Motherwell
RCAF was the pilot of Halifax NA629, and although it was his 14th op,
it was his crew's 13th! Sergeant Joe Hickson RCAF was in the rear turret:

We had been allotted a brand new Halifax that had just come on to our
squadron and we joked with the ground crew before take off whether we
would bring this new plane back. Well, we didn't!

As we neared the target from the west at 18,000 feet, searchlights were
streaking the sky and bursts of flak were coming up directly in front of us.
I was keeping a keen lookout for night-fighters while the bomb aimer was
giving our pilot instructions during the bomb run.

We must have been hit by flak, for as we pulled away I could hear Vic
talking to the engineer Jack Porter that all was not well. It appeared that
we were losing fuel and hydraulic fluid so we could not raise our bomb
doors, but I was feeling safer now that we had left the target area and had
once again been cloaked in darkness. But we were losing altitude and falling
way behind the rest of the force. Soon we were down to 1,000 feet and Jack
was wondering if we had enough fuel to get us over the North Sea. It was
even discussed if we should try for France, but that was ruled out as no
airfield was available for a bomber to land on, especially at night, and in
our shape we would surely crash. We decided to chance it to England.

It wasn't long before Jack reported our gas was going fast as we had to
use extra gas to keep us in the air, with our bomb doors, wheels and flaps
hanging down. Our wireless operator was sending out SOS on emergency
procedure as I continued to watch out for night-fighters, knowing that
ditching in the North Sea had become a reality.

We were about three quarters across the North Sea when Jack said we
had only 15 minutes of fuel left. Shortly after that, the Skipper told me to
get out of the turret and with the others, take up a crash position. Our
wireless operator gave our last position, then clamped the key down. I then
heard the Skipper say, 'We are going in!' and turned on the landing lights.
'Where is the water,' he asked, 'we are at 200 feet and no water?' But then:
'I see the water – hold on – this is it!'

I felt the plane hit the water just lightly, then hard, and at the same time
the round bomb-inspection door popped open between my legs. Water shot
up just like a fire hose, then a big wave of water came over my head – then

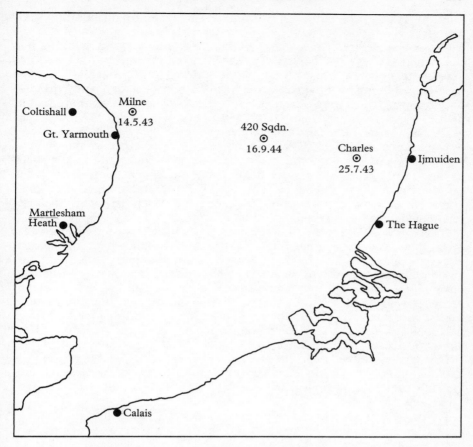

it was pitch dark. When finally I was able to get up, the water was up to my chest. I saw our mid-upper just going up the ladder through the top hatch, so gave him a push and scrambled up after him, pulling the dinghy release handle as I went (as it was my designated responsibility), and it came loose. I knew then that the dinghy must be inflating and as I came out the hatch I could see in the dim, early morning light, the Halifax floating perfectly, with the wings awash and the props bent back.

The dinghy was floating just off the edge of the wing with the rest of the crew already in it. I jumped down on the wing, grabbed the dinghy just as someone shouted that the Skipper was getting out up front. I stretched out flat in the water, holding onto the dinghy with my hands, and my toes anchored in the compartment from which the dinghy had emerged. The strong wind and high waves were trying to pull the dinghy away and seeing the Skipper making his way across the fuselage, I called out to him that I couldn't hold the dinghy for long. One of the boys told me not to worry, they'd grab the tailplane. I pulled myself into the dinghy, which did drift to the tail, and the Skipper walked the rest of the way down the fuselage, climbed in, all nice and dry!

We drifted away, all pretty cramped and sitting on each other's legs as the wirless operator cut the line, freeing us from the Halifax, which was still afloat despite what we had been told – that it would sink in a couple of minutes. It was now well over 10 minutes since coming down and it was still there.

Our navigator, Ian McGowan, had then to admit that he had lost all his gear when the wave of water swept through the machine, so we had no Verey pistol or flares. Still, we were all safe and well, but then within minutes we were all being sick over the side of the dinghy – except our wireless operator, who hailed from Saskatchewan – the only real 'landlubber' amongst us!

We had ditched at 4:10 a.m. and we knew that by 9 a.m. or so the ASR boys would be looking for us. We sat up to look for planes but within minutes we would be doubled up and sick again even though we had nothing left to throw up. About 10 a.m., we heard some planes and spotted them far off to the north, but we could not attract their attention and we knew that within an hour the search would be called off, as we had been on ASR missions before and knew the routine.

At about 5:30 p.m., the Skipper roused us all and we started to talk to each other. I was warm enough but wet from the chest down and we all had our legs cramped up. Later we put up the sail thinking we better head for Holland, but within a short time we spotted three Halifaxes in the distance, low over the water, but they soon turned for England and we settled down on our journey to Holland. Suddenly, three Halifaxes were heading straight for us, bomb doors open, and out fell three smoke bombs which looked at first as if they would hit us. We could see plainly the squadron code letters – they were from 420 Squadron!

One 'Hally' climbed while the other two circled over us, and they dropped two containers which inflated when they hit the water, giving us two more life rafts and some supplies. We managed to retrieve one but the second floated away.

We divided ourselves between the two dinghies and then three Avro Lancaster arrived, then a Warwick, and later still, a Hudson which had an airborne lifeboat slung beneath it.

It was now getting dusk, but then on the horizon a Walrus seaplane appeared, circled once, then came down to land in the rough sea – and disappeared. I felt sure we would then have to rescue him but up he popped on top of another wave, then disappeared again below the waves. In this way he slowly made his way to us and upon reaching us we were lifted out of the dinghy by a strong-armed airman into the nose of the Walrus. I was second to be lifted and followed the mid-upper to the tail of the machine. The others all followed, the Skipper being the last, in true to the Navy/Air Force tradition.

With the Walrus crew of two and eight of us, it made it impossible for a take-off. I could feel the plane moving through the water, but it was dark now and closing my eyes I was soon asleep, but not soundly. We must have been taxying about an hour when the motor of the Walrus revved, then shut down abruptly – with the plane hitting something with a shuddering bang. I could not imagine what we'd hit; I thought at first it had been a mine. The motor revved again for about a minute, then again shut down and another bang. This happened a couple of more times, then I looked out of the hatch and found there was an MTB and we had bumped into the back of it, and then a couple of sailors grabbed our arms and hauled us on board.

We were put into bunks and given a glass of rum although I didn't want mine, but a sailor gladly drank it for me. In a few moments we were on our way again, towing the Walrus behind us.

Getting out of my wet clothes, I put on a pair of navy blue overalls and in the bunk I closed my eyes.

It only seemed like a few seconds when a flash lit up the sky outside the cabin. A sailor came in and said a German E-boat had just shot off a star-flare, lighting up the whole sky. They cut the Walrus loose and the MTB opened up, full throttle. Did we ever move then! I guess the Germans had come out to see what all the commotion had been about off the Dutch coast.

We got to the port of Great Yarmouth at 2 a.m. on 17 September and eventually got back to our base that afternoon, only to find our beds stripped, our gear stowed away and a new crew had moved in. We quickly soon sorted that lot out, remade the beds and got our belongings back.

We learned later that the Navy had gone back out and retrieved the Walrus – the Germans had not found it. Our Skipper was recommended for a DFC for ditching a disabled aircraft successfully, thus saving the lives of his crew. The wireless operator was recommended for the DFM for staying at his set and sending the SOS until the last minute. We were all given 10 days' survivors' leave, starting the 21st.

Sergeant J.L. Hickson, No 420 (RCAF) Squadron

Flight Lieutenant Vic Motherwell, Joe Hickson and the others went on to complete their 30-Op tour by early February 1945. The crew at the time of the ditching had been, in addition to those already mentioned: PO Al MacDonald (bomb aimer); Sgt Lyle Engemoen (wirless operator); Sgt Jim Wigley (mid-upper gunner); and Sgt Joe Bibby (mid-under gunner). The Walrus crew had been Lieutenant N.C. Langdon FAA and Leading Airman R.Atkins, in Walrus HD926. Because they were Fleet Air Arm men, Joe Hickson believed they had been rescued by the Royal Navy! The 'MTB' had been *RML 512*, and they had picked up the Walrus just a few miles off Den Helder.

As well as Joe Hickson's splendid account above, Al MacDonald also says:

We were not originally scheduled to be on this raid to Kiel, but as the stand-by crew we were called upon to go due to illness of the other crew. Our aircraft was a new one which had aborted two previous raids due to malfunctioning equipment! In fact our direct compass became u/s, making it necessary for us to fly by magnetic compass. Over the North Sea our GEE became partially u/s, so that I had to jiggle the antenna continuously in order not to lose the blip in the 'snow' on the screen.

About 20 minutes after leaving the target, things began to happen to our aircraft. First one wheel came down, then the other, followed by the flaps and bomb doors. We did not recall hearing the sound of being hit by flak, but we lost all the hydraulic oil pressure. We also knew that with our reduced height and increased fuel usage, we were not going to make it back.

At 4 a.m. we had no recourse but to come down in the sea. What helped our landing was that the waves were high, and fortunately we were able to get the aeroplane almost into a stall so that the belly hit the water before the wheels dug in.

We had not been picked up by noon, even though we could see aircraft out searching for us. We had put up the sail, although with a missing line and due to our numbers, it took us three hours.

We were finally spotted at around 5 p.m. Anyone who has looked for a dinghy in the North Sea knows that they can readily be lost again. All kinds of flares were dropped around us and soon it seemed we had an armada of aircraft circling us. When we got aboard the Walrus the pilot told us he'd been waiting for a launch to arrive, but since it was getting dark they could not take the chance of losing us so he landed. We had also drifted far to the east, having originally come down within 50 miles of the English coast.

The following day the Walrus pilot came to say goodbye. A pal of his was going to fly him out to see if they could find his plane which had been cast adrift. We received a signal the next day telling us that they had found it and he flew it back.

Flying Officer A.J. MacDonald, No 420 (RCAF) Squadron

★   ★   ★   ★   ★

Arnhem trade

The Arnhem operation began on 17 September, and Pilot Officers Meeklah and W. Trust of 278, in Walrus HD912, picked up a pilot off Orfordness on this day. The next afternoon, Warrant Officer F.J. Bedford and Sub-Lieutenant Felice (W2735) picked up four survivors from a Waco glider off Aldeburgh. There were several other gliders down in the North Sea, and a ditched Liberator, survivors being picked up by HSLs. Bedford taxied his 'customers' to the beach near Matilla Tower, half a mile south of Aldeburgh. The squadron were kept busy over the next few days, mainly helping to guide HSLs to downed gliders.

While flying Spitfires with 278, I flew cover over the North Sea for the glider fleet going to Arnhem on 17 September. I was also involved in the rescue of an He 111 crew that had been shot down at night, bringing over a 'buzz-bomb' (V1) to release near the east coast.

Warrant Officer R.C. Whittaker, No 278 Squadron

In October the CO of 278 Squadron changed, Squadron Leader Ben Bowring leaving, Flight Lieutenant R. Whitcombe DFC taking over, although Bowring was later to return.

Bedford and Leading Airman Westbrook took off in a Walrus at 12:15 p.m. on 5 October, to search for a missing Mustang pilot from the 339th Fighter Group. They were escorted 40 miles out by Spitfires and found the survivor clinging to a dinghy, but the sea was far too rough for the man to pull himself in. Bedford landed and tried to rescue the man, but due to severe buffeting they were not having much success. Westbrook managed to retain a line hold on him until the trawler HMS *George Adgell* arrived, which lowered a boat and got the pilot out of the water.

With the man safe, Bedford went to take off but lost his port float, so the Walrus (HD933) was taken in tow by *RML 547* which had also arrived. Westbrook was out on the starboard wing, and *RML 547* came alongside and took him off, then got Bedford off. Soon after the tow was taken up, the Walrus turned turtle and sank. Nevertheless, it had been a good rescue in a Force 4 sea and the Walrus crew, by getting a line to the exhausted pilot in such difficult circumstances, certainly saved his life.

On 7 November, with the war now going inland on the Continent,

278 moved from Martlesham Heath to Hornchurch, and some of 277 Squadron were transferred to 278.

Walrus rescues now tailed off dramatically – the war had moved on into Europe. However, there were a few more before the war came to an end. On 12 December, Robertson, Walker and Flight Sergeant W. Shaw of 277 at Hawkinge, found a P-47 pilot from the 259th Fighter Squadron – First Lieutenant O'Quinn – 356 Fighter Group, 30 miles off Margate. Robertson landed despite seven-foot waves and then had to taxi back, but later managed to get off.

The squadron had, like the others, had more than their share of American airmen rescued. Some US decorations had been received from time to time, but on 13 January 1945, Squadron Leader Jack Brown was presented with the American DFC by none other than General James H. Doolittle, Commander-in-Chief of the US 8th Air Force. The citation stated that Brown had been on 68 rescue sorties resulting in 26 men being saved.

Two of the four Walrus squadrons, Nos 277 and 278, were disbanded in February 1945, the final Ops being flown on the 14th. This left just 276, which was in Holland, and 278, which was left to cover the Channel.

I took my Flight to Ghent, via Amiens, on 30 September and the rest of the squadron assembled there over the next day or two. A period of chaos, as it was, more or less continuously, until I left the squadron on 8 February 1945. Looking back, I really don't know why we were there. We used to do patrols and searches from the Scheldte–Ostend–Dunkirk, but once airborne all radio communication usually ceased, and no one even seemed to know whether there actually was anyone down in the sea – perhaps it improved after my departure.

From 24 October to 6 November we were based at St Croix, and then at Ursel till 20 December. From there we moved to Knocke on the coast. Here we were billeted in hotels on the sea front and I was driving up to the airfield for dawn readiness on 1 January 1945, when a squadron of Me 109s flew over the airfield; but they did not attack. That, of course, was the day of the Luftwaffe's last major offensive.

Flight Lieutenant J. V. Renvoize, No 276 Squadron

The 300th rescue by 276 Squadron was finally achieved on 17 February. Flying Officer F.G. Beagle, Flying Officer W. McNeil and Flight Sergeant F.J. Daniell searched for a lost B-17 off Ostend in Walrus W3081. It was the first rescue flown by the squadron from the Continent, and they found one survivor, the navigator, Lieutenant Keelan. The Fortress, from the 390th Bomb Group, had exploded in the air. Beagle taxied into Ostend after meeting an HSL on the way, to which they transferred the survivor.

March 1945 saw the last flurry of activity, which began with the Rhine Crossings. On the 2nd CPO Bartley, Butler and Flight Sergeant E. Cartwright were sent out to find a glider which had parted from its tug aircraft south of Eastbourne. They found it still afloat, its pilot sitting on a wing, seemingly quite happy, his Mae West in his hand. Bartley landed, but an RML was fast approaching so they left them to do the necessary. This was the first rescue involving 278's new Flight at

Hawkinge under Ron Wallens, the other two Flights being at Thorney Island under Flight Lieutenant M. Allanson and Beccles under Flight Lieutenant Robertson.

On 12 March, Ken Butterfield of 276, now a Flight Lieutenant, was flying Spitfire BL379 with a 'Number Two', when he sighted a *Biber* Class U-boat off Domburg. He attacked and sank the midget submarine with cannon and machine gun fire. The following day, Warrant Officer Eddie Lloyd sighted a motor boat, landed his seaplane and took off the sole occupant, a Sudeten German. The prisoner was handed over to the authorities in Ostend and was able to supply important information.

On this occasion I was Scrambled in one of the squadron's Spits, along with Sergeant Lamb, to attack a midget submarine off Walcheron. I went straight in and sank it with cannon fire. I was given the photo reel from the camera gun which showed a cluster of direct hits.

I had no qualms about sinking this sub, as on the 8th November 1944 I was Scrambled in a Walrus with W/O Cameron and Badger, for a search off Ostend. During the night, a transport craft carrying a whole signals unit had hit a mine laid by a German sub. There were no survivors; bodies were drifting ashore east of the harbour, and to the west the sea was thick with bodies. Being November, they could not have lasted long in the cold water.

Flight Lieutenant K.S. Butterfield, No 276 Squadron

The last Walrus sortie of note by 276 occurred on 20 March. Warrant Officers Bowe, G. DuRose and N. Cameron were Scrambled in Walrus L2220 and found a dinghy off the Dutch coast. They landed, but due to a rough sea were unable to reach it, and then they came under shell fire from the shore. Being unable to take off, the squadron's Spitfires gave them covering fire as the Walrus taxied out to sea. An American Catalina then arrived, landed and took off the three men, while its gunners sank the Walrus. Unable to get off itself, the Catalina spent the whole night taxying back towards England, but the next morning it transferred the Walrus crew to a Naval launch which landed them at Great Yarmouth. On 1 April, Squadron Leader N.E. Hancock DFC took command of 276.

The last recorded wartime Walrus rescue went to 278 on 24 March, when Squadron Leader Wallens DFC, with Squadron Leader Bowring and Pilot Officer Winfield, patrolled Folkestone to Gris Nez while the Rhine Crossings were underway. They located two gliders which had ditched in the Channel, vectoring HSLs to pick up the pilots and soldiers, the squadron being credited with eight of the 16 men picked up.

The ASR squadrons continued flying right up till VE-Day and beyond, but with the war over, the Walrus swiftly passed into history. Yet there was at least one immediate post-war rescue. Flight Lieutenant Bill Land had returned after a rest to command a Flight of 278 based at Exeter. On 31 August 1945, Pilot Officer Meeklah, from Exeter, successfully rescued an F4U Corsair pilot from the Bristol Channel in a Sea Otter. Bill Land and M.J. Peskett were both recommended for DFCs, but these became AFCs and were announced in the New Year's Honours List on 1 January 1946.

Postscript

Although this book has covered the RAF Walrus squadrons, the Fleet Air Arm had Walrus units round the UK and one interesting rescue occurred on 25 November 1942.

A Sunderland of 119 Squadron – DV972 – flown by two Canadians, Flying Officer D.B. Agate and co-pilot Flight Sergeant B.A. Harper was flying a low practice sortie over the Bristol Channel and dropped some depth charges. Exactly what happened is unclear but either one exploded prematurely or it hit something on or just below the surface. Due to the severity of the blast, there was even some speculation that it had hit a mine.

The flying-boat was severely damaged, forcing Agate to land on the water almost immediately. Its damaged hull immediately let in the sea and the Sunderland began to sink, the crew rapidly taking to their dinghies.

There had just been time to send off a Mayday and after some delay, the distress call was passed to the local Naval Seaplane Station, which had Walrus aircraft in the shape of No. 764 Squadron FAA. They were at Lawrenny Ferry, a couple of miles from Pembroke Dock, which was also the home of 119 Squadron. It immediately sent out two Walrus aircraft, one flown by Lieutenant M.B.P. Francklin – L2230 – the CO of 764, a unit responsible for Naval Seaplane Training, with his TAG, Bob Allerton (Telegraphist/Air Gunner) and Lieutenant R. MacWhirter, the Senior Pilot.

After flying some seven miles, with the light rapidly failing and the sea looking decidedly rough, two dinghies were seen which had been lashed together. The wind was now blowing over 20 knots, and knowing it was a mined area, the Navy flyers were only too aware how difficult it would be for a ship to get to them. Philip Francklin decide to land, telling his Senior Pilot to wait until he found out what it was like.

Sitting in the rear turret of the Sunderland, and now in the dinghy, was Sergeant Ted Karran:

We were found by two Walrus aircraft. One landed – much to my surprise, as the sea was pretty rough – and a wave seemed to buck right over the top mainplane. She bobbed up with her engine popping and crackling and taxied right up to us. The pilot stopped his engine and reaching out, someone grabbed Doug Agate by the hand. 'Sorry to have been so long,' he said. He told us we should be more comfortable aboard the Walrus but first he let us go to restart his engine and to call the other Walrus that it was too rough to land so to return to base. There were nine of us altogether. We climbed into the Walrus, making a total of 11 bodies within the hull, but after the dinghy it seemed quite cosy.

The pilot was a Naval Officer and the Walrus was very buoyant, overloaded or no, and she rose up to the peak of every wave. Most of our crew were seasick, I think, although I was fortunate.

After three hours, an ASR launch arrived. It was dark by then. We transferred to the launch via our dinghies, most of us not even getting our feet wet; and I don't think the launch bumped the Walrus at all. The pilot and his crewman opted to remain in the Walrus while we were all taken below and greeted by a very brave medical orderly. He encouraged us to partake of hot cocoa and to get bedded down, whilst, at intervals, he turned aside to vomit.

Although I did not see it, the launch then took the Walrus in tow but the seaplane rose up and crashed against the stern of the boat. The two Navy men quickly transferred to the launch and the Walrus was sunk by machine-gun fire.

None of us were hurt at all, although I suffered a minor wound, some object having grazed my back in the explosion and exited through my clothing. We never knew what had caused the explosion although I passed the jagged piece of metal to the Court of Enquiry which I later found embedded in the sole of my flying boot. I thought it would be a prime clue.

Sergeant E.B. Karran, 119 Squadron

The launch in fact was a pinnace from Padstow, No. P.1228 of No. 44 ASRMC Unit. This had departed Padstow harbour at 4.57 p.m., sighting the distress flares at 7.55. It made the rescue at 8.15, had transferred the men by 8.54 and arrived back at Padstow at 2.15 a.m. the next day.

My memory of the event is that Bob Allerton and I flew out and if I am correct, the GPO picked up the presence of the Sunderland and that is why Bob and I were able to locate the dinghies. They and Robert MacWhirter also alerted the RAF High Speed Launch in order to take off the crew, for it was obvious to Robert that I was not going to have the slightest chance of taking off with that load.

Lieutenant M.B.P. Francklin, 764 Squadron FAA

This case was one of close operation, success coming by liaison between both air and sea rescue services to save the lives of men at risk in the sea.

Awards to Air-Sea Rescue Personnel

For the record, the following is a list of all known awards to the RAF men of the Air-Sea Rescue Service. It was not enough.

Distinguished Service Order

Squadron Leader W. Sterne	283 Sqdn	LG 28 Sept 1943

Officer of the Order of the British Empire

Squadron Leader A.S. Linney	277 Sqdn	LG 2 Jun 1943

Distinguished Flying Cross

Warrant Officer G.F. Brown	293 Sqdn	LG 21 Jul 1944
Squadron Leader L.J. Brown	277 Sqdn	LG 25 May 1943
Warrant Officer W.L. Butler	277 Sqdn	1943
Flying Officer K.S. Butterfield	276 Sqdn	LG 16 Nov 1943
Flight Lieutenant M.F. Dekyvere	277 Sqdn	LG 1 Oct 1943
Flying Officer F.O. Dimblebee	276 Sqdn	LG 30 Jul 1943
Flying Officer M.N. Durrell	276 Sqdn	LG 17 Aug 1945
Squadron Leader E.E. Fitchew	279 Sqdn	LG 1 Oct 1943
Pilot Officer T. Fletcher DFM	277 Sqdn	LG 26 May 1944
Wing Commander A.D. Grace	277 Sqdn	LG 26 Oct 1943
Warrant Officer K.G. Hall	284 Sqdn	LG 1 Oct 1943
Flight Lieutenant R.F. Hayes	284 Sqdn	LG 1 Oct 1943
Pilot Officer L.R. Healey DFM	277 Sqdn	LG 8 Aug 1944
Flying Officer T.E. Hilton	277 Sqdn	LG 4 Dec 1942
Flight Lieutenant R. Van Den Honert	275 Sqdn	Jun 1944
Flying Officer T.R.G. Jones RCAF	280 Sqdn	Aug 1943
Flight Lieutenant N.D. Mackertich	277 Sqdn	LG 14 Jul 1944
Flying Officer D.R. Martin	276 Sqdn	Apr 1943
Flight Lieutenant D.J. McBrien	276 Sqdn	LG 25 May 1943
Squadron Leader R.H. McIntosh AFC	280 Sqdn	LG 9 Jul 1943
Pilot Officer J.A. Miller	276 Sqdn	Sept 1945
Flying Officer A.B. Moribito RCAF	283 Sqdn	LG 30 Nov 1943
Pilot Officer T. McN. Ormiston	277 Sqdn	Aug 1943

Warrant Officer C.I.A. Paterson	283 Sqdn	LG 25 Aug 1944
Warrant Officer N. Pickles	284 Sqdn	LG 3 Mar 1944
Warrant Officer G.B. Reeder	278 Sqdn	LG 3 Oct 1944
Pilot Officer P.J. Roy RCAF	278 Sqdn	LG 3 Oct 1944
Pilot Officer A.K. Saunders RNZAF	277 Sqdn	LG 7 Jul 1944
Flight Lieutenant E.W. Seabourne	275 Sqdn	LG 23 Jun 1942
Pilot Officer D.G. Shepherd	277 Sqdn	LG 25 May 1943
Flight Lieutenant J.A. Spence	277 Sqdn	LG 19 Mar 1943
Pilot Officer W.G. Tomkins	292 Sqdn	Jun 1945
Flight Lieutenant S.A. Trevallion	278 Sqdn	LG 20 Jul 1943
Lieutenant K.B. Walker SAAF	293 Sqdn	1945
Squadron Leader R.W. Wallens	277 Sqdn	LG 11 Aug 1944
Flight Lieutenant R.G. Whitcombe	280 Sqdn	LG 14 Apr 1944

Bar to Distinguished Flying Cross

Flight Lieutenant J.A. Spence DFC	277 Sqdn	LG Jul 1943
Flight Lieutenant R.F. Hayes DFC	284 Sqdn	LG 25 Aug 1944

Distinguished Flying Medal

Sergeant L.G. Badger	276 Sqdn	LG 13 Jul 1943
Flight Sergeant J.L. Barber	277 Sqdn	LG 2 Oct 1942
Flight Sergeant J.R. Berry RNZAF	284 Sqdn	LG 7 Jan 1944
Flight Sergeant A. Divers RNZAF	283 Sqdn	LG 25 Jan 1944
Flight Sergeant W. Elder	276 Sqdn	LG 13 Jul 1943
Sergeant T. Fletcher	277 Sqdn	LG 3 Nov 1942
Sergeant W.T. Gregory	277 Sqdn	LG 18 Aug 1944
Flight Sergeant A.W. Hammond	278 Sqdn	LG 14 Jul 1944
Sergeant L.R. Healey	277 Sqdn	LG 3 Nov 1942
Flight Sergeant E.J. Holmes	284 Sqdn	LG 25 Jan 1944
Flight Sergeant C. Horne	283 Sqdn	LG 30 Nov 1943
Flight Sergeant V.H. Jarvis	277 Sqdn*	LG 21 Oct 1941
Flight Sergeant E.E. Keeble	284 Sqdn	LG 25 Aug 1944
Sergeant P. Kirby	276 Sqdn	LG 13 Jul 1943
Sergeant W.S. Lambert	283 Sqdn	LG 28 Sept 1943
Sergeant D.J. Lunn	284 Sqdn	LG 1 Oct 1943
Flight Sergeant K.R. Pugh	283 Sqdn	LG 1 Oct 1943
Flight Sergeant J.B. Snell	277 Sqdn	LG 29 Dec 1942
Flight Sergeant C.S. Taylor	293 Sqdn	LG 21 Jul 1944

*Actually awarded when 277 was still a Flight.

Bar to Distinguished Flying Medal

Sergeant T. Fletcher DFM	277 Sqdn	LG 14 Jan 1943

Air Force Cross

Pilot Officer A. Dunhill	278 Sqdn	
Squadron Leader R.F. Hamlyn DFM	276 Sqdn	1 Jan 1943
Flight Lieutenant W.A. Land	278 Sqdn	LG 1 Jan 1946
Pilot Officer M.J. Peskett	278 Sqdn	LG 1 Jan 1946

Air Force Medal
Flight Sergeant J. Sainsbury   276 Sqdn   June 1942

American Distinguished Flying Cross
Squadron Leader L.J. Brown DFC   277 Sqdn   20 Nov 1944
Warrant Officer W. Greenfield   277 Sqdn   LG 20 Jul 1943
Flight Lieutenant R.F. Hayes DFC   284 Sqdn   LG 25 Aug 1944
Flight Sergeant C. Horne   293 Sqdn   LG 25 Aug 1944
Squadron Leader W. Sterne DSO   283 Sqdn   LG 28 Jul 1944

American Air Medal
Flight Sergeant G.N. Leighton   277 Sqdn   LG 20 Jul 1943
Pilot Officer T. McN. Ormiston   277 Sqdn   LG 20 Jul 1943
Pilot Officer A.K. Saunders RNZAF   277 Sqdn   LG 20 Jul 1943
Squadron Leader S.A. Trevallion   278 Sqdn   LG 20 Jul 1943

Polish Cross of Valour
Flying Officer P.C. Standen   277 Sqdn   March 1944

Norwegian St Olav's Medal & Oak Leaf
Flight Lieutenant N.D. Mackertich   277 Sqdn   LG 28 Jul 1944

British Empire Medal
LAC H. Burke   276 Sqdn   June 1942

Mention in Despatches
Flight Sergeant T. Roberts   277 Sqdn   Oct 1942
Squadron Leader E.W. Seabourne DFC 275 Sqdn   Jun 1944
Flight Lieutenant A.T. Webster   276 Sqdn   Nov 1945

Main UK-based Walrus Rescues: Nos 275, 276, 277 & 278 Squadrons

W hen the war ended, the Air-Sea Rescue squadrons operating from the UK and in the Mediterranean had saved more than 2,000 men from the sea, the vast majority being Allied aircrew. They were proud of their record and each unit kept a total of successful rescues, whether they had been picked-up by Walrus or Sea Otter, or if they had been involved in a rescue by guiding surface craft to the pick-up position. 277 Squadron topped the list with 598 live rescues or assists.

The following tables record those rescues which involved landing Walrus or Sea Otter amphibians.

Main Walrus Rescues by No 275 Squadron

1942

7 Jan F/L R.F. Hamlyn & crew (Valley) — Walrus — Crew of Anson (N9822) of 9 AOS, RAF Penrhos, missing 6 Jan. Sgt E.W. Peacock and three others picked up in two sorties. 09:10-? hrs.

9 May F/L R.F. Hamlyn & crew (Valley) — Walrus — Four men of an Anson crew by semi-afloat aircraft. Landed and awaited arrival of HSL.

26 Jun P/O R.W.V. Jessott F/Sgt Bryan (Valley) — Walrus — P/O P.A. Day & Sgt E.W. Mitchell, 456 Sqn Beaufighter (T3014) brought down by return fire from a Ju 88, 30 miles W of Bardsey. Located by W/Cdr W.M. Churchill DSO DFC, Stn Cdr RAF Valley, in a Spitfire. 12:50-15:10 hrs.

8 Jul F/L E.W. Seabourne F/Sgt B. Cordinley F/L R. Van Den Honert (Valley) — Walrus — Five men of an Anson from No 3 (C) OTU ditched off Bardsey Island. Picked up despite a very rough sea. 12:10-13:10 hrs.

3 Aug F/L O.H. Furlong F/Sgt B. Cordingley — Walrus — Halifax crew in Rhoscolyn Bay. Four men taken aboard and three others

	F/Sgt D.J.R. McClellan (Valley)		put into dinghy. Awaited arrival of help as unable to take off. p.m.

1944

23 May	Sub-Lt J.S. McIvor Sub-Lt N.N. Bornw LA W.D. Pinching (Warmwell)	Walrus HD930	F/O F.J. Crowley, Typhoon pilot of 181 Sqn (MN637), hit by flak during attack on radar site near Cherbourg. Baled out 32 miles from coast. 17:20-18:40 hrs.
" "	W/O L.G. Fisher F/Sgt D.F. Glass W/O E. Cole (Warmwell)	Walrus HD929	S/L J.G. Keep, Typhoon pilot and CO of 181 Sqn (JR381) ditched 10 miles off Cherbourg after being hit by AA fire attacking radar position. 17:30-23:40 hrs.
2 Jun	W/O R.B. Davies F/O H.C. Beckman W/O M.N. McGillivray (Warmwell)	Walrus HD930	American P-47 pilot baled out 20 miles off Swanage. Rescued him in a rough sea. Unable to take off and later transferred to a French ship and Walrus towed into Calshot. 21:15-00:30 hrs.
5 Jun	F/L R. Van Den Honert F/O T.A. Harper F/O W.S. Dixon (Warmwell)	Walrus L2282	F/O W. Smith, Typhoon pilot of 245 Sqn, hit by flak on radar station at Auderville. Baled out 30 miles from Cherbourg. Circling Typhoon pilot also had to bale out.
" "	P/O T.F. Murray F/L S.H. Britton P/O D.L. Forster (Warmwell)	Walrus HD908	F/L W.E. Reynolds, 245 Sqn, baled out due to engine trouble. Walrus unable to take off and later had to be abandoned and sunk when transferred to a minesweeper.
6 Jun+			Eleven survivors picked up by the squadron's Walrus crews during this period, making 15 in all for June.
11 Jun	Lt L.F. Plant F/L J.R. Irvine F/O J. McAleese (Warmwell)	Walrus R6548	2/Lt Herrera, P-47 pilot from the 404th Fighter Sqn, 371st Fighter Gp; nine miles SE of The Needles.
22 Jun	? (Warmwell)	Walrus	Lt G.M. Dumars, P-47 pilot seen to bale out by Spits of 278 Sqn while searching for another dinghy. Dumars did not have dinghy. 509th FBS, 405th FBG. Eight miles N of Cherbourg.
24 Jul	F/O C.G. Eaton F/O J.S. Barker Sgt S.J. Broadway (Warmwell)	Walrus HD823	Seven men from a 401st Bomb Group B-17, hit during attack on St Lo. Had to taxi back into Weymouth. 13:35-14:45 hrs; taxied until 18:30 hrs.
" "	P/O T.F. Murray F/L S.H. Britton	Walrus R6548	Rescued eighth man from the above B-17. Seven: Lt W.E. Coleman, 2/Lt

F/O D.L. Forster (Warmwell)		E.K. Stout, F/O D.L. Forster, 2/Lt H.E. Kron, T/Sgt C.A. Carrow, Staff/Sgts A.J. Meaney, E. W Anderson and Sgt W.D. Kitman; Eighth: T/Sgt Lindholm.

Main Walrus Rescues by No 276 Squadron

1942

18 Jun	Sgt R.C. Yeates F/Sgt W. Smith Sgt L.G. Badger	Walrus W3026	Crew of 58 Sqn Whitley (Z9161) came down in the sea 3 miles SW of Bude, returning from convoy patrol. Walrus unable to take off so taxied into Bude. Sgts K.W. Craig, W.D. Ryan, D. Gay-Cummings, Wallace & J.D. Vassello. 13:40-14:25 hrs.

1943

23 Feb	P/O F.O. Dimblebee F/Sgt R. Davies P/O R. Hughes (Predannock)	Walrus W2784	Sgt R.J. Gourlay, pilot of 602 Sqn Spitfire (EE616), baled out after hitting the sea SW of the Lizard. (*see text*) 11:25-12:50 hrs.
14 Apl	F/O D.J. McBrien Sgt Sothern-Estcourt Sgt L.G. Badger (Harrowbeer)	Walrus W2271	Crew of 103 Sqn Lancaster (W4318) ditched after raid on Spezia, 50 miles from Falmouth. Picked them up then took off after transferring three men to a launch. 276 Sqn's 100th live rescue. Sgts S. Dixon, T. Stanley & J.S. Stoneman; P/Os D.C. Elder & C.E. Bryan; F/Sgts J. Flynn & J.H. McMahon. 08:50-11:40 hrs.
15 Apl	F/O D.R. Martin P/O R. Hughes F/Sgt G. Paxton (Bolt Head)	Walrus W2785	Crew 276 Sqn Walrus (W3029) which hit an underwater obstruction during a sea landing. One later transferred to a rescue boat. P/O K. Butterfield, S/L B. Bowring, Sgt O. Evans & Sgt R. Churchill. (*see text*) Late p.m.
18 Apl	F/Sgt Hall P/O Porter F/Sgt W. Elder (Warmwell)	Walrus L2335	Sgt S.J. Fowler, Spitfire pilot from 616 Sqn, ditched after engine trouble while on ASR search.
" "	F/O D.R. Martin P/O R. Hughes (Bolt Head)	Walrus W2784	Sgt G.F. Eames, pilot of 602 Sqn Spitfire (EE633), shot down by an FW 190 while on shipping recce from Perranporth on 11 April. (*see text*) 21:00-03:30 hrs
7 Jun	P/O K. Butterfield Sgt G. Douglas Sgt R. Churchill	Walrus L2271	P/O R.W. Thatcher, pilot of 412 Sqn Spitfire (EE769), hit by flak during *Rhubarb* sortie. Rescued 10

			miles N of Les Sept Isles. (*see text*) 16:35-19:00 hrs.
17 Jun	P/O K. Butterfield Sgt L.G. Badger Sgt R. Churchill	Walrus L2271	F/O H.A. Cooper, pilot of 266 Sqn Typhoon (R7915), engine trouble 25 miles S of Start Point. Walrus unable to take off due to heavy sea and later transferred pilot to launch and taxied back.(*see text*) 20:40-01:20 hrs.
21 Jun	F/L D.J. McBrien F/O A.B. Hill Sgt A.H. Kyle	Walrus L2271	P/O N.V. Borland, pilot of 266 Sqn Typhoon (EJ931), due to engine failure 12 miles E of Berry Head. 14:10-16:40 hrs.
24 Jun	F/L J.V. Renvoize F/O T. Vacquier Sgt J. Frisby	Walrus L2335	Sgt C.S. Wright, pilot of 504 Sqn Spitfire (EE621) hit by flak while on bomber escort. Baled out 45 miles S of The Needles. Walrus unable to take off so had to taxi to Isle of Wight. (*see text*) 11:05-16:05 hrs.
2 Sep	F/O K. Butterfield F/Sgt L.G. Badger Sgt R. Churchill (Harrowbeer/Exeter)	Walrus	F/L G. Holloway, pilot of 16 Sqn Mustang (AP263) shot down by FW 190 on 30 August. (*see text*) 07:10-? hrs.
1944 **16 Mar**	F/L P. Rosser W/O L.G. Badger W/O G. Douglas (Harrowbeer)	Walrus P5658	Crew of 466 Sqn Halifax (LW521) that ditched 30 miles S of Portland Bill while returning from Stuttgart. Navigator missing. Rescued: F/Sgts J.C. Bond, B.L. Sheean & J.N. Keys; Sgts C.Y. Warren, D.K. Messenger & J.A. White. 08:00-10:40 hrs.
24 Mar	F/L J.V. Renvoize F/O T. Vacquier F/O D. Dring	Walrus	Crew of 276 Sqn Anson: P/O Feeny, F/Sgt Lane & W/Os Musket & Hussey.
10 Jun	F/O A. McIntosh W/O L.G. Badger P/O A.H. Kyle (Bolt Head)	Walrus P5856	F/L M.A. Graves DFC, Spitfire pilot of 616 Sqn, due to engine trouble after *Rhubarb* sortie. Ditched 40 miles S of Start Point; slightly injured.
12 Jun	W/O A. Symons W/O F. Cake W/O B. Evans (Bolt Head)	Walrus W3083	F/O M.A.L. Balasse (Belgian), pilot of 41 Sqn Spitfire (M8842) ditched after *Rhubarb* sortie, 12 miles S of Bolt Head.
18 Jun	F/L D.R. Martin F/O L. Gayler W/O J. Partridge	Walrus L2335	F/Sgt J.P. Ware, pilot of 41 Sqn Spitfire (EN231) and F/L T.A.H. Slack of the same Sqn. Slack was hit by flak on a shipping recce and Ware ran out of fuel. (*see text*) 07:30-10:30 hrs.

23 Jun	F/L A.B. Hill F/O C. Rolls P/O A.H. Kyle	Walrus W3081	F/Sgt I.D.M. Dunlop, pilot of 263 Sqn Typhoon (MN300) hit by flak during attack on radar station. (*see text*) 13:30–14:35 hrs.
19 Jul	F/L D.J. McBrien F/O C. Rolls F/Sgt F. Perry (Harrowbeer)	Walrus W3083	Oblt Ulf Lawaetz, CO of *U-672*, who had scuttled his submarine after it had been damaged by HMS *Balfour*. Rest of survivors picked up later by ship.13:35–15:10 hrs.
31 Jul	W/O E. Lloyd & crew	Walrus L2246	Four survivors of 53 Sqn Liberator (EW306) on training flight which hit the sea. F/O J. Osborne plus 3 crew. Off Trevose Head.
5 Aug	F/L G.R. Johns F/S E. Perry W/O Evans (Bolt Head)	Walrus W3038	F/O A. Thorpe, pilot of 64 Sqn Spitfire (MK895) hit by flak from an armed trawler in Lezardrieux, after escort sortie. 12:15–? hrs.
1945 **17 Feb**	F/O F.G. Beagle F/O W. McNeil F/S F.J. Daniell	Walrus W3081	Lt Keelan, 390th BG B-17 navigator and sole survivor, rescued 20 miles off Ostend. Walrus taxied into Ostend Harbour having put the man aboard an HSL. 276 Sqn's 300th live rescue. 12:55–19:30 hrs.
13 Mar	W/O E. Lloyd F/O H. Estho W/O P. Speed	Walrus W2774	Picked up German in motor boat and took him to Ostend as a prisoner. 12:45–14:20 hrs.

Main Walrus Rescues by No 277 Squadron

1942 **1 Jun**	Sgt J.S.G. Arundel Sgt Markey F/Sgt N. Pickles (Martlesham)	Walrus W2735	F/Sgt R.L. Stillwell DFM, pilot of 65 Sqn Spitfire (P8789), baled out on *Circus 179* after engine trouble. Rescued after two hours, at approx 7 p.m. 19:00–21:45 hrs
3 Jun	Sgt J.S.G. Arundel Sgt Markey Sgt W.G. Bunn (Martlesham)	Walrus W2735	F/Sgt T.A. Gibbs, Havoc pilot of 85 Sqn, shot down by 'friendly' aircraft on a night sortie during enemy raid upon Canterbury. Navigator, Sgt M.S.J. Waller, was killed. a.m.
5 Jun	F/Sgt K.A. Creamer F/Sgt G.D. Neale F/O Jones (MO) (Shoreham)	Walrus W2736	Sgt A.J. Edwards, Spitfire pilot of 129 Sqn, shot down by FW 190 during *Circus 188*. Picked up after nearly 2 hours in the sea, 45 miles off Selsey Bill. 15:55–17:55 hrs.
1 Aug	Sgt T.E. Hilton F/Sgt G.N. Leighton F/Sgt N. Pickles (Martlesham)	Walrus	Crew of 107 Sqn Boston (AL280), down on a raid to Flushing. P/O L.J. Skinner & Sgt B. Bernstein rescued, but Sgt B. Quinn (navigator) killed p.m.

6 Sep	F/Sgt J.L. Barber Sgt L.R. Healey (Shoreham)	Walrus W3076	F/Sgt G.A. Mason, pilot of 64 Sqn Spitfire (BR980) shot down by FW 190 during *Circus 214*, on the 5th. In sea for 37 hours off French coast. (*see text*) 17:30-19:15 hrs.
2 Oct	Sgt T. Fletcher Sgt L.R. Healey F/Sgt T. Roberts (Hawkinge)	Walrus L2315	F/Sgt M.H.F. Cooper, Spitfire pilot from 616 Sqn, shot down by FW 190 while on *Circus 221* off French coast. (*see text*) 18:20-19:00 hrs.
6 Oct	F/Sgt T.M. Ormiston P/O L.L. Nault F/Sgt N. Pickles	Walrus X9526	Sgt Forrestal, sole survivor of a 418 Sqn Boston that crashed during a training flight, off Bradwell Bay. Rescued from shallow water E of Denghie Flats. 15:25-16:25 hrs.
31 Oct	P/O T.E. Hilton F/Sgt L. Seales (Shoreham)	Walrus W3076	F/Lt J.E. Van Shaick DFM, pilot of 137 Sqn Whirlwind (P7064) brought down by flak during *Rhubarb* sortie. Rescued from a minefield off French coast. (*see text*) 11:45-12:10 hrs.
11 Nov	F/O M.F. Dekyvere Sgt E.C. Quick F/Sgt L. Seales (Shoreham)	Walrus L2246	P/O B. Sheidhauer, French Spitfire pilot with 131 Sqn, baled out after collision 20 miles off English coast. (*see text*) 12:40-14:40 hrs.
14 Dec	Sgt T. Fletcher Sgt L.R. Healey Sgt R.C. Glew (Hawkinge)	Walrus X9521	Three German sailors rescued under very difficult circumstances. Had to taxi back to Dover. (*see text*) Take-off: 16:45 hrs.
1943 **27 Jan**	F/O L.J. Brown P/O D.G. Sheppard (Martlesham)	Walrus X9526	W/O W. Greenfield & F/Sgt J. Horan of 277 Sqn, who ditched their Defiant (N3392) 25 miles off the Suffolk coast after engine trouble. 12:10-13:40 hrs.
20 Feb	F/O L.J. Brown F/O D.G. Sheppard F/Sgt W.A. Rance (Martlesham)	Walrus X9526	Crew of a 415 Sqn Hampden torpedo-bomber shot down on the 18th. F/O A.B. Brenner, F/Sgt E.L.L. Rowe, Sgt A. Glass & Sgt E.A. Vautier. 45 miles off coast. 15:30-18:45 hrs.
28 Feb	F/Lt J.A. Spence F/Sgt W. Butler Sgt P. Graham (Hawkinge)	Walrus W3024	F/Sgt R.W. Lamont, pilot of 416 Sqn Spitfire (AD560), hit the sea on low-level *Rhubarb* sortie and had to ditch 20 miles off Dungeness. 08:15-09:45 hrs.
11 Apl	P/O N. Mackertich Sgt H.H. Teillett (Shoreham)	Walrus W2773	Crew of a 75 (RNZAF) Sqn Stirling (BF455) ditched on return from Frankfurt raid, four miles off English coast. Mackertich picked up seven,

" "	Sgt T.Fletcher F/O MG Chamberlain (Shoreham)	Walrus W3010	while Fletcher rescued the 8th man who had started to drift away. F/Sgt C.A. Rothschild, F/Sgt G.K. Sampson, Sgt R.E. Tod, Sgt R.D. Tod, Sgt J.L. Richards, Sgt W.A.M Hardy, Sgt E. Grainger & Sgt H.E. Moss. (see text) 07:10-08:55 & 07:35-08:30 hrs.
14 Apl	P/O R. Hayes Sgt A. Kelly F/O M.G. Chamberlain (Shoreham)	Walrus W3097	P/O J.L. Barber & P/O L.R. Healey whose 277 Sqn Walrus (W2772) was shot down by Me 109s over English Channel. (see text) 16:35-18:25 hrs.
15 Apl	W/O A.K. Saunders F/Sgt R.C. Glew F/Sgt F. Gash (Martlesham)	Walrus W3024	Lt Col C. Peterson, commander of the 4th Fighter Group USAAF, ditched his P-47 during Rodeo 204, 30 miles out. (see text) 18:20-19:50 hrs.
17 Apl	S/L A.D. Grace F/L M.F. Dekyvere F/Sgt L. Seales (Shoreham)	Walrus	F/O M.F. Armytage, pilot of 132 Sqn Spitfire (EM974) shot down by FW 190 while on bomber escort to Caen. Slight wound, and dinghy failed to inflate.
11 May	P/O M. Mackertich Sgt H.H. Teillett (Shoreham)	Walrus	P/O H.M. Pattullo, pilot of 197 Sqn Typhoon, located by P/O R. Eccles and P/O Walker in a Defiant. Pattullo had engine trouble and baled out off Selsey. p.m.
31 May	W/O T.M. Ormiston Sgt Mann F/Sgt V. Errington (Martlesham)	Walrus	Searching for a missing Spitfire pilot, a dinghy was located and upon rescue it was found to be a Luftwaffe pilot, Ltn Arlois Harlos who had been in the sea for two days. 18:15-20:05 hrs.
12 Jun	W/O W. Greenfield W/O W.A. Rance F/Sgt N. Leighton (Martlesham)	Walrus	P/O C.R. Abbott, pilot of a 198 Sqn Typhoon (DN587) with engine trouble, so baled out. He was 277's 99th live rescue. (see text) a.m.
" "	W/O W. Greenfield W/O W.A. Rance F/Sgt Stirling (Martlesham)	Walrus	Lt E.D. Beatie, 336th FS, 4th FG USAAF, baled out of his P-47 after engine trouble while on a Rodeo. (see text) 20:25-20:50 hrs.
15 Jun	Sgt T. Fletcher P/O L.R. Healey Sgt E.G. Green (Shoreham)	Walrus	Located Lt Deacon Hively, 334th FS, 4th FG USAAF and directed an HSL to him. Hively was to become a 14-victory ace with the 8th Air Force. a.m.
16 Jun	F/Lt J.A. Spence Sgt J. Humphreys (Martlesham)	Walrus	Sgt E. Ticklepenny, 3 Sqn, whose Typhoon (DN948) was shot down by flak off enemy coast while on

night shipping recce. Walrus had to taxi back to Dover despite an air fight overhead between Spitfires of 91 Sqn and 20 FW 190s, four of which were shot down for two Spitfires; one pilot was picked up by an HSL, the second was lost. Sgt Ticklepenny was killed on 27 June while returning from a sortie, hitting a balloon cable. 06:10-08:00 hrs.

22 Jun	W/O W. Greenfield F/Sgt J. Horan F/Sgt N. Leighton (Martlesham)	Walrus X9526	Crew of 102 Sqn Halifax (JD206) ditched after a raid on Krefeld. Sgt G.S. Honey, Sgt R. A. Ward, Sgt J. Brennan, Sgt F.R. Hayward, Sgt D.A. Wagar, Sgt A.J. Dick & Sgt R.O. Tudberry. Came down off Dutch coast. One Walrus took off but the other had to taxi back. Air battle was taking place overhead.(*see text*) 18:37-21:10 hrs. Second Walrus abandoned; it later beached itself.
" "	W/O T.M. Ormiston F/Sgt V. Errington Sgt Mann (Martlesham)	Walrus X9563	
27 Jul	F/Sgt J. Brodie F/O F.E. Wilson Sgt J. Mallinson (Hawkinge)	Walrus	S/L G.C. Keefer DFC, CO of 412 Sqn, whose Spitfire (EN784), developed glycol leak on a *Rodeo*. Baled out off French coast. (*see text*) 20:50-22:30 hrs.
" "	F/O J.L. Barber F/S E.C. Quick F/Sgt H. Bruck-Horst (Shoreham)	Walrus	F/Sgt Pittock, 65 Sqn, 15 miles SSE of St Catherine's Point.
28 Jul	S/L A.D. Grace W/O J. Butler Sgt J. Humphreys (Hawkinge)	Walrus	S/L R.W. McNair DFC, CO 421 Sqn, whose Spitfire (MA586) developed engine trouble while on *Ramrod 165*. Baled out, but burnt. Given first aid in Walrus. 13:00-15:20 hrs.
30 Jul	F/O D.R. Hartwell F/O F.E. Wilson Sgt J. Mallinson (Hawkinge)	Walrus X9526	Crew of B-17 from 335th BS, 95th BG USAAF, ditched after raid on Kassel. Five crew baled out over Holland but Lt R.B. Jutzi, Lt R.D. Paterson, Lt W.W. Collins, Lt R.V. Luinzber & T/Sgt H.R. Knotts all rescued, although Walrus had to taxi back. 08:42-11:15 hrs.
" "	F/Sgt J. Brodie W/O J. Butler W/O J. Rose (Hawkinge)	Walrus	Lt Paul H. Lehman, 82nd FS, 78th FG USAAF, went down in his P-47 after escorting Kassel raid bombers. 11:20-13:30 hrs.
4 Aug	S/L A.D. Grace F/O F.E. Wilson	Walrus	Four members of the SBS returning from commando raid in two canoes.

	Sgt J. Humphreys (Hawkinge)		Captain Livingstone, Lt Sidders, Sgts Salisbury & Weatherall. 10 miles off Gravelines. 11:55-13:20 hrs.
17 Aug	S/L A.D. Grace W/O W.L. Butler W/O J. Rose (Hawkinge)	Walrus	Crew of B-17 from 401st BS, 91st BG, captained by Lt E.M. Lockhart on his 21st Op. Grace collected all 10 crewmen, then began to taxi back to Ramsgate. (*see text*) 19:50-05:30 hrs
19 Aug	Sub Lt R. Mander F/O F.E. Wilson Sub-Lt E. Hall (Hawkinge)	Walrus L2298	P/O G.D. O'Callaghan, 174 Sqn. Engine trouble to Typhoon (JP550) and baled out off Le Touquet. 16:35-17:35 hrs.
31 Aug	Sgt T. Fletcher Sub-Lt Gardner P/O C.G. Gardner (Shoreham)	Walrus HD908	Sgt T.A. Wilder of 29 OTU ditched his Wellington after raid on St Omer. Rest of crew were killed. Walrus taxied to Newhaven. 10:30-? hrs.
3 Sep	F/O A.K. Saunders F/O C. Walker F/Sgt E.C. Quick (Shoreham)	Walrus W2735	Three Walrus aircraft escorted by 277 Sqn's Spitfires located and rescued the 10-man crew of a B-17, 57 miles off English coast. Saunders took four, Dekyvere three and
" "	F/L.M. Dekyvere F/Sgt H. Bruck-Horst Sgt E.G. Green (Shoreham)	Walrus W3097	Fletcher the last three. Fletcher was unable to take off so had to taxi back. Ran out of petrol and towed back by *HSL 2548*. 10:00 and 10:50-12:15 hrs.
" "	Sgt T. Fletcher F/O M.G. Chamberlain W/O L. Seales (Shoreham)	Walrus HD908	
4 Sep	S/L A.D. Grace Sgt J. Snell Sgt J. Humphreys (Hawkinge)	Walrus L2271	F/Sgt J.A.W. Quinton, in a 165 Sqn Spitfire (EE619), baled out when engine stopped nine miles off French coast at 9.30 a.m. 09:35-11:15 hrs.
" "	F/O W. Smith W/O Hughes F/S D. Campbell (Hawkinge)	Walrus W2282	F/O D.F. Prentice of 416 Sqn after he had baled out of his Spitfire (W3456) off Le Touquet, following damage by Me 109 while on *Ramrod S.31* to St Pol. 18:55-20:25 hrs.
13 Sep	S/L A.D. Grace W/O J. Rose Sub-Lt E. Hall (Hawkinge)	Walrus	Sgt G.A. Whitman, 3 Sqn, whose Typhoon (EJ958) had engine trouble and ditched off Zeebrugge. 16:50-19:45 hrs.
17 Sep	Sgt T. Fletcher W/O L. Seales (Shoreham)	Walrus W2735	F/O R.W. Osborn, navigator of a 141 Sqn Beaufighter (V8803) on night intruder sortie on the 15th.

Engine trouble, so baled out.
Rescued after 36 hours in dinghy.
His pilot, F/L R.W. Ferguson, was
killed. 11:10-12:15 hrs.

18 Sep	F/S J. Brodie W/O L. Butler Sgt J. Humpherys (Hawkinge)	Walrus W2289	F/O J.W. Fiander, pilot of 401 Sqn Spitfire (BM199); engine trouble on *Ramrod 228* to Rouen, baled out 20 miles W of the Somme Estuary. Later, Walrus was towed into Dover Harbour by *HSL 149*. 10:30-01:00 hrs.
19 Sep	F/S J. Brodie P/O J.B. Snell Sgt J. Humphreys (Hawkinge)	Walrus X9526	Sgt J. Krzysztopinski, pilot of 302 Sqn Spitfire (W3631) on *Ramrod 233* to Bethune. 18:05-20:40 hrs
20/21 Sep	P/O P.C. Standen F/O F.E. Wilson F/Sgt H. Bruck-Horst (Hawkinge)	Walrus W3076	P/O T.S. Turek, pilot of 609 Sqn Typhoon (JP745), ditched after being hit by AA fire while on a *Rhubarb*. Rescued on the 21st. (*see text*) 07:15-13:35 hrs.
26 Sep	P/O P.C. Standen P/O J.B. Snell W/O J. Rose (Hawkinge)	Walrus X9526	S/L I.C. Ormiston DFC, pilot of 401 Sqn Spitfire (BM627), had engine trouble and baled out while on *Ramrod 247* to Rouen. Walrus had to be towed back by an HSL. (*see text*) 09:35-17:25 hrs.
3 Oct	F/O J.L. Barber F/Sgt H.H. Teillett W/O L. Seales (Shoreham)	Walrus HD908	F/Sgt M.E. McGrath, sole survivor from a 467 Sqn Lancaster (ED530) that ditched after a raid on Munich – their 29th Op. a.m.
" "	W/C A.D. Grace W/O J. Rose Sgt J. Humphreys (Hawkinge)	Walrus W3010	F/Sgt N.E. Frehner, NZ pilot with 485 Sqn whose Spitfire (MH351) suffered engine failure on escort sortie. Baled out 12 miles S of Dungeness; Walrus taxied back. 15:10-16:35 hrs.
" "	Sgt T. Fletcher P/O L.R. Healey (Shoreham)	Walrus W3097	Crew of 88 Sqn Boston (BZ316) shot down on raid to Distre. F/S G.G.K. Gray and Sgt J. Addison rescued; body of Sgt R.J. Bickel (navigator) also brought back. 15:55-? hrs.
" "	F/O J.L. Barber Sgt E.G. Green (Shoreham)	Walrus HD908	Crew of 88 Sqn Boston (BZ322) shot down on raid to Distre. F/S W.D.D. Davies & Sgt J. Bateson safe; F/O R. Christie the navigator, missing. 16:10-17:05 hrs.
4 Oct	F/Sgt T. Fletcher P/O L.R. Healey (Shoreham)	Walrus W3097	F/Sgt C.J. Sheddan, NZ pilot of 486 Sqn Typhoon (EK272), ditched on the 3rd while on Boston escort. (*see*

text) 08:05-? hrs. Walrus towed and later sank.

24 Oct	F/O A.K. Saunders F/Sgt H.H. Teillett F/Sgt R. Birch-Hurst (Shoreham)	Walrus W2735	F/Lt Welch, 528 Sqn, ditched his autogyro (V1186) off Worthing after its engine failed. 11:30-12:00 hrs.

1944

28 Jan	Sub Lt R. Mander W/O J. Rose Sub-Lt E. Hall (Hawkinge)	Walrus X9562	F/Lt D.C. MacKay, pilot of 412 Sqn Spitfire (MJ302), baled out following engine trouble. Dinghy only partly inflated and Mander landed on rough sea to make the rescue. Pilot located by 277 Sqn Spitfire, flown by F/Sgt A.M. Rollo. 12:05-12:15 hrs.
29 Jan	P/O P.C. Standen F/O F.E. Wilson Sgt J. Humphreys (Hawkinge)	Walrus L2289	Capt G.E. Preddy 487 FS, 352nd FG, baled out of his P-47 after hits by AA fire. Future ace with the 8th AF, with 31 kills. Walrus towed into Ramsgate Harbour. (*see text*) 13:05-17:30 hrs.
13 Feb	S/L R.W. Wallens W/O J. Rose Sgt R.N. Smith (Hawkinge)	Walrus W3042	Crew of B-17 from the 94th BG. Wallens picked up one man while Barber picked up eight. 16:20-18:20 hrs.
" "	F/O J.L. Barber Sgt W. Gregory (Shoreham)	Walrus L2315	Damaged float on take-off, so put eight men aboard an HSL which then towed them home. 16:40-? hrs.
25 Feb	W/C A.D. Grace W/O W.L. Butler Sgt J. Humphreys (Hawkinge)	Walrus X9563	F/Sgt D. Moultrie, navigator of a 226 Sqn Mitchell shot down, but he died soon after rescue. Rest of crew picked up by an HSL. Walrus towed into Dover next morning. (*see text*) 12:55-01:00 hrs.
5 Mar	P/O A.K. Saunders F/O L.R. Healey F/Sgt E.G. Green (Shoreham)	Sea Otter JM770	Crew of a 704 BS, 446th BG B-24: 2/Lt Gilman, Staff Sgts Grimes & Marrow; F/Sgts E.G. Green, Macklin, Nilson; T/Sgt Sichow. Other four missing. Several men injured. (*see text*) 14:00-16:50 hrs.
6 Mar	P/O W. Greenfield W/O G.N. Leighton F/S L.A.G. Carpenter	Walrus W3072	Two survivors from a 453rd BG B-24 that ditched returning from Berlin. One died later. (*see text*) 14:30-18:05 hrs.
16 Mar	S/L L.J. Brown P/O P.W. Weeden (Gravesend)	Sea Otter JM745	Survivors from a 457th BG B-17 returning from Augsburg. Rescued one man; HSLs picked up three others. (*see text*) 14:30-15:10 hrs.
" "	S/L R.W. Wallens	Walrus	Five men from a 458th BG B-17,

Sub Lt E. Hall Sgt J. Humphreys (Hawkinge)	X9526	60-65 miles out. Walrus took off despite sea mines! 16:25-18:45 hrs.
" " P/O T. Fletcher F/O L.R. Healey F/Sgt T. Gregory (Shoreham)	Sea Otter JM796	F/O T.M. Saunderson, pilot of 412 Sqn Spitfire (MJ149). Lost engine on *Ramrod 661* and baled out off Somme Estuary. (*see text*) 14:30-16:55 hrs.
" " Lt D.V. Robinson F/O H. Archer W/O E.C. Quick (Shoreham)	Walrus HD917	Crew of 457th BG B-17. Five picked up by Robinson who could not get airborne, so began to taxi. Fletcher arrived in Sea Otter (JM796) and took off three of the men, allowing Robinson to take off. 15:00-20:00 hrs.
18 Mar F/Lt M.F. Ogilvie-Forbes Sub Lt P. Ellis F/Sgt L. Carpenter (Martlesham)	Walrus W3072	2/Lt Allan D. Singleton, P-38 pilot from 55th FS, 20th FG. 16:55-17:50 hrs
" " S/L L.J. Brown W/O J. Rose Sgt R.N. Smith (Hawkinge)	Sea Otter JM745	Crew of 320 (Dutch) Sqn Mitchell (FH180) hit by flak and ditched four miles W of the Somme Estuary. Sgts J.H. Ot, F. Gans & J.J.G. Lub, and Cpl J H Postaumus. (*see text*) 14:30-20:45 hrs.
" " S/L R.W. Wallens Sub Lt E. Hall Sgt E. Cartwright (Hawkinge)	Walrus X9526	Crew of 320 (Dutch) Sqn (FR177) hit by flak and ditched in Channel. F/L H.J. Voorspuy, Sgt J Vink, and Cpls K. van Nouhuis and M. Engelsma. (*see text*) 13:35-15:25 hrs.
24 Mar P/O T.M. Ormiston W/O G.N. Leighton Sgt R. Mullins (Martlesham)	Walrus W3072	2/Lt Donald Gerber, of the 356th FS, 354th FG. 08:30-09:30 hrs.
28 Mar S/L R.W. Wallens Sub Lt E.C. Hall Sgt R.N. Smith (Hawkinge)	Walrus L2315	Two men of a Marauder crew who had been in the sea for four days. 16:55-18:10 hrs
29 Mar P/O T.M. Ormiston Sub Lt E.C. Ellis W/O G.N. Leighton (Martlesham)	Walrus W3072	Lt F.L. Edwards, a P-47 pilot from the 353rd FG, on escort to B-17 raid on Brunswick. 14:35-15:40 hrs.
" " W/O D.C.O. Campbell F/L D.G. Sheppard W/O V. Errington (Martlesham)	Walrus HD867	Lt Glen Smart, 335th FS, 4th FG, baled out after the Brunswick mission. Walrus unable to take off and had taxi back to Felixstowe. 15:30-20:00 hrs
5 Apl Lt A.B. Edgar W/O G.N. Leighton (Martlesham)	Walrus W3072	Captain R.D. Hobert, 336th FS, 4th FG, baled out but failed to inflate his dinghy. Died of exposure next

day. He had two air and three ground kills. 17:50-? hrs.

Date	Crew	Aircraft	Details
12 Apl	Lt A.B. Edgar F/S J.W.E. Lawrence Sgt R. Mullins (Martlesham)	Walrus L2289	Rescued four survivors of 730th BS, 452nd BG from Halle & Leipzig: 2/Lt E.M. Kaminsky (pilot), Sgts W. Gunnila, M.S. Hunter and R.G. Givens. 12:00-12:50 hrs; off Caister.
13 Apl	F/L M. Mackertich F/L D.G. Sheppard Sgt R. Mullins (Martlesham)	Walrus W3072	P-38 pilot, Lt Haws, of the 55th FG. 100th live rescue by Martlesham Flight. 17:15-19:10 hrs.
21 Apl	P/O T. Fletcher F/O B. H Willson W/O E.C. Quick (Shoreham)	Sea Otter JM796	F/O J. Moreau, Belgian pilot of 349 Sqn Spitfire (MH371) hit by ground fire W of Abbeville, baled out 20 miles S of Beachy Head. 10:35-11:53 hrs.
24 Apl	W/C A.D. Grace Sub Lt P. Ellis F/S J.W.E. Lawrence (Hawkinge)	Walrus L2315	Three crew members from the 550th BS, 385th BG, off Dungeness. Walrus taxied to Dover. 17:00-19:55 hrs.
" "	F/L M. Mackertich W/O J. Rose W/O W.L. Butler (Hawkinge)	Walrus X9526	Four crewmen from 351st BG B-17 off Ramsgate. Six others picked up by an HSL. 18:15-19:10 hrs.
25 Apl	P/O A.K. Saunders F/O B.H. Willson W/O G.N. Leighton (Shoreham)	Sea Otter JM798	W/O J.W. Haugh, navigator 464 (RNZAF) Sqn Mosquito (MM400) that hit the sea on return from attack on V1 site. The pilot, F/O L.J.S. Fittock, died of his injuries. (*see text*) 15:05-15:55 hrs.
30 Apl	P/O T. Fletcher F/Sgt S.W. Gregory F/Sgt R. Birch-Hurst (Shoreham)	Sea Otter JM796	W/O G. Warrington, Spitfire pilot from 132 Sqn, baled out after unsuccessful transfer of fuel tanks. Rescued from the Solent. 09:10-10:20 hrs.
" "	Lt A.B. Edgar Sub Lt E.C. Hall Sgt E. Cartwright (Hawkinge)	Walrus L2289	2/Lt Schreiber, P-51 pilot from 357th FG, baled out after flying accident near French coast. Walrus and P-51 pilot fired at by coastal guns; 277's escorting Spitfires returned fire. 08:55-10:45 hrs.
3 May	P/O A.K. Saunders F/Sgt E.G. Green Sgt W. Shaw (Shoreham)	Sea Otter JM798	F/Lt W.G.M. Hume, Spitfire pilot of 403 Sqn, baled out after hit by ground fire while dive-bombing V1 site. Landed 12 miles off Le Treport. Sea Otter taxied back but subsequently had to be abandoned. (*see text*) Take-off: 20:55 hrs.
4 May	Sub Lt R. Mander W/O W.L. Butler	Walrus L2735	Crew of a 320 (Dutch) Sqn, Mitchell (FR184), hit by flak on

	Sgt R.N. Smith (Hawkinge)		*Ramrod* S of Abbeville. 2/Lt G.O.J.A. Nuesink, 2/Lt L.T. Limbosch & Sgts C.H.V. Offeren and P. de Haan. 10:50-12:30 hrs.
8 May	P/O A.K. Saunders F/S S.W. Gregory W/O R. Birch-Hurst (Shoreham)	Sea Otter JM759	Lt Karl Kuba, 547th BS, 384th BG. 18:40-21:10 hrs.
" "	P/O W. Greenfield P/O R.L. Kennedy F/O H.J. Archer (Shoreham)	Sea Otter JM770	S/Sgt Ghyeager, 547th BS, 384th BG. 19:30-22:25 hrs.
9 May	P/O A.K. Saunders F/Sgt T. Gregory F/O H.J. Archer (Shoreham)	Sea Otter JM770	Major Drukl, Marauder captain from the 323rd BG. 277's Spitfires also located other crew members and directed HSLs to them. 10:50-12:50 hrs.
10 May	S/L R.W. Wallens Sub-Lt P.M.W. Ellis Sgt R.N. Smith (Hawkinge)	Walrus L2315	Rescued a pilot, seven miles NE of Gravelines. 09:55-12:20 hrs.
11 May	S/L R.W. Wallens W/O W.L. Butler Sgt R.N. Smith (Hawkinge)	Walrus L2315	W/C A. Barker & F/Lt R.J. Frederick, 418 Sqn Mosquito crew, hit the water on return from intruder sortie at low level, off Dieppe. 18:35-20:15 hrs.
12 May	W/C A.D. Grace F/L G.I. McNamee F/O N.J. Probert (Hawkinge)	Walrus L2315	Crew of B-17 from the 709th BS, 447th BG. Seven men picked up, four by Grace, three by Mitchell. 15:40-17:55 hrs. Both aircraft fired on by coastal gun positions.
" "	F/L J.V.C. Mitchell W/O V. Errington Sgt J. Humphreys (Hawkinge)	Walrus L2735	2/Lts Moses, Mitchell & Gilbert, Sgts Roesch & Pole, S/Sgts Dumm & Clarke. 16:20-17:55 hrs.
13 May	F/L C.G. Robertson F/O H.J. Archer P/O R.L. Kennedy (Shoreham)	Sea Otter	F/O J.T. Marriott, 442 Sqn. Spitfire hit by flak on *Ramrod 881* near Dieppe. Baled out 10 miles off Beachy Head. p.m.
20 May	F/L M. Mackertich Sub-Lt E. Hall Sgt L.J. Mullins (Hawkinge)	Walrus L2315	Lt Lawson, 369th FS, 368th FG, 30 miles off N Foreland. 16:30-17:25 hrs.
21 May	Sub Lt R. Mander W/O R. Harvey Sgt R.N. Smith (Hawkinge)	Walrus W3072	Walrus damaged during take-off, but it brought Capt Shurles of the 513 FBS, 406th FBG back from the sea off Cap Gris Nez. 12:10-14:05 hrs.
22 May	W/C A.D. Grace W/O K.E. Rhodes	Walrus W2735	Rescued airman from a very rough sea, but had to be towed back by an

	W/O J. Rose (Hawkinge)		HSL. 15:10-15:45 hrs.
" "	F/L M. Mackertich Sgt J.C. Humphreys Sgt R.N. Smith (Hawkinge)	Walrus	W/C E. Haabjoern DSO DFC, OC 124 (Typhoon) Wing, in the sea one mile off Dieppe Harbour. 15:45-RTB.
" "	P/O W. Greenfield P/O L.R. Healey F/Sgt E.G. Green (Shoreham)	Sea Otter JM796	2/Lt Dixon, 56th FG. 20:15-22:20 hrs.
23 May	Lt D.V. Robinson F/O B.H. Willson F/Sgt E.G. Green (Shoreham)	Sea Otter JM770	W/C R.E.P. Brooker DFC, OC 123 (Typhoon) Wing, baled out of (MN143) after engine trouble on Ramrod to St Valery. Baled out 25 miles S of Beachy Head. 11:10-12:35 hrs.
" "	F/L C.G. Robertson F/Sgt L.A. Carpenter Sub-Lt A.W. More (Shoreham)	Sea Otter JM770	F/L J.D. Furneaux, 2 Sqn, Mustang FD557. Brought down by flak and baled out five miles off Cap D'Artifer. 15:55-17:35 hrs.
27 May	P/O T.M. Ormiston F/Sgt E.G. Green Sub-Lt P.F. Mariner (Shoreham)	Sea Otter JM770	Capt Nuff & 2/Lt Lever, 640th BS, 409th BGp, two miles off Le Treport. 277 Sqn's 500th live rescue. 13:55-16:00 hrs
" "	F/L J.V.C. Mitchell Sub Lt E. Hall Sgt L.J. Mullins (Hawkinge)	Walrus X9563	F/Sgt A.C.H. White, pilot of 127 Sqn Spitfire (MK696) hit by flak during raid on V1 site. Ditched 10 miles W of Ault. 19:00-20:40 hrs.
28 May	F/L C.G. Robertson F/O L.R. Healey Sub-Lt P.F. Mariner (Shoreham)	Sea Otter JM770	F/O A.A. Watkins, Canadian pilot of Typhoon (MN583) shot down by flak on 22 May. Drifted six days off French coast. (see text). 09:30-11:45 hrs.
" "	Lt J.D. Nunn Sgt W. Shore F/Sgt E.G. Green (Shoreham)	Walrus HD877	F/O J. Ester, Belgian pilot of 349 Sqn Spitfire (MK302), hit by flak and baled out 10 miles off Le Treport. Second time he'd been rescued, having been picked up by HSL 127 on 19 May 1942. 11:25-13:25 hrs.
" "	S/L R.W. Wallens W/O W.L. Butler F/Sgt J.W.E. Lawrence (Hawkinge)	Walrus	S/Sgts Crept & Timmens from the 567th BS, 389th BG, six miles N of Gravelines. 17:25-19:25 hrs.
2 Jun	F/L J.V.C. Mitchell W/O K.E. Rhodes F/S J.W.E. Lawrence (Hawkinge)	Walrus L2289	S/Sgt Walgrem, USAF, in a rough sea from which Walrus could not take off. Taken in tow by HSL 96 to Dover after taxying for 40 minutes. 20:05-01:00 hrs.

7 Jun	CPO C. Barley F/Sgt E. Humphreys Sgt J.A.W. Smith (Hawkinge)	Walrus X9563	2/Lt Day, P-47 pilot. 15:00-18:20 hrs.
11 Jun	F/L M. Mackertich W/O V. Errington Sgt E. Cartwright (Hawkinge)	Walrus HD923	Watched aircraft 491st BG B-24 ditch six miles E of Beachy Head. Picked up two men; an RN cutter picked up three more and two bodies. 08:05-10:25 hrs.
" "	Lt A.B. Edgar Sgt R.N. Smith Sgt J.A.W. Smith (Hawkinge)	Walrus HD914	Lt Ralston, 369th FS, 359th FG USAAF, badly wounded. Walrus couldn't take off so taxied until towed into Dover by HSL. 10:40-12:05 hrs.
24 Jun	F/L W.B. Dobree P/O R.L. Kennedy F/Sgt E.G. Green (Shoreham)	Sea Otter JM764	Capt L. DeLong Martin, P-51 pilot, hit by flak baled out in the Channel and was found by pure chance. 15:50-19:08 hrs.
4 Jul	F/L C.G. Robertson W/O E.C. Quick P/O E.W. Coop (Shoreham)	Sea Otter JM776	P/O G.T. Emery, 66 Sqn, engine trouble. Unable to take off, towed back by HSL after spending night in the Channel. 16:25-06:00 hrs.
13 Jul	CPO C. Barley W/O R. Harvey LAC Winfield (Hawkinge)	Walrus W2766	2/Lt C.W. Dungan, P-38 pilot from the 77th FS, 20th FG, in Thames Estuary. 09:35-10:25 hrs.
16 Jul	CPO C. Barley W/O W.L. Butler F/Sgt E. Humphreys (Hawkinge)	Walrus W2766	Lt John E. Clark, P-38 pilot from the 55th FS, 20th FG, off Margate. 11:35-12:35 hrs.
9 Aug	F/L L. Field F/O R.L. Kennedy F/Sgt E. Green (Shoreham)	Sea Otter JM770	Crew of 320 (Dutch) Sqn Mitchell, 70 miles off Shoreham. Lt L. Vanderburg, 2/Lt G.A.G. Pieters, Sgts G. Hofman & Sgt A.J. Wams. 11:55-13:30 hrs.
25 Aug	FO J.R.E. Driscoll W/O R. Harvey LAC Woods (Hawkinge)	Walrus L2766	F/O A. Keith-Thomas, pilot of 122 Sqn Mustang (FZ114) hit by flak six miles off Somme Estuary. Baled out 24 August; rescued next day. 08:35-10:35 hrs.
" "	Lt J.D. Nunn F/O C.G. Walker Sub Lt A.W. Moore (Shoreham)	Walrus L2183	F/O Hodder, 2 Group HQ Sqn, who was badly injured eight miles S of Newhaven. Three dead bodies in the water. 12:15-15:15 hrs.
17 Sep	Lt R. Mander Sub Lt E. Hall Sgt E. Cartwright (Hawkinge)	Walrus L2766	Crew of Halifax, two miles off shore at Hardelot. Transferred to *HSL 190*. Walrus crew later helped in the rescue of a glider crew, picked up by *RNL 22*. 09:45-11:45 hrs.

| 12 Dec | F/L C.G. Robertson
F/O C.G. Walker
F/Sgt W. Shaw
(Hawkinge) | Walrus
K8554 | Lt O'Quinn, 359th FS, 356th FG. Rough sea, so had to taxi most of way back before being able to take off. 277 Sqn's 598th live rescue. 11:00-12:45 hrs. |

Main Walrus Rescues by No 278 Squadron

1942

| 23 Jun | P/O S.A. Trevallion
Sgt T. Templeton
(Coltishall) | Walrus
L2238 | Five airmen rescued after being guided to a dinghy by a Wellington and a Hudson. Walrus took three attempts to take off. 10:30-12:20 hrs. |
| 19 Aug | F/L P. Smith
F/O J. Chase
F/Sgt S. Hurrell
(Coltishall) | Walrus
L2238 | German airman from a Do 217 shot down by 137 Sqn that morning. 11:45-13:15 hrs. |

1943

24 Feb	F/Sgt G.B. Reeder P/O A. Dunhill (Coltishall)	Walrus L2238	F/Sgt E.A. Buglass, pilot of 118 Sqn Spitfire (EN969), ditched after being hit by flak on a *Rhubarb* sortie. 17:30-18:20 hrs.
15 Mar	F/O W.F. Sims F/Sgt F.J. Hall (Coltishall)	Walrus L2268	S/L V. Pheloung, CO of 56 Sqn, whose Typhoon (DN374) was hit by flak from a ship. Baled out 35 miles off Norfolk coast. 17:30-18:50 hrs.
14 May	F/O S.A. Trevallion F/O W.A. Land F/O A.E. Peill F/S C.W. Rolls (Coltishall)	Walrus L2268	P/O R.H. Milne, 245 Sqn pilot whose Typhoon (DN599) had engine failure on patrol.(*see text*) 20:00-21:00 hrs.
13 Jun	F/L S.A. Trevallion F/Sgt F. Nall (Coltishall)	Walrus L2268	Eight men from the crew of a 351st BG B-17. Picked up all eight, but could not take off. Later put all survivors onto an HSL. 20:40-23:00 hrs.
22 Jun	W/O F.C. Perry Sgt D.R. Swindell (Coltishall)	Walrus L2238	Crew of a 35 Sqn Halifax (BB368) that ditched off Cromer coming back from Krefeld. Four of the seven men later transferred to a second Walrus. (*see text*) 07:30-09:15 hrs.
" "	F/O W.A. Land P/O P.J. Roy	Walrus K8549	Sgts D.H. Milne, A.G. Cox, P.R. Lisoner, J. Jolly, K. Wolstencroft, T.R.M. Smith & R.A.H. Bowring. 09:00-10:00 hrs. (This crew failed to return from a raid on Cologne on 3/4 July.)
17 Jul	F/Sgt T. Humphrey P/O A. Dunhill (Coltishall)	Walrus L2307	Crew of a 511th BS, 351st BG B-17, located by Sqn Anson. Picked up five men while other four picked up

" "	F/O V.A. Hester F/O H.R. Cawker	Walrus L2238	by second Walrus. Had to taxi back in a rough sea. HSLs later arrived and took off all survivors. (*see text*) 12:45-13:20 hrs.
25 Jul	F/O V.A. Hester F/Sgt J.F. Neal P/O A. Dunhill (Coltishall)	Walrus L2307	S/L E.F.J. Charles DFC, CO of 611 Sqn, who baled out of his Spitfire (AR610) on *Ramrod 154*. (*see text*) 19:05-21:25 hrs.
26 Jul	W/O G.B. Reeder F/S C.W. Rolls	Walrus L2307	Both Walrus crews landed and picked up crew of a B-17 off Norfolk coast. Neither able to take off. Later put men aboard an HSL. Reeder then took off, but Land had to be towed into Great Yarmouth Harbour. 8th Air Force raid on Hamburg. 322nd BS, 91st BG crew: Lts J. Hargis, C.N. Smith, C.R. Simons & W.H. Turcroft; S/Sgts J.A. Bowcock, R.A. Thigpen, A. Di Menno & G. Tucker; T/Sgts J. Allen & V. Ciganek. (*see text*) 18:40-21:30 and 18:25-04:25 hrs
" "	F/O W.A. Land P/O C G Scott	Walrus K8549	
20 Aug	F/O W.F. Sims P/O A. Dunhill (Coltishall)	Walrus L2268	Crew of 320 (Dutch) Sqn Mitchell (FR147) shot down during attack on Flushing. H. Nienhuis, J.P. Oele, F.A.J. Prinsen & D.H.J. Born. 17:20-19:45 hrs.

1944

22 Apl	F/Sgt A. W. Hammond W/O E.K. Dineen	Walrus	Seven US airmen from a 452nd BG B-17 lost on 20 April after attack on V1 site at Calais. 90 miles off English coast. Walrus had to taxi back until towed into Harwich Harbour by HSL.
23 Apl	W/O R.C. Whittaker F/O P.J. Roy	Walrus HD918	Lt P.J. Trudeau, 351st FS, 353rd FG P-47 pilot. Unable to switch fuel tanks and baled out previous afternoon after Hamm mission. Off Scheldt Estuary; Walrus taxied for over four hours until taken in tow into Felixstowe Harbour by HSL.
29 May	Sub Lt R. Carr-Gregg & crew (Martlesham)	Walrus HD933	Airman being circled by two USAAF P-47s. 13:45-14:50 hrs.
11 Jul	W/O R.C. Whittaker F/O P.J. Roy (Martlesham)	Walrus HD912	Sole survivor from USAAF B-24. Walrus towed back by *RML 547*. 16:53-18:00 hrs.
30 Aug	P/O M.J. Peskett P/O E.K. Dineen (Martlesham)	Walrus W2715	Airman in the sea off Den Helder. 11:15-14:35 hrs.

9 Sep WO G.B. Reeder   Walrus   1/Lt Earl C. Walsh, 334th FS, 4th
Sgt D.R. Swindell   FG P-51D (QP-Z). Walrus
(Martlesham)   damaged by heavy seas and later
                                    sank. All three men rescued by RNL
                                    547.

13 Sep P/O M.J. Peskett   Walrus   Airman in Mae West. Walrus taxied
LA R.H. Westbrook   HD912   until met by RML and taken in tow
(Martlesham)   to Felixstowe Harbour. 10:00-11:05
                                    hrs.

14 Sep P/O J.E. Meeklah   Walrus   W/O H. Ross, pilot of 80 Sqn
Sub-Lt J. Felice   HD830   Tempest (EJ695). Engine trouble on
(Martlesham)   an armed recce to The Hague. Baled
                                    out. (*see text*) 17:20-19:10 hrs.

16 Sep Lt N.C. Langdon   Walrus   Crew of 420 Sqn Halifax (NA629)
LA R. Atkins   HD926   that ditched returning from Keil.
(Martlesham)   Later towed back by *RML 512* and
                                    transferred survivors: F/L V.G.
                                    Motherwell, F/Os A.J. MacDonald
                                    & I.E. McGown, Sgts L.K.
                                    Engemoen, J.A. Wigley, J.L.
                                    Hickson, J. Porter & T.J. Bibby. (*see text*) 18:10-19:30 hrs.

17 Sep P/O J. Meeklah   Walrus   Pilot off Orfordness. 16:55-17:20
P/O W. Trust   HD912   hrs.
(Martlesham)

18 Sep W/O F.J. Bedford   Walrus   Four survivors from a Waco glider
Sub Lt J. Felice   W2735   off Aldeburgh. Walrus taxied back
(Martlesham)   and beached near Matilla Tower.
                                    12:15-13:45 hrs.

5 Oct W/O F.J. Bedford   Walrus   USAAF 339th FG P-51 pilot found,
LA R.H. Westbrook   HD933   but unable to get him into the
(Martlesham)   aircraft. Held onto the man until
                                    trawler arrived and picked him up.
                                    Walrus damaged; towed, but then
                                    sank. 12:15-? hrs

1945
31 Aug PO J. Meeklah   Sea   Lt R.D.I.C. Henderson, FAA in
F/O L. C Murray   Otter   Corsair (JS498) from the Naval
W/O R. Brierley   JM957   OTU, St Merryn. Collided during
                                    formation aerobatics with Lt Cdr
                                    P.J.E. Nicholls and baled out N of
                                    Bude (Nicholls returned to base).
                                    11:55-13:05 hrs.

The UK-based Walrus Squadrons

No 275 Squadron   *Non Interibunt*   **Squadron Code: PV**
Formed at RAF Valley, from detached Flights at Valley and Andreas, on 15 October 1941. Equipped with Lysander III, Walrus II and Defiant I aircraft. Rescued 58 survivors by Walrus, guided launches to a further 62.

BASES:

Valley, with detachments at Andreas and Eglinton	Oct 1941–Apr 1944
Warmwell	Apr 1944–Aug 1944
Bolt Head, and detachment at Portreath	Aug 1944–Oct 1944
Exeter, detachments at Portreath and Bolt Head	Oct 1944–Jan 1945
Harrowbeer, detachments at Portreath and Bolt Head	Jan 1945–Feb 1945
Disbanded at Harrowbeer, 15 February 1945	

COs:

S/Ldr R.F. Hamblyn AFC DFM	Oct 1941–Dec 1942
S/Ldr E.W. Seaborne DFC	Dec 1942–Feb 1945

MAIN EQUIPMENT:

Lysander:	V9737; V9738; V9749/'N'.
Walrus:	L2207/'Z'; L2282; W2746/'K'; HD823; HD923/'S'; HD925; HD927; HD929/'Z'; HD930.
Defiant:	N3423; T3920.
Spitfire:	BL294; BM448.
Anson:	AX645; EG492/'F'; LT952/'O'.

No 276 Squadron   *Retrieve*   **Squadron Code: AQ**
Formed at RAF Harrowbeer from detached Flights at Harrowbeer, Fairwood Common, Perranporth, Roborough and Warmwell, on 21 October 1941. Equipped with Lysander and Walrus aircraft. 'A' Flight detached to Roborough under F/Lt P.R.P. Fisher. Rescued or helped to rescue 301 survivors.

BASES:

Harrowbeer, and detachments at Fairwood Common, Perranporth, Portreath and Warmwell	Oct 1941–Apr 1944
Portreath with detachment at A23/Querqueville	Apr 1944–Sep 1944
Querqueville, detachment at Portreath	Sep 1944–Sep 1944

Amiens Glissy, detachment at Portreath   Sep 1944–Sep 1944
St Denis Westrem, detachment at Portreath   Sep 1944–Oct 1944
St Croix, detachment at Ursel   Oct 1944–Dec 1944
Knocke-le-Zoute   Dec 1944–Jun 1945
Disbanded at Dunsfold, 14 November 1945

COs:

S/Ldr N.J. Hulbert	Oct 1941– ? 1942
S/Ldr P.R.P. Fisher	? 1942–Dec 1942
S/Ldr R.F. Hamblyn AFC DFM	Dec 1942–Sep 1943
S/Ldr J.M. Littler	Sep 1943–Jul 1944
S/Ldr A.F. Sunderland-Cooper	Jul 1944–Apr 1945
S/Ldr N.E. Hancock DFC	Apr 1945–Nov 1945

MAIN EQUIPMENT:

Lysander: T1620/'F'; V9310; V9444; V9505; V9710/'K'; V9743/'L'; V9820.

Walrus: L2220; L2246; L2271/'X'; L2335; P5658/'N'; W2774; W2784; W3026/'N'; W3029; W3081; W3083/'W'; X9522/'W'.

Defiant: N3372/'T'; N3430; T3929; T3939; T4051/'N'; AA296.

Spitfire: P7366; P7616; P7732; P8131/'C'; P8232; P8265; P8565/'H'; P8584; P8667; P8674/'J'; P8727; BL379; BL495; BN474; EN841.

Anson: R3443; EG499; EG505.

No 277 Squadron   *Quaerendo Servanius*   **Squadron Code: BA**
Formed from detached Flights at Hawkinge, Martlesham Heath, Shoreham, and Stapleford Tawney, on 22 December 1941, equipped with Lysander and Walrus aircraft. Rescued or helped to rescue 598 men from the sea.

BASES:

Stapleford Tawney, detached flights at Shoreham,
   Hawkinge and Martlesham Heath   Dec 1941–Dec 1942
Gravesend, detachments at Hawkinge, Martlesham
   Heath and Shoreham   Dec 1942–Apr 1944
Shoreham, detachments at Hawkinge, Hurn and
   Warmwell   Apr 1944–Oct 1944
Hawkinge, detachment at Portreath   Oct 1944–Feb 1945
Disbanded at Hawkinge, 15 February 1945

COs:

S/Ldr D. deB. Clark	Dec 1941–Mar 1942
S/Ldr W.P. Green	Mar 1942–Aug 1942
S/Ldr A.S. Linney OBE	Aug 1942–Jul 1943
S/Ldr L.J. Brown DFC	Jul 1943–Feb 1945

MAIN EQUIPMENT:

Lysander: V9288/'X'; V9364; V9431/'S'; V9487; V9547; V9545/'C'; V9583.

Walrus: L2223; L2246/'L'; L2271; L2282; L2289; L2298; L2313/'T'; L2315; W2735; W2736; W2766; W2773; W3010; W3024; W3072; W3076/'Y'; W3077; W3097; X9503; X9521; X9526; X9563/'A'; HD867/'F'; HD908; HD917/'U'.

Sea Otter: JM745; JM764; JM770; JM776; JM796; JM798.

Defiant: N1561; N3392; N3443/'L'; N3445; V1117; AA254; AA312; AA315.

Spitfire: P7321; P7325; P7359; P7490; P7605/'G'; P7828; P7734; P7775; P7994; P8030; P8032; P8072; P8179/'T'; P8261; P8322; P8375; P8441/'R'; P8479; P8508; P8509; P8705/'C'; AB975; AD185; AD199; AD366/'Z'; AD377; AD815; BM510; BM522.

No 278 Squadron   *Ex Mare Ad Referiendum*   **Squadron Code: MY**
Formed from No 3 ASF Flight at RAF Matlaske on 1 October 1941, with Walrus and Lysander aircraft. Detachment at North Coates. Live rescues totalled 296.

BASES:

Matlaske, detachment at North Coates	Oct 1941–Apr 1942
Coltishall, with detachments at North Coates, the north of England and in Scotland	Apr 1942–Apr 1944
Bradwell Bay, with detachments at Martlesham Heath and Hornchurch	Apr 1944–Feb 1945
Thorney Island, detachments at Hawkinge, Beccles and Exeter	Feb 1945–Oct 1945
Disbanded at Thorney Island, 14 October 1945	

COs:

F/Lt P.R. Smith	Oct 1941–Apr 1943
S/Ldr S.A. Trevallion DFC	Apr 1943–
S/Ldr B.H. Bowring	Oct 1944
S/Ldr R. Whitcomb DFC	Oct 1944–Oct 1945

MAIN EQUIPMENT:

Lysander: V9431; V9451; V9538; V9609; V9817/'E'.

Walrus: K8549/'W'; K8554; L2238; L2268/'A'; L2271/'S'; L2307/'G'; R6548/'E'; W2715; W2735; W3049/'A'; HD830; HD912; HD917/'A'; HD918; HD926; HD933.

Sea Otter: JM826/'O'; JM885/'U'; JM957/'M'.

Spitfire: R6951/'P'; AD652/'V'; BM491; BM532.

Ansons: DG809; EF985/'F'; EG496; EQ540; LT592.

WE ARE THE AIR-SEA RESCUE

We are the Air-Sea Rescue,
No earthly good are we;
The only times you see us,
Is breakfast, lunch and tea.

And if we sight a dinghy,
We shout with all our might,
'Per Ardua ad Astra',
Blow you chum, we're all right.

Epilogue

During the Second World War, the rescue services had rescued hundreds of airmen from the waters of the Channel, North Sea, Irish Sea, off the south-west coast of England, and so on. The four main ASR squadrons which operated Walrus and Sea Otter seaplanes had creditable totals themselves. Top scorers were, of course, 277, which had a final total of 598 'live' rescues. Next came 278 with something in the region of 304, followed by 276 with 302 and finally 275 Squadron with 120. Not all were pure Walrus rescues, naturally. For instance, 275's score of 120 was made up of 58 Walrus rescues plus a further 62 found by the squadron's aircraft and rescued by boats.

In the end, however, it was not how they were rescued, just so long as they had been. But for the Walrus and Sea Otter – the old 'Shagbat' with more than 1,000 rescues or assisted rescues – it was a considerable achievement.

The Walrus crews were out in all weathers and all conditions . . .

Glossary

1/Lt	First Lieutenant (USAAF)	MASB	Motor Anti-Submarine Boat
2/Lt	Second Lieutenant (USAAF)	N	North
AA	Anti-Aircraft	NCO	Non-Commissioned Officer
A/C	Air Commodore	NE	North-east
AFC	Air Force Cross	OBE	Officer of the Order of the British Empire
AFM	Air Force Medal	Oblt	Oberleutnant (German)
AOC	Air Officer Commanding	OC	Officer Commanding
ASI	Air Speed Indicator	Op	Operation
ASR	Air-Sea Rescue	OTU	Operational Training Unit
AVM	Air Vice-Marshal	PFF	Pathfinder Force
BEF	British Expeditionary Force	P/O	Pilot Officer
Circus	Fighter-escorted bombing raid to attract enemy response	RAAF	Royal Australian Air Force
		Ramrod	Day bomber raid escorted by fighters
CO	Commanding Officer	RCAF	Royal Canadian Air Force
Cpl	Corporal	RDF	Radio Direction Finding
CPO	Chief Petty Officer	Recce	Reconnaissance
D/F	Direction Finding	*Rhubarb*	Low-level attacks by pairs of aircraft on road and rail traffic under low cloud conditions
DFC	Distinguished Flying Cross		
DFM	Distinguished Flying Medal		
DSO	Distinguished Service Order	RN	Royal Navy
E	East	RNAS	Royal Naval Air Station
FBG	Fighter-Bomber Group (USAAF)	RNL	Royal Naval Lifeboat
FBS	Fighter-Bomber Squadron (USAAF)	RNVR	Royal Naval Volunteer Reserve
FG	Fighter Group (USAAF)	RNZAF	Royal New Zealand Air Force
F/L	Flight Lieutenant	*Roadsted*	Fighter operations against shipping
Flak	Flieberabwehrkannonen – German anti-aircraft fire	*Rodeo*	Fighter sweep
		R/T	Radio Telephone
F/O	Flying Officer	S	South
FS	Fighter Squadron (USAAF)	SBS	Special Boat Service
F/S	Flight Sergeant	S/L	Squadron Leader
FW	Focke-Wulf Flugzeugbau	S-Lt	Sub-Lieutenant
GCI	Ground-Controlled Interception	SSE	South-south-east
Gee	British navigation aid using ground transmitters and an airborne receiver	S/Sgt	Staff Sergeant (USAAF)
		SW	South-west
HE	High Explosive	TAF	Tactical Air Force
HSL	High-Speed Launch	T/Sgt	Technical Sergeant (USAAF)
JG	Jagdgeschwader – German fighter group	U/S	Unserviceable
Jim Crow	Reconnaissance by fighter aircraft (over English Channel)	USAAF	United States Army Air Force
		VC	Victoria Cross
Ju	Junkers Flugzeug und Motorenwerke AG	VHF	Very High Frequency
		V1	Vergeltungswaffe 1 – the Fiesler 103 flying bomb
LAC	Leading Aircraftsman		
LACW	Leading Aircraftswoman		
LT	Lieutenant	WAAF	Women's Auxiliary Air Force
Me	Messerschmitt AG	W	West
MO	Medical Officer	W/C	Wing Commander
MP	Military Policeman	W/O	Warrant Officer
MTB	Motor Torpedo Boat	W/OP	Wireless Operator

Index